250,000 M
What Women *REALLY*
Want to Know

WTF

are men thinking?

Christopher Brya and Miguel Almaraz

sourcebooks
casablanca

Published by Sourcebooks Casablanca, an imprint of Sourcebooks, Inc.
P.O. Box 4410, Naperville, Illinois 60567-4410
(630) 961-3900
Fax: (630) 961-2168
www.sourcebooks.com

Library of Congress Cataloging-in-Publication Data

Brya, Christopher.
  WTF are men thinking? : 250,000 men tell the truth about what women really want
to know / Christopher Brya & Miguel Almaraz.
    p. cm.
  Includes bibliographical references and index.
  (pbk. : alk. paper) 1. Man-woman relationships. 2. Men--Psychology. 3. Mate
selection. I. Almaraz, Miguel. II. Title.
  HQ801.B8739 2012
  306.82--dc23
                              2012022153

Printed and bound in the United States of America.
VP 10 9 8 7 6 5 4 3 2 1

DEDICATION

For Pilar—the strongest and most amazing woman I know.
Thank you for being my best friend, for making my life happen,
and most especially for Evan & Ella. My love for you is endless.
—Christopher Brya

Carol, Miguel, and Lauren—I wish I could find words
that would exhibit my love and admiration to you.
—Miguel Almaraz IV

CONTENTS

Acknowledgments...xiii

Introduction..xvii

Communication...1

When will he call me?...2

Why doesn't he call?...4

Should I call?..7

What's the deal with lame pickup lines?.........................9

Why won't he open up?..12

Why is it so hard for men to express their feelings?...........15

Why is asking to talk a big deal?..............................18

How do men justify lies?.......................................21

He gave in, so I "won," right?.................................24

Do men even value our opinions?................................27

Why can't men say what they mean?..............................30

Why doesn't he always believe me?..............................33

Why do men lie about the little things?........................36

Omit ~~needless~~ words...38

What really moves him?..41

Why do men always want to fix things?................43

Why do men flirt so much?.....................................46

Why does he want to fight?.....................................49

Why does he always side with his mother over me?...52

Why do men talk differently around "the guys"?..........56

Is he listening?..59

Is there stuff he won't talk about?........................62

Why do I have to spell it out for him?..................65

If I don't nag him, will he ever do anything?..............68

Does he think I'll never discover those lies?..............71

I'm mad. How do I tell him?....................................74

When is the best time to bring up a heavy subject?......77

Who does he talk to?..79

Dating...83

Can I make the first move?.....................................84

What is the best first date?.....................................86

What do guys think will impress me?..................89

Does he "take care of business"
before we go out on a date?....................................92

First date kiss: yes or no?.......................................95

Would you kiss a date you are not attracted to?..........97

What will cost me a second date?..........................100

What makes a woman worthy of a second date?........103

He doesn't want to date me.
Will he still sleep with me?......................................106
Why doesn't he just say it's a booty call?....................109
Can I ask for favors?...111
Can I date more than one guy at a time?....................113
When should I talk about my ex?..............................115
When should I tell him I'm a parent?........................118
At what point do men expect sex?............................120
How long will he wait for sex?.................................122
How many girls does he have?..................................124
Will he gossip about me?..126
Does he compare me to her?.....................................128
Good looks or good personality?..............................131
What personality traits are important to men?..........133
What is the number-one
physical feature men look for?.................................136
How important are my clothes?................................138
Do men really prefer blonds?...................................140
Cougars: yes or no?...143
What habit drives men away?...................................145
What grosses men out about women?........................148
What does he look for in a long-term partner?..........151
The official relationship starts—when?....................154
What makes him commit?...157
Why are men so afraid to commit?...........................160
Money: more or less important?...............................163

Will he cheat on me?...166

Why not leave, instead of cheating?.........................168

What bothers men about being in a relationship?.......171

What signals you that it's time to break up?..............174

Romance...177

Is love at first sight possible?..................................178

How does he know he's in love?...............................180

Are there any romantic men?...................................183

What do guys really think about cuddling?...............186

Dirty talk: romantic or vulgar?...............................189

Is sharing his interests romantic?............................191

How do guys feel about PDA?..................................193

What's his idea of a romantic getaway?....................195

Would he rather hang with me than the guys?...........197

Why does he forget important dates?........................200

Dancing: does he like it or just tolerate it?................205

Do men appreciate the women they are with?...........208

Can I call him Schmoopy?.......................................211

What's the hottest lingerie?.....................................214

What's the most romantic thing he's done?...............217

Attractive, sexy, or erotic?......................................220

Is it romantic if I make the first move?.....................224

More romantic: massage or oral?..............................227

What does he want for Valentine's Day?...................230

New Year's Eve: what's best?...................................233

Sex...237

   Who initiates?..239

   What turns men on?..242

   Do men really enjoy foreplay?...........................244

   Foreplay versus sex..246

   What positions does he prefer?..........................249

   What is so appealing about anal sex?..................252

   Will he care if I am experienced?.......................255

   Do all men like to experiment?..........................257

   Do men ever not want sex?.................................260

   What does he think about performance issues?........263

   What's he staring at during sex?........................266

   How often does he want it?................................268

   Does he fake it?...270

   Can he tell if I fake it?......................................272

   What are his fantasies?.....................................275

   Can fantasies be deal breakers?.........................277

   Does he fantasize about two women?..................279

   Do all men look at porn?...................................282

   But will he look at porn if he's got me?...............285

   Are condoms uncomfortable?.............................288

   Tightness: does it matter?.................................291

   Can my weight push him away from sex?..............294

   How important is oral sex?................................297

   Why doesn't he perform oral sex for very long?........300

   Does he like a screamer?...................................302

Sensual or rough?..304
Shaving: yes or no?..307
What can I do to make sex better for him?..............310

Marriage...**313**
When does he think about marriage?....................314
What is the best age to get married?.......................316
Does he see marriage as a trap?............................318
What's he scared of?..321
Living together: yes or no?....................................324
How would he pop the question?...........................327
Do men want to help plan the wedding?................330
Does he believe marriage is forever?......................332
Are men happy being married?..............................334
Should the man be the spiritual leader?.................337
Will he expect me to work?..................................339
Will he feel insecure if I earn more than him?...........341
What role am I expected to play?...........................344
Will he do some chores?......................................347
Why are men so messy?......................................350
Do men feel an obligation to make wives happy?......353
Do men think their wives are
less attractive with age?.......................................355
Does love change in a marriage?...........................358
Does he think about his exes?...............................361
Children: yes or no?..363
Would he cheat if he could get away with it?...........365

What would he consider unforgivable?......................367
Why do men cheat?...370

Work...375

Can he take a boss seriously if
she dresses provocatively?...................................376
What does he think about appropriate dress?...........379
What does he think about office hookups?.................382
Can you cry at work?...384
Can I be too opinionated?....................................386
Am I professional or cold?...................................389
Can you be too friendly?.....................................392
Can I be too strong?..395
What is the best way to be
assertive without being offensive?..........................398
Are men intimidated by women
in a higher position?...400
Can my success be a threat?.................................402
Who's more qualified?..404
Equal cash?...407
Would a man choose a man's
idea over a woman's?...409
How can a woman make her
boss take her more seriously?................................411
Is he tempted to cheat with someone from work?......413
How can a woman ask a man
to tone down his guy talk?...................................415

Men Sound Off...417
  The Top Five Mistakes.................................417
  Miscellaneous...433

Conclusion...435

Methodology..437

About the Authors..439

ACKNOWLEDGMENTS

First things first: to our friends, family, and colleagues who worked, dealt, or lived with us during the writing and production of this book—we're deeply sorry, but very appreciative. We really couldn't have done it without you.

Secondly, all the people who purchased the book you're now reading. (We hope it was you.) Thank you very much. Enjoy this one and others to come!

We would also like to thank the thousands of women and men who submitted questions and answers and who provided the detail for this book.

Lastly, it might take a village to raise a child, but to publish a book, it might take more. Like most things in life, this was a team effort. We would like to personally thank the following people on our team for their brainpower, friendship, and skills.

Stephany Evans, our literary agent (and all the people at FinePrint Literary Management). Thanks for having the faith in us and guiding us on our first literary endeavor. We look forward to many, many more mutual congratulations we'll share over the next decade and beyond.

Shana Drehs, editorial manager at Sourcebooks. Seriously, you need to be cloned. You're like our editorial spouse; you diligently kept us on time, on track, and in line. The result was an amazing product that exceeded everything we imagined.

Dominique Raccah, CEO of Sourcebooks, and her team who were involved in our project, even at the most detailed of levels. It meant a lot to us. Thanks for sharing your passion, guidance, expertise, and ideas.

Jeff Yanovitch and *Chip Allison* at Yanocreative.com. You guys are the best. Whether it was creative, graphic or brand design, concept layouts, a soundboard for idea creation, or just helping us through any creative dilemma, you were always there and made it happen. Thank you, gentlemen. You rock.

Kasia Jezuit, who helped us this whole way. We appreciate all your faith, effort, creativity, and hard work throughout this project. You helped us in ways that made this crazy effort possible. (And thanks for all of the sugary treats along the way!)

Nali Giliana, our brother in nearly every way except blood and the founder of the WTFIGO business principle. You have a remarkable business mind and always gave us insights into where we could take this project and everything else for that matter. But more importantly, your friendship is the gift that keeps on giving. We look forward to strategically thinking about more future projects with you over good food, wine, and laughs.

Brittni Payne, who gave us the extra spark of effort when it was needed and for all the work you did on the spreadsheets. Ugh, the spreadsheets! Thanks for all your hard work and diligence when we asked for it. You never disappoint.

Jennie Brya and *Karen Linkins* are not only two of the smartest women we know, but they're also core family. We thank you for the generous use of the mountain retreat, the desert sanctuary, and for your love and support.

Gaurav Parekh and the team at Parsus. You have always been an advocate in everything we did. We love your enthusiasm, generosity, and all the time you made for us over great coffee, lunch meetings, or happy hours. Your support and counsel is only surpassed by your friendship.

Lance Faulkner, for all of your technical and SEO guidance, as well as being the rare straight shooter in this very wavy modern world. You are the man!

Holly Jonas, our web design guru. You always made the website better than we thought possible and were always a big advocate of the book, of the concept, and of this project. Thank you for making our web world happen.

The Solavista team, for tireless hours on this project to make this material available to everyone.

And here is a group of people (in no particular order), some we know and some we don't, who we'd like to thank. They were our muses who inspired us and helped us in various ways: Richard Dawson, Chris Gardner, Larry David, Rick Normali, Albert Brooks, Pink Floyd, Connie Mableson, Howard Stern, Mark & Trish, Steve Jobs, Carmen Hernandez, Pablo Picasso, Richard Branson, Claudia Hill, Seth Godin, Mark Goodson, Bill Todman, Bob Barker, Brett Schiefelbein, Timothy Ferris, Craig Zahn, and nearly everyone working at every Starbucks in the greater Phoenix metropolitan area.

INTRODUCTION

Can you handle the truth?

In *WTF Are Men Thinking?*, we provide female readers the real truth about how men think, plus the real truth about the mistakes and problems women unknowingly make when interacting with men. In this book, more than 250,000 men provide the answers to hundreds of questions that women have supplied us regarding communication, dating, romance, sex, marriage, work, and the things that bug them the most.

The answers revealed in our book are not based on opinions or theories of any one specific author, columnist, or therapist, but instead come from a powerful crowdsource of real men.

The result is a truly fresh and empowering understanding of the male-female dynamic. The unbiased, research-based information is a unique twist on relationship, sex, dating, or communication books you might have encountered in the past. This book contains more than 150 questions and answers that will provide you with an inside look from the man's perspective on how men view women, approach relationships, and think about their interactions with them.

After reading our book, you'll have a better understanding not only of how men think, act, and react, but also how you can use this understanding to improve your own life and your relationship with the opposite sex for years to come. You'll know how to avoid any of the potential mistakes you might be making. And you'll be secure in the knowledge that even if your man behaves differently from majority opinions we've offered here, it's just the way he is, and the problem is not with you.

So how did we get into this business of writing a book about men for women?

This book was not our idea. Never in the course of our business and marketing research careers did we ever conceive of writing a book—about men, no less. We're men. What do we know about the male-female dynamic outside of fooling our once-girlfriends into becoming our wives? Not much. So a book about men geared for women was not on our radar. At Solavista, we conduct market research to develop brands. For us, research is not simply data collection; it's a revelation about people and their behaviors. But because we are researchers, we know how to get answers. Looking back, the premise of this book and its data make perfect sense, in that it was born from the research mentality and not the author mentality. In a sense, we are the perfect men to compile this type of data. It's what we were trained to do all along.

It started out simply enough. All we were doing was meeting with an existing client of our marketing research services. We had been performing marketing research for her company for a few years, but we hadn't seen her in a while. She was one of our first clients and certainly one of our best. We were looking forward to seeing her again, catching up, and finding out what sort of market research project she had in store for us.

We remembered her as being the picture-perfect, modern executive. She was always well put together, with her Louis Vuitton briefcase, fresh-from-the-salon hair, Christian Louboutin power pumps on her feet, and Chanel in the air.

But on this day, she walked in and was a shell of the person we knew.

We knew she was different, no question. But what happened? What could morph the powerful woman we knew, who had the world by the tail, into someone we could hardly recognize? She just wanted to get down to business, so we let go of our curiosity and concern for the moment and got to the subject at hand, the next research project.

As we were wrapping up details at the end of our brainstorming session, she asked us a question out of the blue:

Client:	*"So I guess as researchers you could probably ask anyone anything on any topic, right?"*
Us:	*"Yes."* (Our witty reply)
Client:	*"It would be great if I could find out stuff about men."*
Us:	*"Why is that? What kind of stuff?"* (We start to sound like psychologists)

Client:	*"I don't know if you heard, but I got divorced recently. Getting back into dating has been a real eye-opener."*
Us:	*"Sorry to hear that. What's the big deal? Has it changed that much?"*
Client:	*"Yes. And the rules are different. I don't know what men really think. And no men I know will give me the straight answer. They sugarcoat the truth. It would be refreshing if, for once, I knew ahead of time why men act the way they do, so I could be more successful in dealing with them."*

At that moment, a light went on. Why couldn't we do that? Why couldn't we find out from women what they wanted to know, ask men, and then deliver the answers back to women? Why not? We're researchers. We have a research panel of male respondents we could leverage. We have the knowledge and the technology.

But, as researchers, we needed validation. We first needed to know if this premise would even work. Would other women be interested in the same type of feedback that our client was talking about?

So what did we do as typical research men presented with an atypical premise? We did a quick online poll asking 1,000 women the following question:

Would you pay for access to honest answers from a national cross-section of men on what they truly think and feel on any topic, based solely on questions you could ask anonymously?

We had 624 answers in less than nine hours, and 92.8 percent said yes.

So we then set off to (a) find out what women want to know about men and (b) ask men those questions to then (c) compile the answers in a book to share what we had found.

This is the book you are now reading.

You'll move through the questions in categories, and we'll start by tackling one of the big ones: communication. After that is the dating chapter, which covers questions and mistakes that might happen before you are in a relationship. Following logically is the relationship chapter, in which we discuss the insights and nuances of being in and managing a relationship with men. Romance is covered next, including how men feel about romance, what they think is romantic, and what they wish you knew about romance. Once romance has been discussed, the next step is sex, and we cover that topic head-on with a no-holds-barred approach that will probably be one of the biggest surprises in the book. Marriage is then discussed, and we reveal how men actually feel about being and staying married. We round out the data with our chapter on work and relating with and to men in the workplace. We finish with some final takeaways that men have for you, including what they say are the top mistakes women make.

So let's get right into it…

Chapter 1

COMMUNICATION

If you want to find a species that really knows how to communicate, relay their thoughts, express their feelings, and explain how they truly feel, it would be the adult male, wouldn't it, ladies?

Wrong.

Hey, we all know that men are somewhat challenged in the communication department. If you need someone to kill bugs, maintain a car, or set up a home Internet network, you could do worse than using a man. But looking to men for in-depth discussions addressing how they really feel? Not the best choice.

So, we took your questions about why men communicate the way they do and asked them to explain themselves. Interestingly, they had no problems communicating to us why they do what they do (and why they don't). Armed with what you're about to learn, you won't take your introspective gent and turn him into an emotional and verbal dynamo overnight. But you'll be closer to understanding why he behaves certain ways. And that's leaps and bounds ahead of most women.

So read on, and let's get to the bottom of one of life's mysteries: how and why men communicate.

When will he call me?

"I've dated my share of men through my share of years. There is always the common debate and game about when men need or want to call you, etc. So of any question I'd like to ask men, I'd like to start with basics: **how long do men really think they need to wait to call a woman after getting her phone number?**" —Raylee, age 28, dating

What the men say

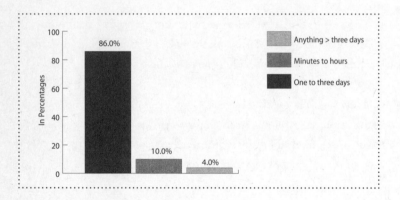

What men are really saying

If a man asks for your phone number, he plans to use it. Even if it's just to tell you that he is thinking about you, he'll call. Although men overwhelmingly said they would call anywhere between one and three days, to a man, just the act of calling means they are more serious about a potential date.

"That depends on what was agreed to at the moment she gave me her number. If nothing was said, then I usually wait one or two days." —Allen, age 27

"I would wait a day or so, depending upon my schedule." —Marvin, age 33

"I would call the next day briefly. This would be just to say I have your number, I am thinking about you, and I will call back to make specific plans." —Vincent, age 31

What to look out for: Hoping that even though it's been over a week and he hasn't called, he may still be interested.

Be patient. He's going to call. Men told us that they will not ask for a woman's number if they don't have any intention of calling. Granted, he will probably wait the obligatory three days, but if he is still interested, he won't let the chance of a date with you slip through his fingers. He wants to time the call so it doesn't appear that he is too eager; however, if it's been a week and there's been no call, there is a very slim chance that you'll hear the phone ring.

Why doesn't he call?

"I've gone out on several dates with various men, and I've found that sometimes, for reasons I don't know, men will simply not call me back after a date. It's not just when we've had sex, although that has happened as well. I'm frustrated about why it always seems to happen, so I want to know: **why don't men call back, even when we have a great time together?**"—Carissa, age 32, single

What the men say

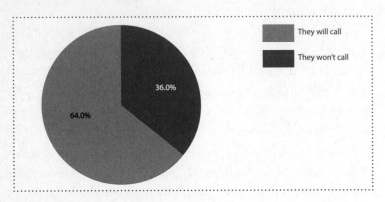

They will call

They won't call

36.0%

64.0%

What men are really saying

The majority of men, 64 percent, say they don't "just stop calling" a woman without reason. Most men feel that if they had a good time, there would be no reason not to call, and even if the good-time feeling wasn't mutual, they would call out of respect.

"I generally don't go out with someone unless I'm fairly comfortable and sure I'm going to have a good time. This gives me incentive to call back. Even if I don't have a good time, I find it to be common courtesy to call back. If this is the case, then I make it a point to establish a friendship and nothing more."
—Kody, age 20

"If I have a good time, I will pursue the woman to either continue advancing in our relationship or become friends. I don't see why everyone can't try to be friends with everyone. I am not losing anything from calling her back." —Jared, age 24

So why don't 36 percent of men call women back? Well, it can be as simple as they really didn't have a good time or they don't feel like being rejected.

"Well, sometimes one person's perception of having fun can vary a bit from another. Maybe I had a good time but was just not interested in anything remotely serious; maybe something was said that evening that flashed warning signs. Or in the case of women who sleep with men on the first date and don't get a call, that's a no-brainer: the game is over." —Marc, age 38

"You had a good time. That doesn't mean I had a great time. Telling someone something unpleasant isn't going to make the date any better. Forget about it and move on." —Jim, age 61

"Having a great time must be consensual. While you might have had a great time, it doesn't mean that he did. A few reasons for not calling back are: (1) he thinks you didn't have a good time and you'll reject him; (2) he just wanted to get laid; (3) he met someone else; (4) you had a good time and he didn't."
—Arnold, age 25

What to look out for: Misreading how well the date actually went. You might think you both had a great time, especially when sex was involved. The problem is men don't equate sex with a great time. For men, sex equals sex. He may very well have sex with you, even if he didn't enjoy the date very much. You should understand that sex doesn't mean you'll hear from him again. (This also can occur when sex isn't in the picture.) You need to read the date from multiple communication angles: Is he laughing? Is he asking you questions? Is he engaged with you on many topics? Take a larger view of how the communication is going, and this will give you a better chance for that callback to take place.

Should I call?

"I'm definitely on the fast track in a very large pharmaceutical company. I've been dating for more than twenty years, but I still get frustrated about protocol in today's dating environment. I want to know once and for all: **is it acceptable for a woman to call for the first date and/or the second date?**" —Danielle, age 38, dating

What the men say

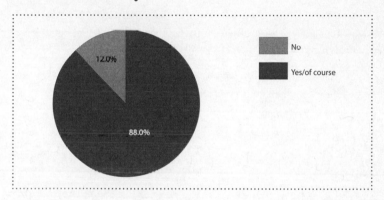

No

Yes/of course

12.0%

88.0%

What men are really saying

Ladies, it's time to man up and make the first move. If you are really into the guy, don't sit by the phone waiting for him to call; pick up the phone and get yourself that date.

> "Why not? It's the twenty-first century. A woman can do what she wants, and it's completely refreshing for her to make the bold move. It's also nice to take the guesswork out of the equation."
> —Darius, age 37

"I'd almost prefer it because it means fewer headaches for me. Plus, women want to pay for dinners and do things men traditionally do, so by all means, let her call." —Chad, age 31

Some men are just plain old-fashioned and don't think it's the woman's place.

"No, because women can't do so. They're passive by nature, and it always comes across as a 'friend' call because they rarely take the initiative or responsibility for what they want." —Jim, age 27

"I know in this day and age it might be okay, but I still want to decide who, when, and how often I date, so I need to make the calls." —Doug, age 43

What to look out for: You haven't taken charge to do what you really want.

The majority of men don't mind you calling them; they actually find it flattering. It has the same effect on men that it has on you. If you make the first move and ask him on a date, it shows him you are into him, and if you call him to ask him out for a second date, it shows that he did something right and you're willing to see him again. Use this to your advantage.

What's the deal with lame pickup lines?

"I've found that the men I date just aren't very serious. It's not the age of the men—I typically date men older than me. It's the fact that I find the corny and cliché stuff men do to be more style over substance. I've always wanted to know: **why do men use lame pickup lines to meet women?**"
—Sara, age 22, single

What the men say

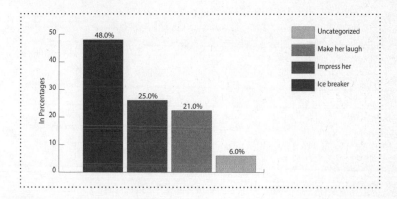

What men are really saying

Men need a tactic to break the ice with a woman and think that pickup lines, poems, and jokes are an easy way to do it. That's why 48 percent of men say they've used or would use this approach.

"It is a way to make a connection. Some men like to do this with humor, some with a flare of sentiment. Both are meant to get noticed a bit and to stand out a bit, and at least make that experience different in a hopefully positive way." —Paul, age 30

"Men need a way to break the ice. We do not like to be rejected, so by coming up with a joke or poem, it makes it easy for us to break the ice and get things started. If they are doomed to fail, we can tell and can avert the situation before we feel rejected." —Fabian, age 31

While it's a similar premise to breaking the ice, impressing a woman came in second, with 30 percent of men responding the same way.

"They are trying to impress the woman by showing that they have a creative side. Most men think that women love to be romanced with cheesy things like jokes or poems." —Ryan, age 23

"It's part of the game. They're doing everything they can to impress you. Men are constantly told that women are looking for men who make them laugh, and poetry has always been something that has been claimed to be romantic." —Keith, age 33

What to look out for: Dismissing the efforts that men go through to impress you.

When a man is interested in you, he will look for an opening, either to impress you or to relate to you quickly. By dismissing his efforts, you are essentially dismissing him. What this does, unfortunately, is close you off to a key way men use to try to communicate with you. What's more powerful for you is not to focus on the tactic of how men approach you, but on the fact that they are approaching you. Embracing the interest they have in you makes the flow of communication that much easier.

Why won't he open up?

"I'm currently dating a man who doesn't like to talk. It's not that he doesn't open up to me, as he's done that. But what's frustrating is that in daily life, he doesn't have much to say. When I ask him how he is, I feel as though my question falls on deaf ears. So I'd like to know: **why is it that most men don't like to talk?**" —Amy, age 39, single

What the men say

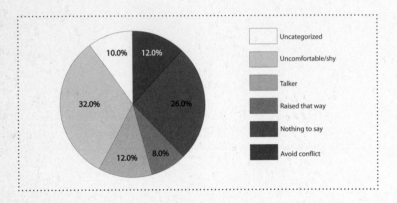

Uncategorized
Uncomfortable/shy
Talker
Raised that way
Nothing to say
Avoid conflict

10.0%   12.0%

32.0%

26.0%

12.0%   8.0%

What men are really saying

From the feedback we received, men believe either they were brought up not to talk about their feelings and/or they feel uncomfortable or weak doing so. The majority of men, 32 percent, said they can't talk about how they feel because they are just too shy.

"Most men, first of all, like to keep things to themselves. We do not like to share problems or how we are feeling because we want to solve those problems on our own and not look weak." —Chris, age 32

"I really don't want to share every problem I have with my wife because I don't think she needs the aggravation of dealing with her problems and my problems. It's better for the relationship that I work these things out instead of stressing her out with my problems." —Rich, age 46

"In the category of men who do not talk a lot, we must keep in mind that they may only seem that way because they are uncomfortable or shy. Maybe when they are around close friends or in the right setting, they will talk nonstop. Perhaps you may need to take initiative and engage him (not aggressively, of course). After that, it's up to him to step up to the plate or not. Men are quiet because they are nervous, mentally occupied, or simply because they don't talk a lot." —Ryan, age 20

While some men just don't feel comfortable talking, 26 percent say they don't because they just don't have anything to say. However, some did qualify this: they are not saying anything because they aren't interested in the woman and don't want to share with her.

"We talk when we have something to say or something really needs to be discussed. Not interested that much in idle chitchat for no reason." —Keith, age 33

Men lose interest in sharing in much the same way that women lose interest in listening.

"She's heard all of my stories because I've told her all my stories. Why discuss the mundane? It's like when I ask my kid how school was today or what did you learn. His response is always 'fine' and nothing. I don't take it that he loves me any less. While my wife and I have great days and some that are bad, most are really average. It doesn't mean that because I'm not gushing over her every word that I don't love her or that I care for her less; it's just an average day, and I don't have much to say." —Barry, age 34

What to look out for: Assuming that his interest in conversation is the same as yours.

The two main reasons men cite for not opening up to you: being so comfortable around you that they can spend quiet time without the feeling of awkward silence, or they don't yet feel comfortable around you to open up. You need to assess where you are in the relationship with the man before making assumptions about why he doesn't open up as much as you'd like. This will give you the information you need to make communication easier for him and deepen your relationship with him.

Why is it so hard for men to express their feelings?

"I've been married to my husband for more than ten years, but over the years of marriage, he has become more and more withdrawn, or so it seems. Over the past year, when he lost his job and his mother passed away, he refused to talk about it and open up to me. I've tried to coax him out of his shell, but he's not budging. **Why can't men talk about how they feel?**" —"Moo," age 45, married

What the men say

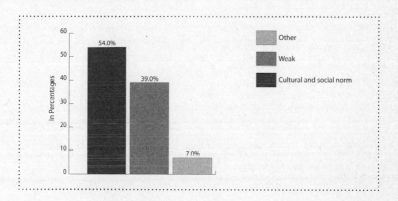

What men are really saying

In fact, 54 percent of men say it's just difficult for them to share how they are feeling. They see it as a cultural and social norm for men.

"Because I tend to keep my thoughts to myself and I cannot open up and freely give information. I was brought up in my family

that men deal with things on their own, and because of that, I have a hard time saying exactly how I feel about some things."
—James, age 27

"It is hard for us to express our feelings because, quite frankly, often times we don't really know how we feel. We're brought up this way. There are other times we do know, but we need to figure it out and process our feelings before we let you know what those feelings are." —Shelby, age 29

Other than just not being able to show their emotions, men perceive being emotional as being weak. Thirty-nine percent of men feel that being a man means being macho, and emotions and talking about how they feel takes away from that.

"We have been conditioned all of our lives that men need to be tough, and expressing feelings is a sign of weakness. Men are very prideful, and when you express your true feelings, it can be a serious blow to your ego." —James, age 39

"Some men find it hard to express their feelings because many of us grew up thinking that it was macho and manly not to cry or show pain. We look weak. This would be one reason. Another would be that a lot of men tend to be very emotional behind this wall they build, and expressing emotion allows someone behind that wall, which gives them the opportunity, whether they would or not, to exploit that and hurt the man. Instead of letting anyone in, many men just clam up." —Logan, age 26

What to look out for: Believing that men will open up only when they're in a relationship.

Unfortunately for "Moo," men tell us they just aren't likely to share their feelings and what they are going through. While most women think this isn't natural because they feel better sharing everything, men tell us that they just don't think the same way. If you want to get a man to open up, try a different approach. Still, you need to respect the fact that he might not want to talk and might only do so when he's ready. Many men told us that this is how they were raised and it's their coping skill. It might not be the way you'd prefer he handle it, but it's how many men do.

Why is asking to talk a big deal?

"I've noticed that every time I want to have a talk with my boyfriend, I get the feeling that he's apprehensive. I've realized it with my current boyfriend, but I recall that it's also happened with my past boyfriends as well. I know I'm not the only one who wants to know: **what is it about being asked to have a talk that turns men off?**"
—Stephanie, age 53, single

What the men say

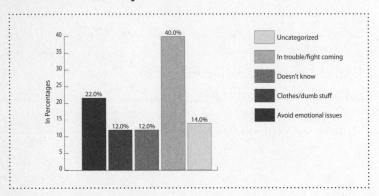

What men are really saying

For men, the biggest turnoff with talking is they always get the feeling they are in trouble or the talk will lead to a fight. In fact, 40 percent of men try to avoid talking to you for just that reason.

"This does not always turn us off. In most cases, from our perspective, a woman asking to have a discussion usually leads to something negative toward us. It may help to clarify the topic when asking for a discussion." —David, age 37

"Usually a 'talk' or 'discussion' is like saying, 'You messed up' or 'Here comes something I probably don't want to talk about.' Try just easing into the conversation. This way you can sneak it in like you're just talking. Men don't like 'scheduled' conversations." —Jonathan, age 38

Outside of dreading the fight that might come out of talking, 19 percent of men don't like to talk because they don't like the emotions involved. Many of the male respondents told us they tried to avoid emotional issues, and thus avoid talking.

"Because usually women want to talk about things that make a man uncomfortable. Things like their mood or their deep feelings." —Jake, age 36

"I think because it's going to involve emotions, and we are not good at talking about them. We can be romantic, but we can't talk about it. We just do it (if at all)." —Webster, age 40

What to look out for: Approaching a conversation with your man the way you would your female friends to get him to engage.

You don't want to start out a conversation with a man by saying "We need to talk" or "Can we talk?" Doing so will automatically put men on the defensive, and certain words like "discussion" just have a negative/serious connotation. If you want to get your man to talk to you, timing and approach are everything. Hone that skill by trying different approaches to see what works with your man, and your world can open up. Really.

How do men justify lies?

"I separated from my husband just over four months ago. Some of our mutual friends are still friendly with my husband and are spilling the beans about some of the aspects of our relationship *he* believed were responsible for our breakup. None of what I've heard from friends were things my ex ever told me. I guess my question is: **would you lie to your girlfriend if you feel the truth would only hurt her?**"
—Mary, age 57, separated

What the men say

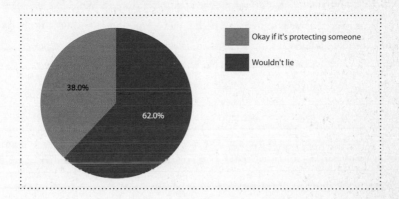

Okay if it's protecting someone

Wouldn't lie

38.0%

62.0%

What men are really saying

Honesty is the best policy, and men abide by this saying. Sixty-two percent of men say they wouldn't lie to their girlfriend just to spare her feelings.

"Lying is never acceptable in a relationship, even if you believe it is protecting your loved one. A true, honest relationship is the only way to know if you are really in love or not. If you feel the need to lie, even if your loved one will never find out, then you are not being a good significant other. Love is entirely about honesty and comfort with one another. Lying goes against everything true love means." —Robert, age 20

"Lying about anything of importance is likely to blow up in your face, because even if she doesn't learn the truth, there's a good chance she'll know or strongly suspect that you are lying. She'll assume that where there is one lie, there are others, and not all of them will be for her own good. If you are lying about a small thing, such as how much you like the way she looks in those blue pants, go ahead and lie, but do your best to believe in the lie yourself." —Al, age 49

But a whole bunch of men think a little white lie never hurt anybody, especially if the truth hurts worse than not knowing. Thirty-eight percent of men think it's okay to lie if you are protecting the one you love.

"Well it really depends on what the lie was about. If it was about cheating on her, well, that's not too honorable, but say someone said something really nasty about her and he doesn't tell her because he doesn't want her to be hurt. Any situation like that, then I can understand." —Marc, age 38

"Men do a lot of lying to protect the ones we care about. It sounds crazy, but in our minds to protect the ones we love it is better to lie than say something we know will hurt them."
—Hunter, age 28

What to look out for: Thinking that all lies are equal.

Most men don't like to protect the feelings of their significant others through lying; however, they don't view all lies the same. To men, "little white lies" are a tool to help keep relationships protected and to avoid confrontation. In Mary's case, though, it wasn't about lying to protect her, it was more lying to avoid problems. But you can take solace that when communicating with men, most men view lies not as a way to hurt you, but to protect you.

He gave in, so I "won," right?

"My husband and I have been having some arguments as of late, and I find it increasingly straining to my relationship. Maybe it sounds a bit devious, but I'd really like to know from the male perspective: **what is the fastest way to settle an argument?**" —Heather, age 41, married

What the men say

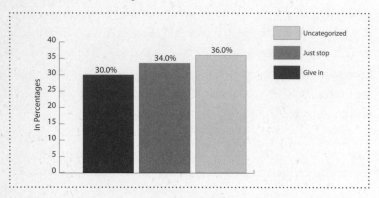

Legend:
- Uncategorized
- Just stop
- Give in

Bar values: 30.0%, 34.0%, 36.0%
Y-axis: In Percentages (0–40)

What men are really saying

The majority of men have a simple method for settling an argument: they just stop. They take some time to let cooler heads prevail and just walk away for a bit.

> "The fastest way to settle an argument is to say, 'Let's agree to disagree,' and exit the room. The statement represents an end, and leaving the room does not allow us to continue to argue with you." —Rolph, age 28

"To get it over with quickly, you have to be prepared to leave it unresolved. You need to decide if you need to win the argument, or just end it. You may find it helpful to choose your battles ahead of time, as well. If the road ahead looks bumpy, decide how important the topic is. If you then decide to proceed, you should stick to the plan and use persuasive language. If you find that you can't win, you can end an unpleasant argument quickly by apologizing, while still keeping the door open for later discussion. Phrases like 'Can we both sleep on this?' indicate that you are accepting that it is unresolved, but that you would still like to pursue an amicable solution." —Stern, age 45

"When just stopping an argument doesn't work, my next plan of attack is to give in. However, one must tread lightly not to piss off the other party by giving in too quickly." —Derek, age 32

"Admit you're wrong. Who is wrong or right is irrelevant because in most cases both people know anyway. Admitting you're wrong (even if not the case) shows ownership of the issue, shows willingness to change the situation, and keeps the peace." —Andy, age 36

"The fastest way to settle an argument is to give up. It isn't the best way (which would be to compromise and understand the position of the other), but simply giving up ends the argument. It can, however, start another argument right away." —Bryan, age 26

What to look out for: Assuming that because he gives in it means you won the argument. In fact, sometimes it doesn't get you anywhere.

Settling the argument doesn't mean the problem is resolved. You need to have a conversation to get both of you to think about the issue, rather than focus on how to end the argument without getting to the bottom of it.

Do men even value our opinions?

"My husband seems to not have any issues talking about our relationship or his feelings toward me, but when it comes to other topics outside our marriage, it seems like he couldn't care less. My question for men is: **other than your relationship, do you even care how women feel about various topics?**" —Sally, age 32, married

What the men say

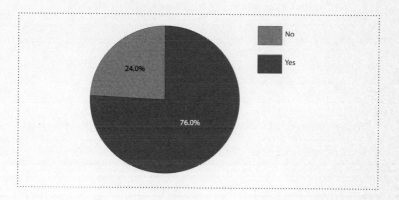

What men are really saying

Make sure you are sitting down, ladies, because we've got a surprise for you. Seventy-six percent of men say they do care and want to hear about stuff going on in your life, even if it doesn't involve them.

> "I would love to know everything, because then that would mean I know more about you...it would be more satisfying to expand

the horizons and get to know everything about you. There will be more to converse over and more to experience in that manner." —Sterling, age 37

"If we were in a relationship, of course I would want to know about how you feel in the other situations in your life as well. Such emotions are fundamental to your character and experience, and properly being shared and appreciated are elements in potential growth for the things that are shared together." —Paul, age 30

While men care about what you are feeling if it directly affects them, there are some who just couldn't care less if it's about anything else.

"Unless it directly affects me, I could care less. If it is something important, yeah, I would like to know, but in general I don't want to hear it at all." —Mark, age 21

"No, we don't really want to hear about how you're feeling, outside of what we have going on." —Matt, age 33

What to look out for: Believing that men put equal value on all topics of communication.

Actually, men can have a short attention span (surprise!), and sometimes, although they care, they just might be at their limit of processing your information. This can lead to their responding with the obligatory "uh-huh" to act like they are listening and not offend you. Keeping in mind how much you are telling your man and whether or not he may be on information overload will lead to better and more engaging conversations.

Why can't men say what they mean?

"When my husband and I are having a discussion, I take him at his actual word. However, when I call him out using his words or wording, he insists that I just know what he means and what he is trying to say. I see this as straightforward, but he's making it complicated, so I'd like to know: **why can't men just say what they mean?**" —Lindsay, age 33, married

What the men say

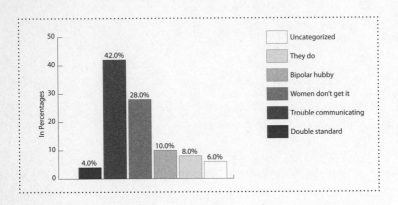

What men are really saying

Bottom line is that men are not great communicators. The majority of men (70 percent) think they either can't say what they want, how they want, or they just don't feel comfortable talking about their feelings and certain things.

"I will be honest: most of the time my brain and my mouth don't always connect. I say something without thinking, and then I have two options. One, correct myself and look like I don't know what I am saying, or two, just go with it, and deal with the consequences. Sometimes I choose the latter." —Thomas, age 33

"Men who cannot say what they mean are talking faster than they are thinking. This could be a sign that they are not fully engaged in the conversation. They may need to have an understanding of how important the topic is to the woman first before they will know that a thoughtful response is necessary. Without that basis, a casual response will often be natural." —Stern, age 45

Twenty-eight percent of men also feel that when they do talk to women about whatever the topic may be, women just don't seem to get the point.

"Why can't women take things the way they are intended? It shouldn't be a battle in accuracy or our grasp of language. The meaning is what matters to men, not the actual words." —Dan, age 30

"They generally do [say what they mean]. It's usually women who construe it as something else and take it another way. The word 'sure' doesn't mean 'yes, but I don't want to.' It means 'sure.' The key is not twisting the words around. If your husband is lying to you, it generally means he's cheating unless it's near your anniversary or birthday." —Darrel, age 25

What to look out for: Cataloging his words to use against him later.

You're not in a court of law. When it comes to communication, it's much more powerful for you to know what he means and not complicate the issue by quoting what he says. Don't overthink his answer. Granted, 8 percent of the men we surveyed said your guy means what he says, and yes, in court, you can prove him wrong, but you need to think what that behavior costs your relationship in the long run.

Why doesn't he always believe me?

"I have been dating a man for over a year. Things are going well. He seems to really care for me and trust me, but I'm sensing that anything I tell him is always viewed skeptically. When I asked him about why he seemed to doubt me, he said, 'All women hide the truth to a degree; I'm just trying to figure out yours.' This stumped me. I want the relationship to progress, but I also don't want to be judged as insincere, and I just find it hard to believe that all men feel this way. I suppose I'm trying to get to the root of what's bugged him in the past, so I'd like to know: **which lies do men hear from women most often?**" —Kathy, age 22, dating

What the men say

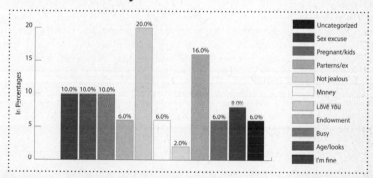

What men are really saying

Hate to tell you, ladies, but men think you lie a lot, and about a lot of different things. The most common lie—20 percent, in fact—just happens to be "I love you."

"I have heard many women say 'I will love you forever,' but they never mean it. :(" —Rusty, age 35

"I guess lies like 'you're the best I ever had,' 'you're the best lover,' 'I will always love you, even though we may not be together,' 'I love you, but I'm not in love with you.' LOL." —Chris, age 30

The second most common type of lie revolves around past relationships. Sixteen percent of men are used to hearing women lying about the number of partners they've had and the status of her and an ex.

"The most common one—the number of men they've slept with previously. It's always at least twice the number she gives." —Emmett, age 21, NY

"When they say that the one guy she hangs out with is just her best friend, you know it's complete bullshit!" —Chris, age 20, CA

What to look out for: Thinking that men don't doubt you.

The reality is that men are skeptical about you and everything you say. Thus they're always trying to figure you out. Think about this: at some point you've probably given men information that wasn't true: your age, weight, sexual history, hair color, fantasies, etc. Men have to weed through all this misinformation to figure out where the truth is. Are you just insecure? Are you shy? Do you have something to hide? What you can do is be up front and honest with your man. Let the chips fall where they may. The truth always comes out eventually, so control the information. This is what modern, progressive, enlightened women do.

Why do men lie about the little things?

"My husband lies about the littlest, stupidest things. Like when he left work, or if he paid a bill on the sixteenth and it was actually the eighteenth. I can't figure out what's in it for him to do this? I get mad at him for this. Not the lies, but the fact that he seems to 'need' to lie to me. I really don't care about if he paid the bill two days after he said he did; it's the little lies that irritate me. But now I have to wonder if he's willing to lie about these little things, could he be lying about bigger things too? I gotta know: **why do you men lie about the smallest things?**" —Kelly, age 32, married

What the men say

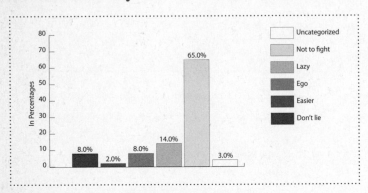

What men are really saying

We get a lot of questions around the topic of lying. For most men, the big reason why they lie is pretty simple. A whopping 65 percent of men say they lie so there won't be any fighting.

"We lie, even about small things, because we want to avoid fights. We don't like fighting with you, so if we think some bit of information will set off an argument, we try to hide it." —Kev, age 25

"We lie because women will flip out sooooooooooo bad over the stupidest little thing. If they didn't do that and were more understanding, we would be more truthful." —Nicholas, age 18

Coming in a distant second with 14 percent is sheer laziness. Men say they are too lazy to do something, and lying is just the easier alternative.

"I lie like that because I'm preoccupied and don't want to do [something], or I'm simply being lazy." —Eric, age 19

"I believe it can be one of two things—laziness or not wanting to let you down. It's ironic that my opinion is so polarized." —Gerald, age 46

What to look out for: Thinking that men lie to cover their tracks. To answer Kelly's question about why men lie about the little things is an easy one: men think lying about something small is the better option than starting a big fight over that little thing. If the little lies bother you, then talk to your man about it and explain that the honest answer won't lead to a fight.

Omit ~~needless~~ words

"Like most women, I've had my share of boyfriends in my past, but I just can't seem to understand why they don't listen when I talk about my day or things of that nature. I sense that men get frustrated when women talk about more mundane, but important topics, but still, I'd like to know what is driving that frustration, so my question is this: **what is the most frustrating thing about communicating with women in general?**" —Jacqueline, age 23, single

What the men say

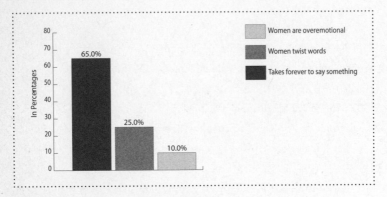

What men are really saying

There are two major issues that men have with women with respect to their communication skills. Sixty-five percent of the men said in one way or another, it takes forever for a woman to say what she wants, and 25 percent said they feel women tend to twist their words around.

"At times, some women can be hard to communicate with because they have trouble getting their point across succinctly. When someone has not taken the time to separate the wheat from the chaff, I get frustrated by the energy I have to devote in order to boil it down to the relevant pieces. A recent example: my wife's description of a work incident. She related the entire concern to me, rather than distilling it down to a specific point. Instead of getting the information or wanting to console her frustration, I had to take the time to hear all of the intricate details of the events that led up to the real reason she was upset." —Stern, age 45

"I'd say the most frustrating thing with women communicating in general is when they twist your words into something you didn't say. Another frustrating thing is when they say 'Can I ask you a question?' Just ask it! You don't need to start the question with a question asking if you can ask me something." —Chris, age 25

Men also get frustrated when it comes to the emotional aspect of communicating. They think that women either assume men are emotionally inept and come into a conversation with that premise, or that women tend to make everything overemotional.

"I think sometimes women have a lot of stereotypical ideas about men—that we're not in touch emotionally, that we're only interested in sex, that we're not intelligent. The usual clichés. It is frustrating to communicate with women who are clearly basing their thought process upon these clichés." —Matt, age 20

"[The most frustrating thing about communicating with women in general is] the emotions women put with everything that we are discussing. For example, I may be discussing a very specific subject involving her that I want to resolve, but when the emotions take over, she immediately sees this as an attack on her as a whole, when really all I'm thinking is 'Can't you do X differently?'"
—Jerrold, age 37

What to look out for: Assuming your particular communication style always works.

If you want your man to engage more willingly with you and not tune you out, there are a few key tips you can follow. Reduce the drama from the conversation and get to the point quickly. If men are interested in the backstory of your situation, they'll ask. Otherwise, use the abridged version to get him interested first.

What really moves him?

"My boyfriend and I live together. I love him dearly and tell him so all the time. But I'm thinking now that perhaps I'm saying it so often that it's losing some meaning. It would be great to find out: **how often do men like to be told they're loved, or do they prefer some other compliment?**" —Tamara, age 27, single

What the men say

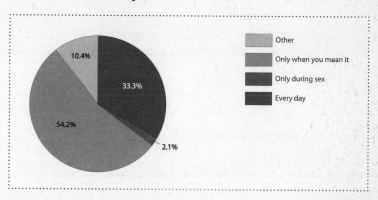

33.3%

10.4%

54.2%

2.1%

Other

Only when you mean it

Only during sex

Every day

What men are really saying

Men love to be loved, but they don't like hearing it just because it seems like the thing to say. The majority of men, 54 percent, say they only want to hear "I love you" when you actually mean it.

"Well if you say it too often and you don't mean it, then there is no value to it, since we are going to know that you're saying it just to try to make either us or yourself feel better by the tone of your voice. Therefore, if you say it when you really mean it, it means a lot more." —Ryan, age 23

"A declaration of love is only meaningful if there is real meaning behind it, so while I like to hear it as often as possible, only when there is true sentiment behind it. And in my opinion, there is no greater compliment!" —Matt, age 20

Deep down most men are hopeless romantics. In fact, 33 percent say they love to hear that they are loved every day.

"I like to hear this every day, but still only want to hear it when you mean it. Most men don't want to be showered with compliments, but knowing what we do that is appreciated by you is appreciated by us." —Paul, age 30

"I like to hear my wife tell me she loves me every day. It's not that I think she doesn't, it's just that I like to be reminded. I would only prefer another compliment if she really meant it. However sometimes too much can be a bad thing." —Brian, age 21

What to look out for: Underestimating how powerfully men view the phrase "I love you."

Everyone wants to know they are loved and appreciated; men are no different from women on that account. So if you love your man, let him know, and share it with him. Just don't say it because you think it's expected. Instead, the real power is saying it when you mean it.

Why do men always want to fix things?

"Every time I tell my husband about a problem I might be having at work, he immediately wants to jump in and tell me how to fix the issue. I love him; don't get me wrong. He's full of advice, but starts giving me suggestions on how to handle the problem without knowing if I've already addressed it. I'm looking to find out: **why is it that when women need to vent about something, men always try to fix it?**" —Erin, age 22, married

What the men say

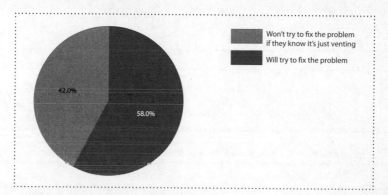

42.0%

58.0%

Won't try to fix the problem if they know it's just venting

Will try to fix the problem

What men are really saying

Men are doers and are inclined to fix things; it's just in their nature. So it should come as no surprise that 58 percent said they will try to solve the problem if they see their significant other is upset about something.

"I like keeping things in the positive balance, and repairing or fixing things is what I'm good at. It's not meant to be mean. Giving a response rather than just listening is my way of showing her that I'm listening and want to help rather than just being selfish and not caring." —Thomas, age 24

"Because that's what we're good at! We rarely vent. We talk about how something has gone wrong to figure out how to make it right. If you don't do that, or don't want us to do that, you need to make it clear from the start. 'I am just venting.' We will listen. Then go back to something else and forget about it." —Blaise, age 40

While most men are fixers, 42 percent say they won't as long as you tell them you are just venting.

"To get him to listen, let him know that you are just venting and that you don't want him to fix it. If you are blowing off steam and he tries to fix it, then the situation becomes more stressful." —Ozzie, age 30

"Tell him to let you have your conversation as a venting process, and just listen and just comment with concern and let you be your own person." —John, age 54

What to look out for: You assume that your man can distinguish when you're venting from times when you need his help.

Instead of getting angry with men when they're trying to help, you should let your man know up front what you want out of the conversation. Set expectations. Doing so is a very powerful communication tool.

Why do men flirt so much?

"I recently met a great man. He is everything I really want in a man, and potentially a partner or husband, except this one tiny habit that absolutely drives me crazy. He flirts. A lot. I don't see why he needs to do this, especially in front of me. I think it's childish and disrespectful. It almost feels like cheating. I'm not insecure about it; it's simply annoying to me, and I just wish he'd stop. But it's also the one thing that I think will hold us back from moving forward. So I'd like to find out: **why do men feel the need to flirt with every chick they see?**"
—Pamela, age 26, single

What the men say

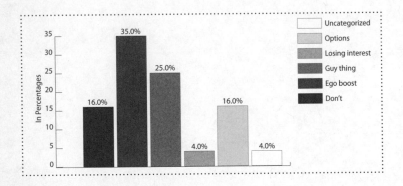

What men are really saying

Everyone wants to feel attractive, and men are no different, so it came as no surprise to us that 35 percent of men say they flirt for the ego boost. Sometimes it just feels good to be reminded you've still got it.

"It makes us feel good about ourselves to make us believe that we still are desired. Sometimes our spouses don't show us that, and we just want a little reassurance that we still got 'it.' Women do it also for the exact same reason." —Matt, age 33

"Flirting when we are in a relationship is just a way to make us feel good. It lets us know that we still got it and look good and our significant other isn't just saying so because she is expected to say that." —Gray, age 27

Men are natural flirts, and 25 percent agree that's it's just a guy thing. They can't help it. They see an attractive woman, and they flirt with her.

"Even being in a relationship, I admit I do flirt with some girls. It's something in my DNA; I just can't help it. I always have done it, and it's always harmless. I never let it progress past just a compliment or two." —Chet, age 18

"Well you see, you have to be a man to understand. It's like asking a woman, 'Why do you want to go into every store at the mall?' It's just how it is." —Leeroy, age 18

What to look out for: Presuming that flirting equals cheating. Most men say that flirting is just something they do, whether the reason is that it gives them a needed ego boost or that it is just something ingrained in men's DNA. While in some cases it might break up a couple, men say that if it's just harmless flirting, women should cut them some slack.

Why does he want to fight?

"Okay, I've always wondered why my ex-husband would rather get into arguments rather than talk about things. This factor alone was the main reason for my divorce. I think if we could have talked things out, it would have been different, but the barriers always got in the way. I'd like to find out if all men do this so I'd love to know: **why do men prefer arguments over discussions?**" —Becky, age 36, single

What the men say

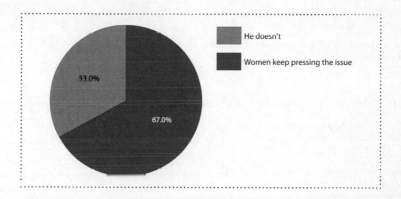

He doesn't

Women keep pressing the issue

33.0%

67.0%

What men are really saying

Women just can't leave well enough alone, say a majority of men. A whopping 67 percent of men felt that instead of just accepting the fact that men don't want to talk, women would nag and press the issue until an argument ensues.

"In my experience, if you just say, 'I don't want to talk about it,' a lot of women will continue to bring things up over and over again. But if these topics come up in a fight, women are more likely to leave it alone for a longer period of time." —Ryan, age 27

"Most of the time when we say we don't want to talk about something, our partner gets mad at us and does not respect our reasoning or consider what may be going on with us at the time." —Dexter, age 37

"Because when [men] 'don't want to talk about it,' they are nagged, badgered, and pushed into talking about it. It is like having a pit bull sink its teeth into a man's emotions." —Arlo, age 61

Why do women assume that men start fights as opposed to talking it out? Many men didn't believe they did. In fact, some said they'd rather talk about problems than fight about them.

"Men actually want to fight and argue? That's too much work. Discuss it like rational people." —Dale, age 35

"I don't think it's fair to generalize that all men like to pick fights rather than talk. The real problem is that sometimes our answer isn't what they want to hear, and if they try to get us to change our view, that has the potential for an argument." —William, age 27

What to look out for: Believing that men would rather argue than talk.

The reality is many men don't have much of an issue with talking. The problems come in when you cannot accept their answer. The empowering move for you is to learn to accept his viewpoint or opinion. You may not agree with it, but accepting it can simmer down some of those arguments. You can more easily communicate with men in that fashion instead of trying to convert him to your line of thinking.

Why does he always side with his mother over me?

"I'm officially tired of arguing with my husband's family. Even when I just disagree with him about his or his mom's opinion, he never seems to support me. I'm to the point where I won't put up with this anymore, but I'm not quite sure if this is typical behavior for all men or if it is just my 'mama's boy' husband. So I'd like the inside opinion of men to find out: **why is it that even if he knows I'm in the right, he sides with his mother?**" —Tennille, age 32, married

What the men say

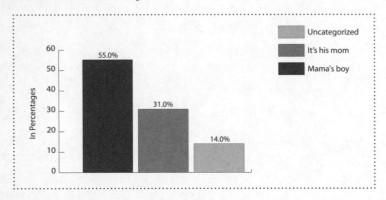

What men are really saying

The majority of men agree that any man who sides with his mother all the time is a "mama's boy." Some men idolize their mothers to the point that they can't disappoint them in any way. Men respect their mother's opinion. Their mothers probably helped them a lot through life, and the men will always remember that she's the one who gave them advice and listened to them and raised them to be the men they are.

> "Men are really mama's boys at heart. Our moms have had our back since we were born. We know that no matter what, they always will. No matter how secure I feel in our relationship, I know my mom is never going anywhere." —Britton, age 29

> "He obviously loves and respects his mother, and it is clouding his judgment as to who is in the right in arguments. Maybe he still seeks her approval." —Jeff, age 41

> "Well, she is the one who raised him, and she has been a molder of who he is, so it is only natural he will side with her. Especially if they are close because he may not want to hurt her." —Terius, age 31

> "He probably has some type of an attachment issue whereby he feels the need to protect his mom and probably does not want her to see that he may disagree with her. Growing up, to him, his mom was the boss and always knew right from wrong…it would seem he never reformed this concept to one that would indicate you, your husband, and your mother-in-law are on more equal grounds." —Marion, age 37

While it may be easy to blindly accuse your man of siding with his mother over you, take into consideration the issues you and he are arguing about. How much does his upbringing factor into the conversation? How much of your position is based on your upbringing? This question was one in which many men offered solutions to the issues as well as their feedback. Some of the most popular are summarized here:

"I'd say that there are two likely situations happening here. One: he is siding with you more than you recognize; and two: he would rather upset you than dare to disappoint his mother."
—Tony, age 37

"Your best bet is to minimize the number of situations where he is having to make a choice between you and his mom."
—Enrique, age 29

"Make your important decisions together without anyone else around." —Sampson, age 43

"I think he needs to get a clue and break up with his mom. Tell your mama's boy husband to stop suckling at his mother's teat and be a man!" —Darby, age 35

What to look out for: Believing that because he's with you makes you automatically correct. Believing that if and when he sides with his mom, it means he's against you personally.

Women have different relationships with their mothers than men do. While the intent isn't to imply that women don't respect or weren't brought up to respect their mothers, the point is that many men have been conditioned to respect their mother's opinion. When it comes to your mother-in-law, pick your battles and try to understand he can be with you and for you and still disagree with you too.

Why do men talk differently around "the guys"?

"I met my husband about three years ago and was married to him recently. Because we met overseas (we work in the same industry that has us working in China for stretches of time), during the first year and a half, we spent a lot of time together. Now that we are back in the States and married, I'm starting to see him interact more often and differently with his friends than I ever saw before. Perhaps I'm overreacting, but I'd like to know: **why does he talk differently when he's with me and when he's with his friends? How can I address this?**" —Sherry, age 33, married

What the men say

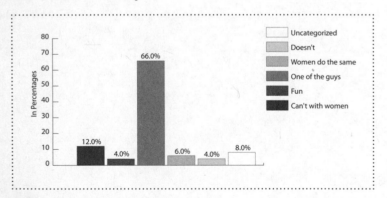

What men are really saying

The majority of men say that as soon as they are surrounded by their male friends, they just become "one of the men."

"They change their pattern of speech because there is a different code of conduct with 'the men' than with you. [It's] the same reason you talk to your boss differently than you talk to [your husband]."
—Carl, age 23

"Men change their speech patterns around other men so that they come off as masculine. Things you would never say in front of a woman because it would be offensive and/or pig-headed make us feel masculine around other men. We need to assert our masculinity in front of other men to feel a part of the pack."
—Marvin, age 31

Women assume that men become someone else when they are with their friends, but men say they really change when they are around women specifically.

"If men spoke to women the way they do to the men, they would get slapped repeatedly!" —Emanuel, age 35

"It's a comfort thing. We're not watching ourselves…When we're around women, we're trying not to offend, at least on some level."
—Robert, age 41

What to look out for: He's a different person when he's around people other than you.

Changing your behavior based on the company you are in is quite common with both sexes. You adapt to the surroundings and scenario, and your comfort level changes accordingly. Women act differently when they are around all their girlfriends, and men do the same. Be assured he's not trying to hide anything from you; he's just going with the flow. You should do the same.

Is he listening?

"I've been married for just over twelve years, and I think that my husband officially doesn't listen to me. For example, I recently told him that our car needed gas (we were taking a short trip together to visit his in-laws, of all places), but after he got into the car and we were on the road, he seemed surprised about the situation of having no gas. I mean, seriously, did he not hear me, or is he going deaf? I have to find out: **do men really listen—not just hear the sounds, but listen and understand?**" —Kimberly, age 47, married

What the men say

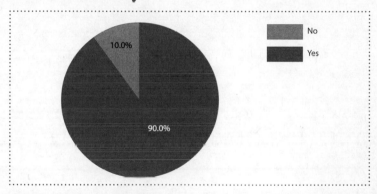

No
Yes

10.0%

90.0%

What men are really saying

Ninety percent of men say they truly try to listen to what a woman says and understand what she is saying. If they are committed in the relationship and want to support their partner, they are focused on the conversation.

"I always listen to my wife. I care about every thought and feeling she has. She listens to me in the same way. I try my best to understand my wife, and if I can't, I let her know, and we try harder to help me understand. It's an important part of a successful marriage." —Daniel, age 23

"If we really care about you and about making the relationship work, we do. I find I'm suddenly bereft of my trademark verbosity, because I can't think of a better, more succinct way of putting it. If your man really loves you, really wants to make things work...he'll make the time to listen to you, to understand you, your needs, and make the effort to address them. If he really, really is into the relationship, then he'll also communicate effectively with you as well. He may just not know how." —Hugo, age 35

Some men, 10 percent, believe that it's not always worth their time or effort to listen to a woman. If she's not saying what she wants clearly or if she rambles, they simply zone out (also see page 39).

"Most of the time [when] women talk, their message is encoded in what they are saying. Since I know I will never fully understand what she is trying to say, I rarely listen. If something is said bluntly and openly, I hear it and understand." —Charles, age 31

"Sometimes it seems like you are telling us the same stuff, or frankly it's just not very interesting to hear about what so-and-

so said at work after you said such-and-such. We wander off. Most of the important stuff I catch, but it's impossible to get it all."
—Lennox, age 40

What to look out for: Assuming when you say it is more important than what you say.

In Kimberly's case, it might be less that her husband was not listening and more that he had a million things going on at the time. If a man is busy, chances are he isn't as focused on what you are really saying. If you want positive results, take into account what he's doing at the time as well as the point you want to make.

Is there stuff he won't talk about?

"I've been through some pretty traumatic situations in my life, and through therapy, I've learned a lot. I've learned to be open and honest about my feelings and not to suppress them. With this in mind, I've tried talking with my boyfriends about various topics in an open manner, but I haven't seen the same returned to me. I want to know if it's my approach or: **are there certain topics that are off-limits?**"
—Vanessa, age 22, single

What the men say

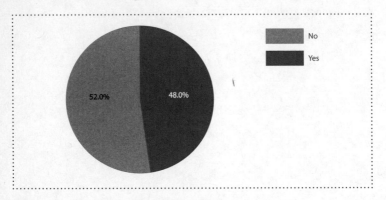

No

Yes

52.0%   48.0%

What men are really saying

Most men don't think there are any off-limit topics. When a man is in a committed relationship, you'll be able to talk with him about anything. In fact, 52 percent of men believe the key to a successful relationship is to be open and straightforward with him.

"In any good relationship there should be complete honesty and openness. No subject should be off-limits. Nothing should be hidden or covered up because it will reveal itself in the long run." —William, age 42

"A relationship, in my opinion, is one that revolves around an honesty-is-the-best-policy notion. Something that is hidden only makes the person feel worse, and keeping your significant one in the dark does not help them either." —Deryck, age 37

The results were close, though, and 48 percent of men said there were some areas that should remain off-limits. Past conquests were chief among the topics that should never be discussed, at least not in detail.

"Don't talk about your ex...ever. That leads a man to believe he is less significant than he thought he was. If your ex is on your mind at all, it causes doubts. Also don't compare us to any other men, especially your friend's boyfriend. Makes us very insecure, though we'd never admit it." —Jonathan, age 38

"No, but that is in large part because I'm a very open person. I do think it is reasonable for people to have some areas they want to keep completely private or don't feel comfortable talking about with a significant other. If you are experiencing this, don't be too pushy in terms of trying to make all subjects open at all times. Some people have to come to terms with what they are comfortable about communicating in their own way, on their own terms." —Paul, age 30

What to look out for: Thinking men want to know everything about everything.

Not so. When a man is serious about his relationship, he will be very open to sharing nearly every aspect of his life. When it comes to you, he doesn't necessarily want to know every intimate detail, but he is still interested in you. This isn't a slight against you or your life; this prioritization is just how he processes and retains important information. The key for you is to go slowly with detail and let him inquire when he's ready, instead of overloading him with everything you've got.

Why do I have to spell it out for him?

"I could never understand why my ex-husband couldn't pick up the signals I was communicating, such as when I was ready to leave when visiting his parents' house or when I felt like his friends were being too obnoxious. It would be great to learn: **why can't men pick up on subtle hints?**" —Alisha, age 30, single

What the men say

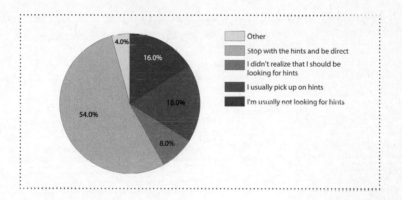

What men are really saying

When it comes to communicating with your man, know that men like to be direct when it comes to anything in life. Knowing this, it should come as no surprise that 54 percent of men feel women should stop giving subtle hints. Your man finds it completely frustrating to decipher whether you are hinting. Men have tried to decode this behavior long enough to learn that they will probably never get it right. Therefore, they find it much more efficient to avoid the game.

If you want something from your man, tell him. Giving hints will leave you disappointed.

> "Women need to realize that men can't read women's minds. They need to be direct with a man and ask for what they want or need. Women tend to have more intuition than men do, anyway." —Scott, age 33

> "Why waste your time on subtle hints instead of just cutting through all the crap and say what's on your mind? Wouldn't it be easier for everyone?" —Keith, age 33

While in the minority, 18 percent of men say they do pick up on women's hints and get it.

> "I am excellent on picking up hints, but generally would prefer if a woman would stop being passive-aggressive and would just be direct about an issue. To drop hints instead of openly discussing an issue is simply a way to eschew responsibility for communication in a relationship." —Paul, age 30

> "I can pick up on the hint, depending on what it is about. When I get the hint of flirtatious behavior, I'll act like I didn't notice, even though I did, just to play along and see where it goes. If they are hints regarding being upset or angry, then I'd prefer you to be direct and not play games." —Thomas, age 24

What to look out for: Thinking that men are on the lookout for hints.

Nope. If there is something you want your man to do, or if you want him to act a certain way, you have to tell him. Beating around the bush wastes both of your time and only serves to get you upset when he doesn't "get it." Stop doing this. In researching this question, there were some pretty interesting discussions as to what the actual question was. Meaning, there was some confusion as to which hints she is using or when she is making use of these hints. Maybe she is in a situation where she can't be as direct in front of other people, like her in-laws or his friends. In these situations, perhaps a private but direct conversation is warranted. You don't have to be rude to get your point across, but as the men point out, you do need to be direct. You'll find that this type of communication is quite liberating because there is no guesswork. Don't assume your man is into mind reading. That's almost always a critical mistake.

If I don't nag him, will he ever do anything?

"Both my husband and I work full time in challenging careers, but I feel like he isn't keeping up with his responsibilities at home. For example, I just do not understand why he has to be reminded that the garbage needs to be taken out or pick up after himself when he gets home from work. I've asked him (multiple times) to pick up what he leaves lying around, but no matter how many times I ask, he gets around to it when he feels like it. My question is simply this: **what is the best way to ask a man to do something without appearing as though she is nagging?**" —Terri, age 54, married

What the men say

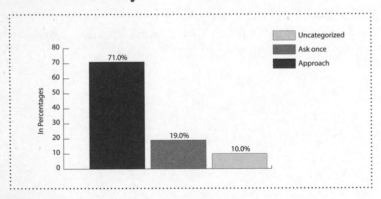

What men are really saying

The approach is everything, and the majority of men say it's all in how you ask that determines whether you are nagging.

"Maybe you can say something like 'Honey, would you please do a small favor for me?' Nagging really gets on a guy's nerves. If the guy is lazy, then you can motivate him to do the task. For example, if the task gets done, you can promise him that you will be intimate with him and please him sexually later that day."
—Scott, age 33

"Your voice tone is important. Try talking to him in a more endearing fashion instead of [sounding like] his mother or his drill sergeant from the Army. Always start with 'hon' or 'dear' and say, 'I would really appreciate it if you...'" —Don, age 55

Another non-nagging tactic is to pay attention to how many times you ask a guy to do something. If he doesn't complete what you asked him right away, leave him alone for a bit. Give him a chance to do it. Your timeline might not be his timeline and vice versa.

"Ask him once, maybe twice. If it's not done, offer your help. After that, do not ask again. Because this is nagging. Simply do it yourself or find an alternate means. The guilt will get to him."
—Alphonse, age 36

"Ask once, and if we don't do it, then just leave it alone. Either we will do the task, like washing the dishes, or once all the clean ones are gone, we will be forced to clean the dishes."
—Darin, age 28

What to look out for: Believing your timeline is his timeline.

Sometimes what is of critical importance for you is only incidental for a man. If you're not sure he knows how important something is for you, tell him so. Most men love to please and make you happy. It's really less about listening and more about how important the task is perceived to be. If you relay how important it is for you, you'll have better success in having him listen to you.

Does he think I'll never discover those lies?

"I've officially started my second life after a divorce, and I don't want to get into a bad situation. My ex-husband and I fought about a lot of things, but he never lied to me. Now that I'm dating again, my friends are telling me that things are different these days and that I need to keep an eye out because men are liars. Worse, my friends are telling me that men think that no matter what lie they tell, they will never get caught. I really need some clarity (or a reality check) on the issue. **Do men really think that women won't find out when they've lied?**" —Jessica, age 48, single

What the men say

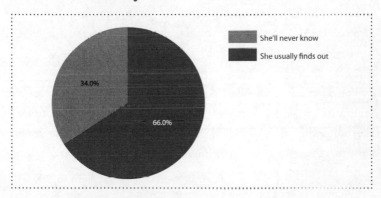

- She'll never know
- She usually finds out

34.0%

66.0%

What men are really saying

Ladies, take some solace in the fact that 66 percent of men know that if they lie, you'll probably find out. However, even though a majority of the men know this fact, they've still lied, if only to avoid arguing or to spare your feelings at the time.

> "I answered no because I believe that women are more attentive to issues when they develop in a relationship. They are excellent in spotting lies from men. Yes, I have been caught telling lies to women." —Abdul, age 34

> "I myself never lie to my wife because honesty is the base of a strong relationship, but I'm sure there are millions of men out there who really believe they won't get caught lying. The truth is, you are most likely gonna get caught lying, because if you truly love the woman you're with, you're gonna tell her the truth later on and just make it even harder on yourself because then she'll be mad at you for lying. But the only reason I think men lie is truly because they believe they won't get caught." —Robert, age 20

The 34 percent who say they can get away with a lie think that either they are skilled enough liars or you haven't figured out how to determine when they were lying. Even of the two-thirds who did lie, many feel they don't have any huge negative repercussions.

> "Whether or not a man feels he can get away with a lie largely depends on the skill of the particular liar. Sometimes, though, lying is in part because perceptions can create jealousy that is unfounded. A good liar will know how to control information and use asymmetries of information to be able to lie and get away with it." —Paul, age 30

"Most lies that men tell are white and don't have any negative consequences. Since they are small, they will never be found out. An example was when I was asked what I had done on a Friday night. When in reality I got fairly intoxicated and went to a gentlemen's club, I told her I was out with the boys, had too much to drink, and headed home early to get some sleep and that was why I didn't call her. It isn't hurtful to her in a real way, so she would never follow up on it, and women usually never find out these things." —Guy, age 31

What to look out for: You overestimate his ability to successfully lie to you.

Jessica's situation seems like a case of bitter-friend syndrome. Her friends are giving her a jaded perception based on their bad experiences. If you go into a relationship with the all-men-are-liars belief, you'll never be happy. The more progressive way to view this is to take one man at a time and take him at his word until he proves in some way that you no longer can. Having this presumption about the attitudes of men clouds your judgment.

I'm mad. How do I tell him?

"Recently, I've been irritated with some of my husband's behavior when we are in public. It's delicate, so I'd like to approach him about it and explain my feelings without him becoming defensive or blowing the situation out of proportion. **What is the best way for me to tell a man that I'm upset about something?**"
—Michele, age 34, married

What the men say

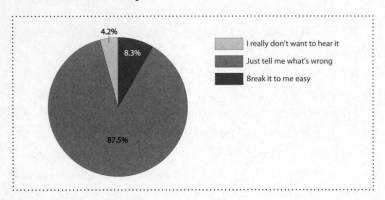

- I really don't want to hear it
- Just tell me what's wrong
- Break it to me easy

4.2%
8.3%
87.5%

What men are really saying

Plain and simple, men just want you to be direct. A whopping 88 percent of men say a woman should just tell them what's wrong. This holds true when you have situations that involve another man. Being straightforward with him is the best way for him to process the information and will leave the smallest chance for him to misinterpret your feelings.

"Men are constantly guessing if a woman is angry based upon her body language, tone, etc. If a woman is upset, we want to know about it and what exactly it is that is wrong. We are not good at guessing, and it angers us when we are supposed to figure it out."
—Blake, age 31

"Just come right out and say that something is bothering you. It does no one any good to keep your feelings bottled up or to beat around the bush; I may not be that bright and pick up on your clues." —William, age 42

Not all men like the direct approach; some men need to be eased into bad news. If you are upset about something, 8 percent of men want to be eased into that news.

"If my lady was upset, I would want to know about it. However, I would also be afraid of hearing bad news. It would be better for her to break the news to me easy, especially if the bad news is that she wanted to break up with me. By telling me this gently, it would hurt my feelings much less than if she was blunt about it."
—Scott, age 33

"I don't like to be overwhelmed with someone's problems. I do not work well under stress or pressure." —Eric, age 32

What to look out for: Acting on the assumption that men always want you to be subtle.

The data says that Michele should be up front with her husband and explain the situation. Most men can handle your grief without getting angry, and if you are honest, it will eliminate his fears or concerns, leaving nothing to be suspicious about.

When is the best time to bring up a heavy subject?

"I've really been fighting my urges to bring up marriage with my boyfriend because everyone tells me not to push it. I'm not sure how or when to do it, but I think that it might be best first thing in the morning, before he's gone through a long day. I really want the conversation to go well, but before I head down that road, can you tell me: **what is the best approach to talking about a tricky subject?**" —Kelly, age 25, single

What the men say

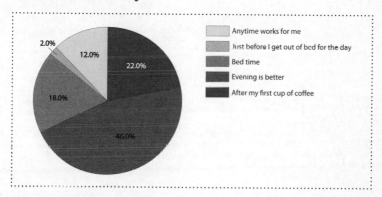

- Anytime works for me
- Just before I get out of bed for the day
- Bed time
- Evening is better
- After my first cup of coffee

2.0%
12.0%
22.0%
18.0%
46.0%

What men are really saying

A "perfect" time may not really exist, but 46 percent of men agree that bringing up more in-depth topics is better done in the evening. It seems to be that ideal time when you aren't stressing over it all day and it isn't the last thing you think about before bed.

"Mornings are too rushed to talk about anything heavy, and bed-time is too late. The evening is perfect, especially if the kids are in bed. Plenty of time and not too tired then." —Everet, age 40

"If it is a heavy subject, don't start the day off with it unless you plan on spending the rest of the day on it. Plan to have this discussion when nothing else will be pressing." —Ari, age 61

If you are going to start the day off talking about something serious, 22 percent of men said at the very least let them get a cup of coffee in them.

"A man needs to feel that he is in control of his mental faculties. First thing in the morning or just before bed when he is tired are the times when a man's brain functions are not at their highest." —Stew, age 57

"Do not tell me first thing in the morning or just before I go to sleep because I need to be awake for this 'heavy' subject." —Trey, age 36

What to look out for: Believing that there is one "best" time to discuss heavy subjects with all men.

Most men say there is no ideal time for a heavy discussion. If you had to choose, maybe as the men say, evening is better. In any case, just be sure both parties are in the right frame of mind and are alert enough to focus on the topic at hand.

Who does he talk to?

"I've been married for over ten years, but I feel that, for the first time, my husband and I are growing apart. I love him dearly, but I don't think he opens up to me. I've been wondering: **do men ever have heart-to-heart talks with their friends? If not me, who does he confide in?**" —Jennifer, age 35, married

What the men say

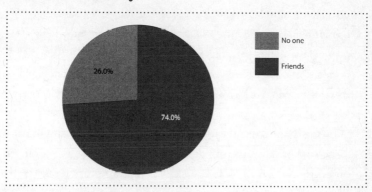

No one
Friends

26.0%

74.0%

What men are really saying

Men, like women, usually have a confidant or two with whom they can share their problems and talk over things. Seventy-four percent of men talk to their friends about anything from their relationship to fears to other problems in their lives.

"My friend and I never hide any secrets from each other. In fact, we love to share secrets. Once my friend had a problem with his wife...he shared with me things from the deepest part of his heart that usually friends don't share." —Hayden, age 29

"First things first, I don't think most men would call a 'heart-to-heart' by that name; largely it's going to be called something else. Guy culture is still pretty steeped in avoiding terms that we view as too feminine. If you think your guy is doing something else with his friends when you would be having a heart-to-heart conversation, chances are that whatever he's doing serves the same purpose for him. Generally, we talk with men about the same things you would with the girls, our feelings about our wife/girlfriend, our goals, our fears, [our] hopes, and our concerns for one another; we just do it in guy ways." —William, age 34

Then there are those men who say they don't have any form of a "heart-to-heart." Twenty-six percent of men just don't open up to their friends, and while some consider it feminine or "weak" to do that, other men prefer to keep their conversations "nice and light" or at a "high level."

"Sports, video games, politics, our work, our families. Basic things that are going on. Food. What we want to do on the weekend. Movies." —Keith, age 33

"We talk about basic things like current events, old memories, and people we know. This usually leads to joking around and teasing each other." —Brian, age 27

What to look out for: Your man only discusses in-depth topics with you.

It's not the case. Both men and women like to bounce ideas and issues off their closest friends before talking to their significant others. This is like a sounding board to make sure they know what they want to say without screwing anything up and ending up in an argument.

Chapter 2

DATING

Dating: equal parts fun, excitement, depression, and anxiety, all wrapped into one. And we're speaking from the male perspective!

Yes, men have the same dating issues you do, but their approach to dating may surprise you. How they think about dating, who they date, and the "game" of dating is fully explored here.

We finally reveal the infamous issue (that we get asked almost daily) about calling after the date. What is the protocol?

What about how men feel about you making the first move? Yep, covered here.

So let's get to the core issues you women ask us all the time about dating and let these men explain themselves (or defend themselves, depending on how you look at it).

Can I make the first move?

"I was talking with 'the girls' recently about why it seems so hard for men to ask us out. Nobody truly knows why, but most of us were brought up that men do all the asking, even though it would be so much easier for us to just do it. So, **is it okay for me to ask him out?**" —Jennifer, age 29, dating

What the men say

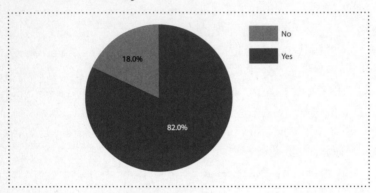

What men are really saying

Men like it a lot when you are up front about what you want.

"Yes. That's just not the case any longer in today's society where men have to make the first move." —Paul, age 27

"Yes. Mostly because to be honest, I don't always pick up on a woman's hints about asking her out. If she does it, she's interested." —Marcus, age 34

"Yes. Waiting for the man to make the first move is real old-school thinking and outdated." —Don, age 43

However, some men still need to be the man and take that first step.

"No! Men ask. Women decide. Why break up what's worked for thousands of years?" —George, age 37

"No. It goes back to chivalry. Is it truly dead? Don't we still open doors for women? Don't we wait to eat until the woman also has been served? If so, then we ask for the dates." —Ken, age 24

"No, unfortunately, but not because we should; it's because women like being pursued." —Steven, age 32

What to look out for: Thinking that you have to wait for him to ask you out because men prefer that he make the first move.

Not really. Men seem to be clear on this one: it's okay by them. While some still have that macho bravado of "it's the man's job," a majority think it's a huge load off if the woman takes the first step.

What is the best first date?

"Dating is hard. I'm getting used to making the call and asking a man out. Lo and behold, it worked! I'm excited, but now I'm in new territory. I assume that since he likes sports that I'd take him to a Red Sox game, but I need some help here. **Where do men like to go out on dates?**" —Dee, age 52, dating

What the men say

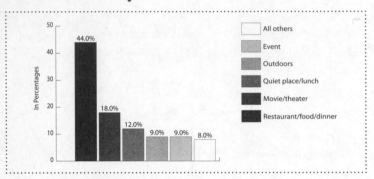

What men are really saying

Food seems to be the common theme when it comes to a date. Granted, it varies from romantic to casual to food combined with some other activity, but food, more often than not, is a part of a good first date. The majority who responded associated food with dinner; most didn't even want to do a lunch date or even meet their date at a coffee shop.

"Food should always be involved, as I think literal tastes are a big part of our personalities and what we look for in other people.

Dinner is always good as long as it's relatively casual. I think going too fancy on a first date can reek of desperation to impress too quickly. First dates should also be limited to you and the other person because you're there to get to know them, not show off to friends or have any opportunity to ignore them." —Larry, age 34

"I like to take dates to dinner because it gives plenty of time to find out about each other." —Jeffery, age 47

Movies were mentioned frequently. Reasons why include:

"I prefer movies, actually. It gives me some insights into what she likes and why. Plus we always have something to talk about before and after." —Chip, age 33

"Movies, restaurants, nature walks/hikes, sporting events, dinner theater. These events provide a variety of ways to learn about my date's interests. We are also able to enjoy each other's company and the company of others at the same time." —Darren, age 32

Not all men felt that dinner and a movie helped their cause.

"I like to have dinner and then do something active—not a movie. The whole point of a first date is to see if there should be a second. This means trying to get to know each other a little, rather than sitting quietly in a theater." —Eric, age 33

What to look out for: Believing you need to be overly creative in deciding where to go on a first date.

Men are more traditional than you might think. Most men, in fact, would prefer the old standard of going out to a restaurant with you. While it's a great idea to do an outdoor or sports event if your man is interested in that, make it more of an exception instead of a norm. Dinner will almost always work!

What do guys think will impress me?

"After getting back into the dating world, I've had some doozy dates. It's become apparent to me that men show their affection and how interested they are by how much they spend on dinner, dates, trips, etc. That said, I've often wondered: **what do men typically do to impress a woman on a date?**" —Suzanne, age 51, dating

What the men say

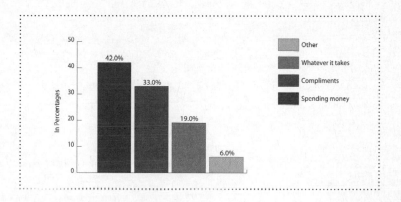

What men are really saying

Okay, so all men want to impress you on a date. How they do so varies, but the most popular responses were spending money (wine and dine you, flowers, candy, etc.), showering you with compliments, and some will go the extra mile to make an impression on you.

"My father had a friend who was friends with the manager at a nice restaurant. I took a date there, and the staff made sure we got first-class service. Why? I wanted to impress my date. Look like a big-shot, if you will." —Matthew, age 48

"Nothing too out there, but the occasional exaggeration of the truth." —Gary, age 37

"Flight lessons; she was worth it—we're still married..." —Chad, age 43

"I have taken a date to a very expensive dinner of sushi. We then drove to Vegas where we stayed for a week in a suite. I did that to show her and myself that I enjoy the finer things in life." —Hoyt, age 36

Other men believe less is more and try to make a big impact with minor details.

"In my opinion here are some things we look for: be confident, but not cocky or conceited; show her that you have goals but have time in your life for her; open her car door and the door to wherever you're going, but don't be obvious. Ask her about herself and actually listen; ask follow-up questions that show you have been paying attention. Here's a tip: know where you are taking her before you go." —Jose, age 29

What to look out for: Concluding that men won't try anything other than spending money to impress a woman.

Men attempt to impress you in many ways. For some, it's just listening more intently and trying to get to know you better. For others, it's with compliments. And yes, some do try to spend money on you. Just keep in mind all of the things men do and not one specific thing. Your noticing and appreciating the effort will go a long way in enhancing your dating life.

Does he "take care of business" before we go out on a date?

"My boyfriend and I were watching the movie *There's Something About Mary*, and there is a scene in the movie where the main character (Ted) was told he needed to masturbate before a date. So I asked my boyfriend if he'd ever done this and he told me no. I believe him, but they say that truth is stranger than fiction, so when a friend told me about your site, I thought this was a perfect venue to get a straight answer. **Do men masturbate before going on a date?**"
—Susan, age 22, dating

What the men say

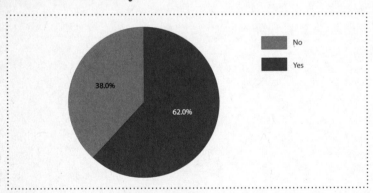

38.0%

62.0%

No

Yes

What men are really saying

Actually, men are trying to impress you by masturbating before a date. Yes, this might be hard to believe from the female perspective, but men view this as sexual chivalry, really. Don't believe us, read on.

"Not too soon before a date, but I want to ejaculate once prior to it in the knowledge that if and when sex does occur, the erection will last longer." —Anton, age 61

"When I was single I used to because if I was to get lucky, I would want to last longer in bed." —Raymond, age 44

"You can't go on a date with a loaded gun." —Forrest, age 31 (note: lots of men used this phrase or variations on the phrase "loaded gun")

"I do so that I can stay calm and not want to blow my load in ten minutes. Plus, if I know I'm going to fuck the chick, I can last longer." —Andy, age 31

Interestingly, even men who say no don't do so for "your benefit."

"You never know if you are going to get some action, and if you do masturbate, then it will take a while for a man to ejaculate, and the woman will feel like they are not doing their job." —Brian, age 25

"I masturbate a lot, like most men, but never before going on a date. Because if it should lead to sex, I want to have an impressive load built up. I don't want to use my supply and have nothing left for when I really do cum." —Mitchell, age 29

What to look out for: Assuming that because men masturbate before a date, they must prefer it to sex while on the date.

This isn't the case. Men do all sorts of things to make sure that they're able to perform and please you. This is just another of them. Maybe it's not the same as bringing you flowers, but to men, it's another one of the things men do for women. A man's work is never done.

First date kiss: yes or no?

"I never know what to expect on a first date. Other dates, it's easier to tell, **but do men expect a kiss on the first date?**" —Robyn, age 28, dating

What the men say

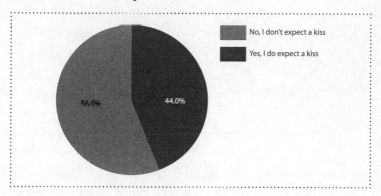

No, I don't expect a kiss
Yes, I do expect a kiss

56.0%   44.0%

What men are really saying

Some men say a kiss at the end of the date is a sign that the date was a success.

"Yes—it shows the date went well." —Clarence, age 29

"Yes, because then I would know if she wanted to see me again; also, even if it is a peck on the cheek, it is a nice way to say thanks for the date." —Sean, age 28

The rest of the men said that the act of kissing is a very intimate act and should not be rushed into.

"No. A kiss is a sign of intimacy, and until this is established, it would be a shallow, meaningless act." —Philip, age 24

"No, because it is the first date. Normally on a first date, you are just trying to get to know a person and see if it is a right fit. For me a kiss is something that should happen naturally." —Chris, age 42

What to look out for: Believing that because he took you out, you owe him a kiss.

Okay, so there are those men who expect a kiss on the first date, some thinking, "Why not?" or "She owes me." Others believe that a kiss gauged how well the date went. Keep in mind that more than half of the men we asked said that they don't expect a kiss. That doesn't mean that men don't want one; it just means they don't expect one.

Would you kiss a date you are not attracted to?

"My question is about kissing. It's so intimate and meaningful. At least that's how I feel and would guess that a lot of women feel the same. When you're on a date with a woman, no matter how it really went, **would you kiss her even if you were not attracted to her?**"
—Roberta, age 56, dating

What the men say

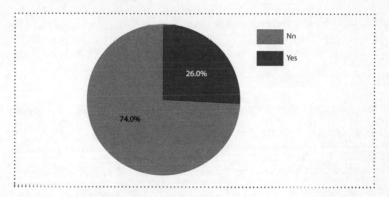

No
Yes
26.0%
74.0%

What men are really saying

Men have standards too. They aren't just going to kiss you to kiss you; there has to be a spark or something else there to make it happen.

"I wouldn't kiss anyone that I wasn't attracted to. There's no point in sending false messages to someone. Furthermore, I wouldn't date someone that I wasn't attracted to in the first place."
—Roger, age 50

"No, I wouldn't. I have always been honest and straight. I wouldn't like to be kissed by someone who feels like she's obligated to do it." —Morris, age 31

"No, I would not kiss her if I wasn't attracted to her. I will only kiss a girl I think I'll have the pleasure of dating again." —Juan, age 43

"No, if I'm not attracted to her, why waste my time?" —Jack, age 29

"No, I wouldn't want to start anything physical with someone that I am not attracted to." —Albert, age 61

However, there is the percentage of men who would do it even if they weren't that into you.

"Yes. All kisses are pleasant, and it is cruel to refuse to kiss a woman with whom you are on a date." —Jonathan, age 36

"Maybe politely in a good night sort of way, but not more than that." —Justin, age 33

What to look out for: Believing that even if your date didn't go well, he is going to want a kiss.

For some reason, kissing is just one of those things that most men have a moral feeling about, even though they're not always so moral about other physical acts. Kissing, to most men, is really intimate, so don't take offense if he doesn't want to kiss you right away.

What will cost me a second date?

"I never have a problem getting a date. It's having a second date. I've got to be doing something wrong but can't figure out what. Maybe it's what I say or do on a date. I've been known to be more of an aggressor type. **I'd like to know: what are the key behaviors women exhibit on a date that turn men off?**" —Kendra, age 47, dating

What the men say

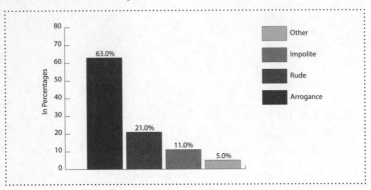

What men are really saying

Men think that being arrogant is far and away the worst thing you can do on a date. The data was really strong on this one. Men were very clear on this topic, as evidenced by their feedback.

"I really can't stand the arrogance that some women show on a date. I remember taking a girl on a date to a pretty nice restaurant, and all night she acted like everyone there was beneath her. It was disgusting to watch. Never called her back!" —Tim, age 51

"When women try to impress everyone by showing how cool they are and how much they have is awkward. To me it's a form of arrogance that comes across as really tacky." —Sal, age 48

Okay, ladies, put those cell phones away during the date if you have hopes of a second one. Your friends will be there after the date to get all the juicy details.

"What's with women using a phone or texting on a date? Forget about being rude. Tells me she's not interested. If she's not, what am I doing here?" —Anthony, age 43

Check your excessive drinking and smoking at the door: (a) Your date won't want to hold your hair while you puke, and (b) he doesn't want to kiss an ashtray goodnight.

"I don't like it when women smoke all night or get drunk. Might seem like it's a great thing, but it's a royal pain in the ass. Turns me off in a big way." —Kevin, age 41

Back to basics; good hygiene is a must!

"As soon as I see a woman's nasty fingernails, or the biting of the nails on a date, I'm out. Worse yet is the gum chewing. It's either fighting off nerves, bad breath, or bad teeth. Any of that, and I'm out." —Jason, age 31

What to look out for: Assuming that when on a date, arrogance and confidence are considered the same behavior.

The reality is that men find being arrogant, rude, and impolite as unattractive as you do. Men really do pick up on and weigh the little things that they see you do. What might be "cute" right now becomes irritating quickly. What you need to be mindful of is that how you act and react is even more important than how you look.

What makes a woman worthy of a second date?

"Here is my typical scenario: I date; the date goes well. We have great conversation, and all is going well. We'll exchange phone numbers, perhaps even email. There usually is a follow-up call, text, or email, but often there is no request for a repeat date. What happened? It all seemed to go well, and yet nothing after date one. **So what makes a girl worthy of a second date?**" —Ruby, age 32, single

What the men say

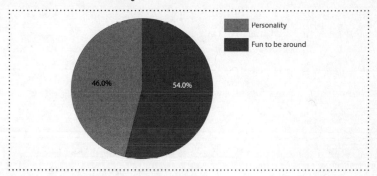

Personality
Fun to be around

46.0%   54.0%

What men are really saying

This question comes to us almost daily, no joke. What's interesting is that all age groups of single women ask this same question, so it's definitely time to expose the results. Men like to have fun with the one they are with, they say, and 54 percent say a woman has to fun to be around on the first date to even consider a second date.

"Pretty much, if they were fun to be with on the first date. If we both had a good time and enjoyed each other's company, I would ask them for a second date." —Kenn, 19

"If she is spontaneous and funny, it's a guaranteed second date." —Fallon, 45

You may be starting to see a trend of what's important to men and the women they are considering for a relationship, and the answers here fit right in: once again, personality comes in the top two. With 46 percent of the men choosing it, personality plays a heavy role in whether or not a woman will get a second date.

"Intelligent, well-spoken conversation with moderate self-image and plans for the future, even if they are not earth-changing or career-oriented." —Jay, 27

"Well, for me, there would have to be something there besides just a physical attraction. My whole life, I've always been over-emotional, so I need more from a woman than just a hot body and a great night in the sack. In order to ask a girl out for a second date, I'd need to find something in her personality and in our conversations that tells me to continue spending time with her." —Robert, 20

What to look out for: Assuming that great conversations and outings lead to repeat dates.

While looks and chemistry certainly play an important role in the first date, men say that it has to be fun and not boring for him to call you again. Being fun to be around is really a mix of everything: your personalities have to click, there has to be a spark of sorts, and you have to be willing to be yourself. Without that, it's just a lot of awkward pauses throughout the evening.

He doesn't want to date me. Will he still sleep with me?

"Everybody knows that men want sex. But my question is, in this day and age, **would men still have sex with a woman they were dating, even if she wasn't their type?**" —Angela, age 19, dating

What the men say

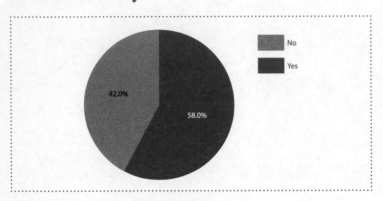

No
Yes

42.0%

58.0%

What men are really saying

Okay, so the majority of men (close to two-thirds) are horn dogs, plain and simple. And while they may balk at kissing you so they don't give mixed signals, when it comes to sex, if there's a hint of chemistry, men rarely pass up a chance.

> "Honestly, yes. Well, because I am a man. If she wants to have sex, why not?" —Joey, age 47

"Yes—get it when I can. If she is pleasant enough, why not?"
—Colin, age 36

"Depends on how much I needed to have sex at the moment. More than likely I would. Hey, I am not going to turn it down."
—Terry, age 27

"Absolutely. We both need sexual fulfillment, and it would meet those needs. This does not mean we would have to go out again."
—Gerald, age 43

"Yes, if she is a consenting adult. What man would pass up sex?"
—Keith, age 21

"Yes, as long as there is some sort of physical attraction or chemistry, no harm done in my book." —Samuel, age 25

Don't go thinking all men are animals; there are those men who would say no to sex if they didn't think the relationship was going anywhere.

"No. That's just using a girl for physical pleasure. If you don't see it going anywhere, there's no point in using the woman for selfish reasons and possibly giving her wrong ideas. Someone will just get hurt or an accident will happen, like a pregnancy."
—Willie, age 31

"No, I don't think so. I have to really like a woman before I can have sex with her." —Ralph, age 39

"No. I prefer to have sex with someone I like. Not someone I do not want to see again." —Lawrence, age 29

What to look out for: Thinking men will believe that you have to "click" first before you have sex.

As we alluded to in a previous question, men think that kissing is more intimate than sex. Sex is something that most men will have with nearly any woman who makes it possible. This means offering sex as a way of moving the relationship to that next level isn't seen in the same way through men's eyes. It's another level, to be sure, but not to the degree that you might think.

Why doesn't he just say it's a booty call?

"I hope men change as I age, but my feeling is they're all the same. I like sex like anyone else, but sometimes it would be great just to hang out and enjoy the company of the guy I'm seeing. Every time he wants me to come over, it's always, always just for sex. I just want some clarity as to **why do you ask a girl over to 'chill' when you really mean 'have sex'?**" —Brittany, age 19, single

What the men say

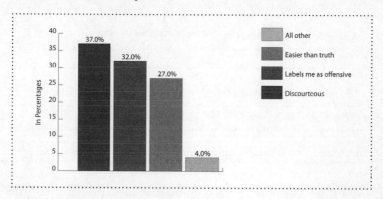

What men are really saying

We have to say that men only speak this way because of how it could be perceived by women. Most men would rather just tell you what they want, but they fear being labeled aggressive, offensive, or worse. So really it's a male version of "courtesy" wrapped up in double talk.

"It's an easy way to break the ice. If we said 'Come over for sex,' you probably wouldn't come over." —Keith, age 29

"Would you come over otherwise?" —Blake, age 38

"Think of it as a gentle, somewhat polite, slightly insecure, yet tactful way of getting you to say yes. It is just a way of trying to act cool, and also to coax you into coming over." —Ned, age 25

"If you ask a girl over just to have sex, she will never come over. Well, most girls, at least. By saying we want to chill, we are getting across the point of what we want without having to say it. It is less stressful for us." —Rowan, age 36

"Because it sounds so less threatening and nonaggressive. Humans always use euphemisms for things they don't want to say directly. Would you rather have him say 'Wanna come over and screw?' I think that would go over like a fart in church." —Silvio, age 61

What to look out for: Assuming that men have no filter for saying what they want.

As modern women of today, you understand that much of the time, men think with things other than their brains. We live in a fairly polite society, and men cater to the social mores by not being overly direct for fear of being labeled or rejected. But it's pretty easy for you to read between the lines. The other social norm is that you get to say yes or no. You hold that power, after all.

Ask men your question at www.wtfarementhinking.com

Can I ask for favors?

"This might seem strange, but every guy I've dated has the ability to help me out with things that have nothing to do with dating. I once dated a plumber, an accountant, and a massage therapist over the course of one year! My question is this: **is it ever acceptable for a woman you are dating to ask you for personal favors (like car or home repairs)?**" —Nancy, age 42, dating

What the men say

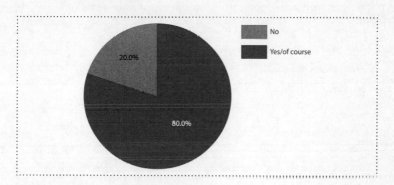

No

Yes/of course

20.0%

80.0%

What men are really saying

When you're in that early dating phase, men like to help you out when they can. Plain and simple, it makes them look good and, depending on the task, it makes them look manly. But remember, just because a guy's willing to help, doesn't mean you should ask him for favors all the time.

"Part of a relationship is doing things for each other. I mean, it should also be reciprocal, but if you care about them, you should want to do things for them." —James, age 33

"Yes. Men like to be helpful. It's something we like to do. Makes me feel needed and important." —Rob, age 26

"Sure, as long as it's not overly excessive and not abusive just to have me do this and that." —Michael, age 29

Surprisingly, some men just don't want to help a girl out.

"No way. I don't like this at all. Puts me in a bad spot. If I don't want to because I don't have time, am I now the 'bad guy'? I don't like the obligation." —Will, age 41

"It's a big turn-off for me. If she's not resourceful enough to fix her own car, set up her own TiVo, or take care of her own personal business, she's too needy for me. After all, we're still just dating..." —Dave, age 28

What to look out for: Expecting that men will always take the "What's-in-it-for-me" approach.

Don't feel bad asking for help if you need it. Most men are more than willing to impress you with some muscle, knowledge, or help if they can. However, keep in mind, relationships are give and take, so if you ask your guy to do something for you, he may expect a little something in return.

Ask men your question at www.wtfarementhinking.com

Can I date more than one guy at a time?

"I've been dating the same man for the past three years. We never had a conversation about exclusivity or not dating others, so I dated other men in addition to him. I know he was dating on and off in addition to me, so I didn't think it was an issue. I recently mentioned that I'd like to be exclusive with him. He freaked at the thought that I wasn't exclusive this whole time. So my question is: **is it okay for a woman that you are dating to date other men?**" —Julie, age 35, dating

What the men say

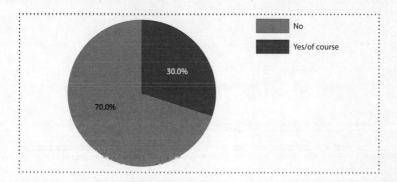

No
Yes/of course
30.0%
70.0%

What men are really saying

Even though times have progressed, men are still as old-fashioned as they used to be.

"No. I can't truly trust a woman who dates around. I don't like to feel that there are secrets between us." —Richard, age 37

"No, because if I'm serious enough to date her and invest my time doing so, then I need her to do the same." —Chuck, age 40

"The focus should be on me. I'm putting my focus on her." —Joe, age 31

Others say that until the relationship becomes serious, all options are open.

"Yes, of course. By her dating other men, hopefully she will see that I'm far and away better." —Thom, age 34

"Yes. Why not? We're only dating. I have options. She has options. I'm not looking for her to answer every one of my needs, and vice versa." —Christopher, age 38

"Yes. I don't feel any obligation toward one woman until I find the woman I want to marry. She should do the same." —Danny, age 29

What to look out for: Presupposing that it's totally acceptable to date multiple men without being clear regarding exclusivity.

When it comes to being exclusive, most men are still stuck on having all the attention focused on them. Quick tip: tell a guy up front if you are seeing other men. This way the lines of communication are open and honest from the get-go, and you'll know if you are hooking up with a conservative guy or a guy who's just as open as you are.

Ask men your question at www.wtfarementhinking.com

When should I talk about my ex?

"I know that politics and religion are no-no's in the playbook of dating conversation, but what are other no-no's? **When is it appropriate for a woman you are dating to talk about her past boyfriends or husbands?**" —Jill, age 36, dating

What the men say

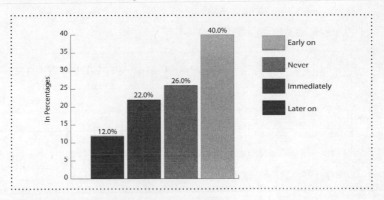

What men are really saying

This is a touchy subject. While men don't really want to hear about your past exploits, eventually three-quarters of them are going to want to know. Most men say it should be discussed before the relationship hits the two-month mark.

"After one month; that way, I know I am in no danger of her getting back with an old lover." —Dean, age 38

"It is appropriate after a month. At that point I would be consider-ing her as a serious girlfriend and would like to know details, such as how she handled previous relationships." —Walter, age 31

"Within a month, as long as she does not go into detail. I would be interested in wanting to know why they broke up; however, he is an ex for a reason, and [I] don't want to know every single detail. I think before that, she would be comparing me to her ex." —Patrick, age 25

Some men never want to know, and others want to know early—really early.

"First date is fine with me. I can find out if I should be looking over my shoulder for psycho exes and can also get a feel for the type of man she usually goes for." —Peter, age 29

"It should be cleared within the first date itself so that we can be more attached mentally and emotionally, and overall I can trust her." —Harold, age 38

"Immediately; I want to know for my own safety." —Douglas, age 28

What to look out for: Assuming he'll be fine with you telling him about details of your past relationship.

Nope. Men want to know about your exes sooner rather than

later, but they don't want to know about your exploits. Save the details, even if pressed. It will make your life much easier. This is a discussion that needs to happen, but at a more general level. Avoid specifics unless he asks for them.

When should I tell him I'm a parent?

"Almost all the women I know who are now dating have kids. Hard to escape that fact, if I've had past relationships and I'm no longer nineteen, but **when is it appropriate for a woman you are dating to introduce you to her kids?**" —Denise, age 29, dating

What the men say

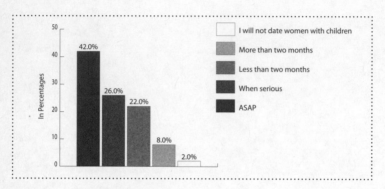

What men are really saying

Okay, take this question as a two-parter.

Part one, you should always be up front about having kids; you'd want to know if he has them, wouldn't you? Most men feel the same way and want to know almost from the moment you meet.

"The sooner the better. I do not like any surprises." —Henry, age 23

"As soon as possible, to break the ice and get rid of any stress leading to the introduction." —Carl, age 28

Part two, men will want to meet your children after you are more serious.

> "A female should get to know me first before she even thinks about introducing me to her children because it helps to keep a lot of extra problems down and her children shouldn't be forced on me and me on them." —Arthur, age 31

> "It's hard to say the exact number of days, but it actually depends on the number of dates you have had. You shouldn't meet the kids of your date if you are not serious, because kids tend to attach emotionally. So it's best to get introduced when you really feel like you want to be a part of the family." —Ryan, age 34

What to look out for: Believing it's best to wait until he knows you better before you tell him about your kids.

For most men, children bring a different element into a relationship. And it's one they take seriously. There are only 2 percent of men who consider kids a deal breaker; all others just need to know up front, so they know how to approach the possible relationship. Take comfort in that and embrace it. He's going to know eventually, so it's always better that he know up front. No man wants to feel tricked.

At what point do men expect sex?

"Sex is important to me. It's important for all women. But I think that men feel it's a need or a conquest they must have or else. So, for men, **after how many dates would you *expect* to have sex with a woman you're seeing?**" —Judy, age 27, single

What the men say

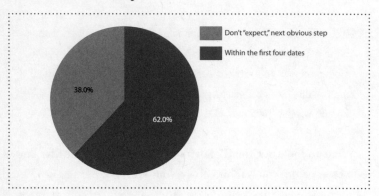

Don't "expect," next obvious step

Within the first four dates

38.0%

62.0%

What men are really saying

The percentage of men who expect sex within four dates is pretty high, with different reasons behind this belief. Some men said that they've lowered their standards to increase their chances of sex.

"Three. I think by that time you're ready to gauge the physical attraction and relevance in the relationship by that point." —Aaron, age 24

"Three, because it should take that long to get to know each other better." —Randy, age 33

Other men didn't necessarily expect sex, but 38 percent said that if things went well, that's the next obvious step.

"It depends on how the night goes and if there is an attraction. I've done it on the first date, if she's open to it. I never expect to get it, though." —Howard, age 48

"Four dates, because this gives me time to get to know what kind of person she is. I don't like to date women who go too fast. (There is no telling what they have.)" —Gene, age 38

What to look out for: Assuming that men have no expectations on when to have sex.

You shouldn't be made to think that sex is all men want when they go out with you. Keep an open line of communication to get a better understanding of what his expectations are (whether they are friendship, companionship, or sex). Men have definite ideas as to when they would like sex to take place; this much is true, but if it is going to happen, they have the expectation that it will happen within the first four dates.

How long will he wait for sex?

"I like to think that dating is the process of getting to know the other person. Yes, sex is important, but not at the expense of getting to know someone. **That said, after how many dates do men give up on dating a woman if they haven't had sex with her?**" —Elise, age 45, dating

What the men say

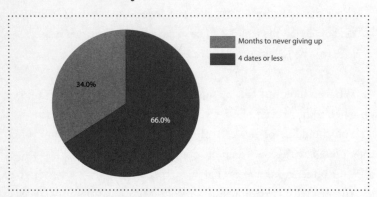

Months to never giving up

4 dates or less

34.0%

66.0%

What men are really saying

More than two-thirds of men out there won't waste the time and effort to pursue a woman if they aren't getting any. Let's face it; men have one thing on their mind—sex. These men have a there-are-more-fish-in-the-sea mentality.

> "It all depends on the first date. If I feel the relationship will not go forward, I would quit dating the woman. So if we hadn't had sex within our first couple of dates, I would stop dating her."
> —Hollis, age 44

"Four dates; that's long enough. If we haven't sex by then, she's obviously not interested." —Giorgio, age 38

But they do say patience is a virtue, and there are those men who have a lot of both. About a third take the following approach.

"I've dated women for months without getting sex. It depends on the connection I make with her." —Louis, age 29

"I really wouldn't mind waiting. My wife and I waited several years before the relationship got sexual—it was worth it." —Jeremy, age 32

What to look out for: Believing that just because he's waiting for sex with you specifically, doesn't mean he's waiting for sex in general.

Most men who answered this question were willing to be patient to a point. While four dates is where a majority of men reached the cutoff point (the same time frame as they expected to have sex, as we saw in the last question), some said they are willing to wait longer. It appears that at the end of the fourth date, there is a decision that needs to be made—whether a more intimate relationship takes place before he moves on.

How many girls does he have?

"I've always assumed that men would try to date as many women as possible at one time, but I'm not sure if that's just what men would like to portray or if it's the reality. **Do men date more than one woman at a time?**" —Mary, age 50, dating

What the men say

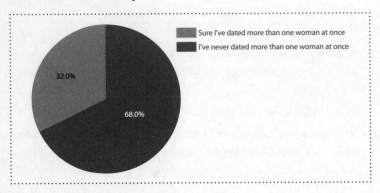

Sure I've dated more than one woman at once
I've never dated more than one woman at once

32.0%

68.0%

What men are really saying

For the men who dated more than one woman at a time, they said they did so only in the beginning, when they were trying to figure out who they're compatible with.

"Yes, but nothing in the way of serious relationships. I was seeing multiple girls at the same time to get to know them better before making any kind of commitment beyond dinner plans." —Danny, age 51

"Of course I've dated more than one woman at a time. I owe it to myself to really see what I want in a woman. And I believe that I'm doing her a favor by doing this. If I'm not sure if I really want to be with her long term, I will just be making her miserable in the meantime." —Mickey, age 23

"What man hasn't dated more than one woman at a time at some point in his life? If you go to a buffet, you try everything before you go back for seconds, right?" —Larry, age 52

The men who don't date more than one woman at a time say that to make a relationship work, or become serious, they (the men) need to focus on and nurture it.

"No, I have never dated more than one woman at a time. I respect the girl I am dating too much to do this to her. I feel that if you get to the point that you are dating someone, then you need to have enough respect to find out if it would work or not." —Tony, age 29

"No, I have never dated more than one woman at a time because dating more can at times be confusing and frustrating." —Luis, age 26

What to look out for: Believing that all men date more than one woman at a time.

Plain and simple, dating more than one woman is hard, and while some try it, they typically do it only in the beginning, when they are trying to find Ms. Right.

Ask men your question at www.wtfaramenthinking.com

Will he gossip about me?

"Everyone knows that women spill the beans about all the ins and outs of their dates with their girlfriends. **But do men give details to their friends about their dates too?**" —Kristen, age 58, dating

What the men say

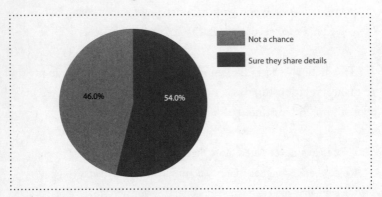

Not a chance

Sure they share details

46.0%   54.0%

What men are really saying

Men are gossips too, and after a date, some just want to call their buddies and go over how the date went. While some say they don't get too personal, others have no problem sharing details with their buds.

> "Yes. I have a select few friends close enough to tell them these things. I find it helpful to get an outside point of view, and everyone needs a friend they can talk to about anything."
> —Johnny, age 51

"Yes, I'll give details to my closest friends in regard to what happened on my first date, second date, etc....However, once I'm in a committed relationship with a woman, I no longer feel the need to discuss all of the details of our relationship with my friends anymore. It no longer becomes an exciting topic for conversation, unless something major happens in the relationship that I would like to seek a friend's advice on." —Earl, age 46

Other men say that what happens on a date is no one's business, and they won't divulge any details to their buddies.

"No. I think what goes on between a man and a woman is their personal business." —Jimmy, age 30

"No, what happens behind closed doors stays behind closed doors." —Antonio, age 28

What to look out for: Thinking that your guy won't kiss and tell. It's important to keep in mind that if men are talking about your date, it was memorable enough to share and get feedback from their friends. This shouldn't be overlooked. In fact, it's a very good sign.

Does he compare me to her?

"I am an older woman and was reflecting on my past relationships, and I noticed the pattern of the men I was with comparing me to past relationships. I always felt that was unfair and wonder if all men do this. My question is: **do men always compare their present girlfriend or wives to old relationships that didn't work out (if so, why)?**"
—Gretchen, age 72, divorced

What the men say

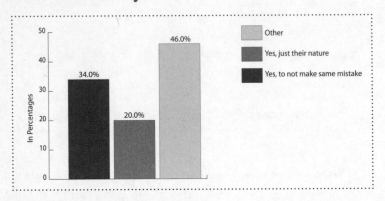

What men are really saying

Men don't like making mistakes, and in a relationship, it's no different. Given that knowledge, we weren't surprised to learn that 34 percent of men said they compare current relationships to past ones so they don't make the same mistake twice.

"This is a common-sense answer. We are trying to learn from past mistakes, so as to avoid them in current relationships. To

not compare to past relationships is to be willfully oblivious or to not care about the current relationship. Would you honestly rather we never looked back or learned from past relationships?"
—James, age 30

"I think it is a combination of a couple of things. First, men in a way are trying to admit where they screwed up in the previous relationship and to find out if what they did would cause trouble in their current relationship. The second reason I think they do it is to find out what they can get away with and what they had better work on if they want the current relationship to continue."
—Michael, age 56

Men also think it's just in their nature to compare. In fact, 20 percent said it's just what men do. They compare everything in life, and relationships are just something they compare as well.

"Men compare everything! There is not much more to it than that. It is our competitive nature, and it never sleeps. Usually it is a good thing, and we men think women do it too!" —Herman, age 29

"Not all men do, but most are guilty of this. I guess it's like comparing anything, sadly. Such as your old car versus your new or your old cell phone even." —Jerome, age 35

What to look out for: Believing that men thinking about the past means they're judging you against women of the past.

To answer Gretchen's question, it's not necessarily *unfair* for a man to compare previous relationships to the current one, as most men say what they are trying to do is learn from past mistakes.

Good looks or good personality?

"I want to know the truth regarding looks versus personality. For example, I know that women don't dress for men, they dress for women. But men are superficial too, especially when being set up on a date, so my question is: **are looks more important than personality when deciding whether to date a woman?**" —Tina, age 52, dating

What the men say

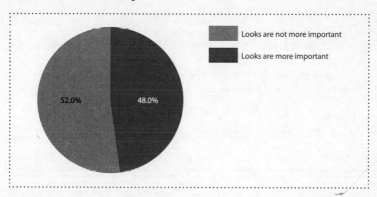

52.0%   48.0%

Looks are not more important
Looks are more important

What men are really saying

For some men, looks are important:

> For some men looks are important because as one said, "Yes…it's the first thing you notice…it opens the door." —Carlos, age 48

> "Looks are more important. You are either physically attracted to the person or not." —Russell, age 32

"I'm somewhat picky about who I'd want to spend my time with. I will admit to having dated women who weren't beauty queens (actually, most of them), but they were at least better than average looking. Just call me superficial." —Bobby, age 38

For men, looks are just as important as personality in a short-term relationship. This means that when men are making the decision as to whether or not to date a woman, her looks are more important than her personality. As the dating process is extended, however, personality becomes more important.

"No, but that doesn't mean looks aren't important. However, personality can make a woman more attractive when her looks aren't great, but a bad personality is not redeemable by any amount of good looks." —Victor, age 54

"No. Personality is what holds a relationship together. That said, attraction is important too, but personality can affect your attraction to someone. Especially over time." —Marty, age 34

What to look out for: Assuming that your looks are more important than your personality.

Looks may fade over the years, and men tend to keep the big picture in mind when deciding how and with whom they are going to progress through their relationships. Looks might be what gets a guy to ask you out, but it's your personality that will keep him around for the long haul.

What personality traits are important to men?

"I know men say that they like women with good personalities. I've tried being outgoing, funny, 'one of the men,' and just can't seem to figure out what men want when it comes to this 'personality' that is so important to them. I need to know, when deciding whom you wish to date, **what personality traits do you look for in a woman?**"
—Sarah, age 22, single

What the men say

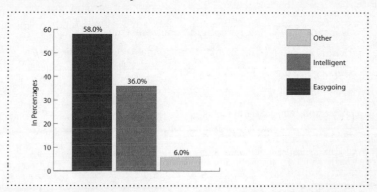

What men are really saying

You probably always heard that "so and so" has a nice personality. Sometimes, this is in lieu of a great physique or physical beauty. When men were faced with this question, however, they almost always seem to say that personality trumps looks.

While a woman may be drop-dead gorgeous, if she happens to be as interesting as a dead fish, men will get bored quickly with her, perhaps seeing her as nothing more than a hookup. When we asked men what personality traits they look for, 94 percent agreed on two: easygoing and intelligent.

Which of the two is more important? Fifty-eight percent of men say a woman being easygoing is the most important trait in her personality.

"I'm a very easygoing person, so I would like my mate to be as well. I don't want her to get jealous when I'm hanging out with the men, and I need space to hang out with my friends as well." —Marshal, age 18

"It means they won't be uptight about everything, usually have friends, are interesting to talk to and connect with, and are able to have a good time." —Jason, age 26

"A person who takes everything seriously is not really going to be compatible with me. And if you aren't easygoing, we will have problems with my sense of humor." —Tyrone, age 37

"Because I want the conversations to be easy and not forced. I also like a woman who is just fun to be around and likes to do the same sort of things that I do." —Craig, age 40

What to look out for: Believing that if you're young and good-looking, men will beat a path to your door.

The answer to Sarah's question is simple. Men love a woman who is easygoing, fun to be around, and intelligent. More than likely you possess these traits. Life shouldn't be taken too seriously; let loose and have fun, and the men will be intrigued and will stick around.

What is the number-one physical feature men look for?

"I'm now divorced, and while this has been tough on me, I really am at the point now where I look forward to getting on with the next chapter in my life. My ex-husband occasionally made comments about me having smaller breasts. So, as part of my settlement, I made a big decision and decided to get breast implants. I just love them. I feel better. It's like a power. However, it hasn't yet translated into finding a new or better man. So I found your site, and I want to ask **what is the number-one physical feature that men look for in a woman?**" —Kat, age 42, divorced

What the men say

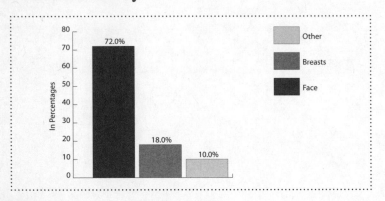

What men are really saying

Men are visual creatures. If an attractive woman walks by, you better believe they are going to check her out. So what feature appeals the most to them? A vast majority, at 72 percent, say a woman's face is what has the biggest draw.

"Specifically in her face, her smile. A nice smile is more important than any other physical feature." —Ash, age 23

"Because I look at [people] in their faces when I talk to them.
They need to have an attractive face if I'm going to be looking at
it for an extended amount of time." —Samson, age 30

Coming in at a distant second are breasts, at 18 percent. This is
probably not a surprise.

"I like a woman with either small or modest-size breasts. If they
are too big or are only implants, then it would probably turn me off.
Since I'm a guy with a healthy sexuality, the first thing I would notice about a naked or topless woman is her breasts." —Bart, age 33

"Breasts are just awesome, and while it might sound totally shallow, they're the first thing I see on a woman. I love women who
have the balls to get plastic surgery and enhance them. They're
fun and sexy for me and make her feel more confident. A win-
win." —Keith, age 33

What to look out for: Assuming that most men are breast men.
While men will always check out a woman's breasts (and have
done so since they were teens), when push comes to shove, it's your
face that draws men to you the most. So perhaps if you're looking to
make some physical changes, you could start with the areas that will
make the most impact from the man's perspective.

Ask men your question at www.wtfaramenthinking.com

How important are my clothes?

"I used to make fun of those women who, after getting married, would sort of let themselves go. You know the type, ponytails and frumpy skirts. It just occurred to me that I've become one of those women. I've actually bought underwear at Costco when I used to shop at Victoria's Secret. It's because of this that I want to know: **does a woman's clothing affect your impression/attraction to a woman?**" —Amy, age 25, married

What the men say

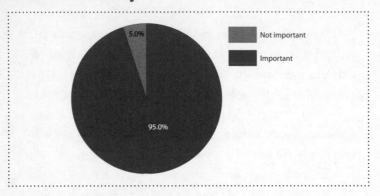

What men are really saying

You are what you wear, ladies. No two ways around this one. Men see how you're dressed and make a personal and sexual opinion instantly. To men: dress like a slut = slut; dress sexy = sexy; dress classy = classy. Women can certainly use this to their advantage, if played correctly, so it's very important *not* to underestimate what you put on your body. Men, believe it or not, don't want to see you in sweats and flip-flops. Your lasting impression depends on it.

"Well, if she dresses like a slut, then she probably is a slut. If she dresses like a normal person, then I would probably talk to her."
—Dennis, age 35

"If they are dressed with skimpy clothes and provocative clothes, I am more likely to think they are sluts, but if they are moderately or conservatively dressed, I'm more likely to think they are nice girls." —Marc, age 21

"Yes, but only to the degree that she looks good in it. There are clothes that scream sexy. There are clothes that scream slutty. And there are clothes that scream 'help me, I need diet and exercise.' Advice to women: there are no clothes that exist that scream 'hey, what a great personality…'" —Bob, age 33

"A woman's clothes say a lot about her. Sexy clothes make you think of her a certain way, sophisticated clothes another way, etc. Either way a woman looks, if she looks well put together in any outfit, it is a big plus. My impression is formed due to what she portrays with her clothing." —Ted, age 36

What to look out for: Thinking he cares more about who you are than what you wear.

For men? Not initially. How you want to be perceived and thought of by men depends on what effort you make.

Do men really prefer blonds?

"I'm considering changing my look and going from brunette to 'all blond.' But before I do, I'd like to know: **is it true that men really prefer blonds?**" —Katrina, age 26, married

What the men say

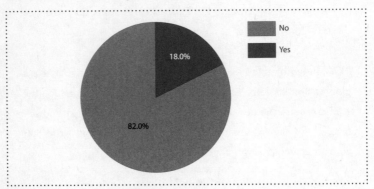

What men are really saying

A majority of men, at 82 percent, say the idea that they prefer blonds is false. Contrary to popular belief, men are not obsessed with blonds and dating them.

"Because a woman's hair is not what she is all about. While some men might prefer blonds (I am not one of those men), just because a woman is blond does not mean she will rock your world emotionally, mentally, and sexually. My wife is Peruvian, so she has black/brownish hair, the exact opposite of blond, but that's not why I think she's so beautiful and sexy. It's all about our personal connection. A blond woman might look amazing with her bright hair, but she might not have it all there for you mentally." —Robert, age 20

"It is not about the hair color, but rather more about the personality! It does no good to hang out with a blond if she has no sense of humor or tends not to smile. Life is too short not to smile and enjoy!" —Les, age 38

So what is the appeal of blonds? Eighteen percent of men who prefer them say blonds are exotic, which makes them more appealing.

"I personally prefer blonds because almost all of them have such a sexy hot body I would love to have sex with." —Dax, age 23

"Because I, like most people, am instinctively attracted to things that are rare and hard to find. Over 90 percent of the human population of the world has black hair and brown eyes, so natural blonds are a tiny minority. So keeping these facts in mind, it's easy to see why an attractive blond woman is more likely to get male attention than a brunette or a black-haired woman can. Because every guy wants to get her before someone else can." —Clem, age 21

What to look out for: Assuming that you're doomed if you're brunette.

While the urban legend exists that most men prefer a blond and "blonds have more fun," it's all false. The majority of men couldn't care less about your hair color, and a lot actually find darker hair more exotic.

Cougars: yes or no?

"I just cannot figure out for the life of me how my boyfriend cheated on me with a forty-two-year-old divorcee. I know that there is this whole attraction to cougars (older women in their forties and fifties interested in younger men), but I find it hard to believe that younger men could ever be interested in older women. Are they? **Are men in their twenties really interested in dating cougars?**"
—Anne, age 28, single

What the men say

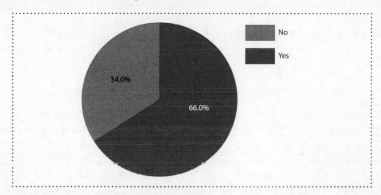

What men are really saying

The times have changed, and age isn't necessarily relevant when it comes to dating. Cougars have become commonplace, and there is even a sitcom named after the phenomenon. So it comes as no surprise that the majority of men, 66 percent, say that they would in fact date an older woman. And the reason? It's simple, really. Experience.

"Older women are more mature and experienced. It does, however, depend on the individual..." —Jeff, age 29

"The thought of an older woman is hot. She has experience and
can show you things never known. She will be more likely to do
adventurous things, and it is sort of a naughty thing, being with an
older woman." —Padraig, age 27

The 34 percent who disagree say that while hooking up with a
cougar is okay, that's all it is; they wouldn't date one.

"Typically, dating, no; sleeping with them, yes." —Jace, age 21

"I don't think twenty-year-old men are interested in dating an
older woman. They are more interested in having a sexual experience with them than anything. They would prefer to date women
their own age, but are drawn in by the sexual experience of an
older woman." —Lancaster, age 28

What to look out for: Presuming that youth trumps experience.
Anne's boyfriend seems to fit into the 34 percent who were just
looking for sex more than anything else. When men are just looking
for sex, age doesn't necessarily matter; men tell us it's all about the
looks and the experience and attitude.

What habit drives men away?

"I realize that I've got some annoying habits. I'm a talker. I'm also a little on the fussy side, but I know what I want. My question is: **what is the one thing women do that drives men away the quickest?**" —Anna, age 28, married

What the men say

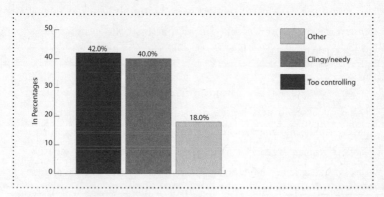

What men are really saying

Overall the results showed that there were many reasons, but two really prevailed. The majority of men, 42 percent, responded that women who were too controlling were not worth their time.

> "A woman can crowd a man's space if she wants to drive him away quickly. Men prize their independence, and a woman invading his space and pressuring every aspect of his life will drive him away very quickly." —Izaak, age 31

"Not allowing him to have any space. A smothered man is a very unhappy man. Allow him to have guy time and hang out with his friends. Allow him to have a night to himself, if he wants. The times you are together will be much better then, and chances are he will be desiring you when he's away, anyway."
—Matt, age 33

Coming in at a close second were being clingy or needy. Forty percent of the men we asked said that any clingy chick was just asking to be dumped.

"Most men do not like a woman who constantly requires contact and questions everything he does. Like every time a man goes out, wondering what he is doing. If he is innocently talking to another woman, even if it's business related, questioning why he was talking to her. Men prefer to have some personal space, and constant nagging and accusing them of doing wrong will drive them away." —Steven, age 25

"Suffocate him. Not only is some distance at the beginning more enticing, if a woman is too clingy and needy at the start of a relationship, then a man is going to run a mile. Give us space; we will crawl to you." —Parker, age 40

What to look out for: Believing that men will always accept you, flaws and all.

Every person has faults, and you all know what you do that is annoying. Eighty percent of men told us that controlling, clingy women are irritating. Maybe the best approach is to warn your man ahead of time, or try to change your behavior if it's one of these two. You can also take comfort that men aren't perfect either!

What grosses men out about women?

"I just moved in with my fiancé, and this is my first live-in situation. I don't think I am different or doing anything that typical women don't do, but I want to avoid totally grossing him out. **Is there anything that women typically do that completely grosses men out that I can avoid?**" —Darla, age 32, engaged

What the men say

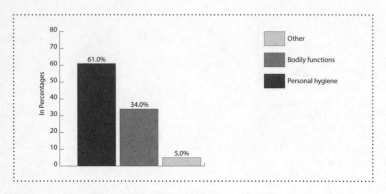

What men are really saying

We know that men can tolerate some pretty gross stuff. From killing bugs to watching slasher movies, it seems that men are quite in their element when it comes to items of the sickening variety. Or are they? We get variations on this question asked of us so often that we knew we'd want to include it in this book. So can something a woman does gross them out? Fifty-eight percent of men say yes. We decided to take that one step further and find out what exactly grosses them out. It should come as no surprise (we don't think) that the majority, at 61 percent, say it's a woman's personal hygiene that really can disgust them.

> "It grosses me out when a woman does not shave or trim her vagina and/or it smells funny." —Wilson, age 35

> "Don't get me started on the whole period and menstruation thing. I don't want to see any of that or evidence of any of that at all. At all! Do you want to handle, see, or deal with the used condoms in the bathroom? I don't want to see your monthly stuff." —Marlon, age 28

> "When I see a woman go to the bathroom and [she] does not wash her hands, that really grosses me out. It makes me sick." —Bernardo, age 30

Ironically, given the farting and burping prowess that men tend to have, 34 percent say bodily functions from a woman, although natural, just bother them.

> "Farting and burping. It's funny when men do it, but gross when women do." —Dave, age 36

> "I think it's kind of gross when women fart or burp, but then again that might be a little bit of a double standard, but that is just how I feel, and I'm not sure exactly why, it just does." —Merrick, age 18

"Farting. I know this is a natural thing for human beings, and I'm not sure why this bothers me about women, but it does."
—Benny, age 49

What to look out for: Presuming that men are tolerant when it comes to a women's hygiene.

Overall, men state that personal hygiene is the number-one issue that grosses men out. It's a standard that men expect to be high for women, and it disgusts most men when they see instances to the contrary. This might be a complete double standard, but remember, this is how men see it, fair or not.

What does he look for in a long-term partner?

"I come from a wealthy family. Growing up, I never saw it as a benefit or a hindrance. I never thought about it much. Now that I'm getting older and dating men instead of boys, I see differences in their behaviors. I never had too many problems getting dates, but I do question at times now what men might want from me. Is money a factor for why I've gotten dates in the past? **What are the elements men look for in a woman for a long-term relationship?**"
—Krysta, age 27, single

What the men say

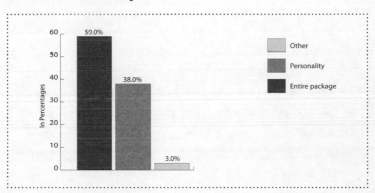

What men are really saying

What do men want from a woman when looking for something serious? Is it looks, money, personality, her body, or all of the above? The majority of men are a bit greedy and want it all. In fact, 59 percent men say they look for the entire package when looking for a long-term partner.

> "[I am] looking for a complete woman. It's not enough to just be beautiful and sexy. I'm also looking for someone I can have a real conversation with and who also has her own career."
> —Casey, age 41

> "Men typically like a woman who has it all together. Obviously, there needs to be some sort of physical attraction, so those attributes are critical. As far as the money is concerned, I don't feel I tend to care if a woman has a lot of money, just as long as I don't feel the woman is going to be a gold digger either."
> —Paul, age 40

> "Because all of these things are important, such as a great body for sex; beauty, so it's not gross being with them; personality, so that you can enjoy the relationship; and money, so you're not completely supporting them. (If you're single, you don't want to have to pay for everything your girlfriend wants.)"
> —Nathan, age 22

What about the men who don't expect the whole package? Personality comes in at a close second, with 38 percent. Looks just aren't everything when it comes to the long term.

"I need the personality to be happy. I'll admit that I'm shallow enough that I almost picked all of the above, but really, without a good personality, all the other things would not be enough."
—David, age 49

"Some of the sweetest women I have known have not had a rocking body. They have not had runway legs. While I prefer women who at least are slender, I have known a few and dated one that had 'too big' of a nose or 'no chest.' But some of them were super nice! On the other hand, I have known many who were no doubt some of the hottest in the area, and again I dated one (prior to the other one), and while she was very attractive and fun in bed, frankly, she was a bitch! It was all about her. In general I have found that the 'hotties' tend to have this attitude more often than one who has minor flaws that prevent others from going 'damn' and walking into a telephone pole." —Gary, age 30

What to look out for: Thinking that money is a major influence for men being interested in you.

Even though the majority of men want it all when it comes to women and are essentially looking for the perfect woman, men say that personality is still the biggest factor. Bottom line, you can't have a long-term relationship on superficiality or money alone. Eventually looks fade, and all you are left with is a boring or bitter woman. Beauty is in the eye of the beholder, and men say that a good smile, attitude, and caring personality will take you further in a long-term relationship than money.

Ask men your question at www.wtfarementhinking.com

The official relationship starts—when?

"I think men prefer the dating life to any type of commitment. They seem to want to drag out the dating for a long time without acknowledging that 'yes, we're a couple.' My question is, therefore: **when do men consider themselves in a committed relationship?**"
—Paula, age 44, dating

What the men say

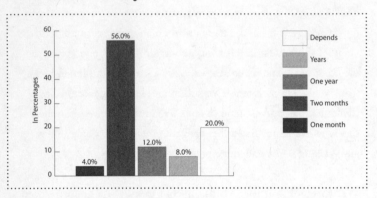

What men are really saying

Men will put a time frame on when they consider themselves in a serious relationship. For many men, it's just a gut feeling. However, there are the men who have it down to a science and base serious relationships on a time frame. Typically, men felt they were in committed relationships after about two months.

"Two months. After two months, I feel like you have really gotten to know someone well..." —Arnand, age 39

"I would say if I have been dating and having a close relationship with a woman for about two months, that is commitment, at my age." —Andrew, age 31

"After a couple of months and both of you are serious." —Raymond, age 36

"After two months of steady dating and intimacy (sex), because by then you should have developed some feelings for the person." —Gregory, age 44

Other timelines were mentioned. Some went from immediately to years to other various benchmarks.

"When she starts sleeping over during the week as well as during the weekend." —Joshua, age 40

"When your partner moves into your apartment." —Jerry, age 35

"After five dates; at this point you either are connecting or it's not worth it." —Dennis, age 26

What to look out for: Assuming that men go by the number of dates to determine their commitment level.

Men don't go by dates. Time is more important. You might have gone out seven times in seven days, but men seem to feel a comfort level at about the two-month mark. Try not to worry about dates or

months, but do what you need to get to know your man. No rush.
This isn't a sprint.

What makes him commit?

"Nobody ever wants to commit. I think that is just how men are wired, but still, I want to know when the dating is actually progressing. So my question is: **what do men say are the key considerations when deciding whether they want to become serious with a woman they're dating?**" —Barbara, age 24, dating

What the men say

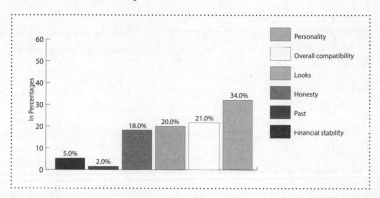

What men are really saying

Surprise, surprise, it's *not* all about the looks. While looks do play a part, since attraction is a big factor in a relationship, personality is what really does it for a guy. Also, another key point worth mentioning is financial stability.

"If I'm in this for the long haul, I want to know she can also take care of herself. This means financially too. In this day and age, you need to cover all bases." —Edward, age 29

Most men interviewed had definitive ideas about what considerations were important, almost as if they had a pre-made list.

"(1) Does she have a good sense of humor, and does she smile? She can't take herself and life too seriously; that type of person is no fun to be around. (2) Does she worry too much about her hair, makeup, etc.? I don't want to compete with a compact for her attention. (3) Do we have similar interests? After the initial attraction wears off, do we have enough in common to stay interested in each other? (4) Does she like opinions that differ from hers? I like discussion and debates that have different points of view. I will always be respectful, but I don't want to have to be careful of every word I say." —Brian, age 30

Most men just wanted compatibility, good personality traits, and a go-with-the-flow attitude.

"Is she fun to be around? Does she nag and try to change the people she dates? If she is unhappy with everything, that is a big turn-off. Does she accept the things that I do and enjoy? If so, I can compromise and do things she enjoys half the time. If I agree to go to an opera, she better be willing to go to a football game!" —Ronnie, age 39

What to look out for: Going under the assumption that you can get by on looks alone.

Men really feel that it's what you bring to the table in terms of personality and attitude that makes them want to commit to you. After all, this is what (usually) doesn't change a lot over time. Looks fade, but attitudes and personality are forever. Just be sure yours are compatible with what your man is looking for.

Why are men so afraid to commit?

"Why won't the man I'm dating commit to our relationship? He seems content to continue along the same path, but will always tell me he isn't ready for marriage. It makes me feel like he isn't taking our relationship seriously. By not committing to our relationship, isn't that saying he isn't committed to me? **What scares men about committing?**" —Krista, age 28, dating

What the men say

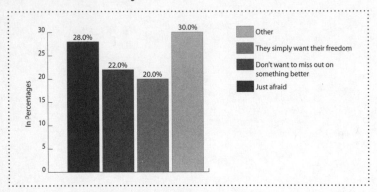

What men are really saying

Commitment-phobic men aren't a new occurrence, but we're trying to get to the bottom of what's driving their feelings. Perhaps not surprisingly, twenty-eight percent of men admitted that they are just afraid.

"There are many reasons, including (1) past experiences with women in relationships; (2) fear of the unknown; (3) cultural expectations of having to provide the money; (4) fear of getting a woman pregnant—and then feeling pressured to marry and be committed or have to break up and then have to pay child support; (5) fear of being falsely accused of domestic violence after divorcing." —Brian, age 25

"Fear of rejection is often mistaken for fear of commitment. If a man is never truly committed, he cannot be truly rejected." —Devereux, age 31

Coming in at a tie for second, 22 percent of men just don't want to miss out on something better. There is always that nagging little voice in the back of their heads that wonders if this is the best out there or if someone better will come along.

"I think it is because men are always looking for something better. When they are younger, they do not want to go with the first girl they meet and always keep their eyes open for the next. Most men do not want to be controlled by a woman also, and commitment makes them under that control." —Matt, age 33

"Because men always have that evil little guy whispering in their ears saying there are so many women out there." —William, age 18

Another 20 percent say they just want their freedom, and it's not something that they really want to or are ready to give up.

"I'm probably a great source for this answer. I've been engaged twice and never married. Simply put, I am afraid of giving up my freedom to the whim of someone who knows that I am legally committed to her. The idea of being sublimated and, to a degree, emasculated, scares me. I treasure my freedom."
—Jeremy, age 35

"For men, marriage often means giving up freedom in exchange for responsibility. It means that some, if not all, of their dreams will have to be given up for the good of others. (Look at older married men, forty to fifty. How many of them seem happy?)"
—Harlan, age 50

What to look out for: Believing he isn't committed to you because of his inability to commit to your relationship.

Men are afraid to commit largely due to fear and the unknown in life. It's not about you specifically. The main takeaway for you, knowing that fear is the driver, is *not* to put pressure on him to commit. We're not saying that you stay on the sidelines waiting for him to make up his mind. Being on the fence is one thing, but a complete lack of commitment is a different story.

Money: more or less important?

"As a couple, you need to buy food, housing, essentials. And don't forget about kids, college, and retirement. Maybe men feel differently. Once you're in a relationship, **how important does money become?**"
—Jane, age 65, married

What the men say

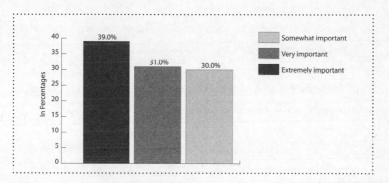

What men are really saying

No matter what anyone says, money does make the world go round. So, in a long-term relationship, how important is money to men? Thirty-nine percent of men said that it is extremely important, 31 percent said it was very important, and 30 percent said it was just somewhat important. The main feedback from men on this issue was that as long as you are responsible and not saddled with big bills, it's not a huge issue.

"As long as there is not a huge amount of debt that someone has, I don't think money is that big of an issue. A large amount of

debt is a red flag that that person is not very good with money and can be a problem in the relationship. I would rather be the breadwinner in the relationship, so income is not that important."
—Matt, age 33

"Money becomes somewhat important in the long run. Love alone can get a marriage through the early stages, but of course money is a factor that is important. Money is not the sole means of happiness and should never be considered so. But of course it is necessary for survival in some way." —Coty, age 18

Thirty-one percent of men also cited that money is fairly important from the angle of what money can do to a relationship.

"I think it is pretty important, and not from the perspective of what it can do to help move the relationship on, but more from the perspective of what damage it can do. A relationship can have its challenges, money not being an issue, but if money does become an issue, all of the other possibly problematic items can be magnified. It is important, on one hand, to have money to be able to live, send kids to school, and engage in entertainment, but it is also as important, on the other hand, that it not become a roadblock in the relationship." —Arnie, age 37

"You need money to do things with one another, and finances are a cause of divorce, if not properly handled to one's liking. In case of emergencies for one or both people, someone is

going to have the relief of knowing you were thinking ahead
in case of something major. There is no wrong or right way to
handle money, though. Have the same bank account or different
ones, but make sure you both are able to support yourselves."
—Blake, age 19

What to look out for: Believing that men are transfixed by money
in a relationship.

While money does pay the bills and buy food, it does not dictate
quality of living. Bottom line: men ultimately feel that it won't be what
makes you happy. If you have a lot of money but aren't happy with the
one you are with, money won't help you.

Will he cheat on me?

"After more than twenty years of dating and thinking I've seen it all, I really want to know about cheating. It seems to me that every man has cheated at some point in their lives. So really, my question is simple: **have you ever cheated on a woman you were dating?**" —Veronica, age 40, dating

What the men say

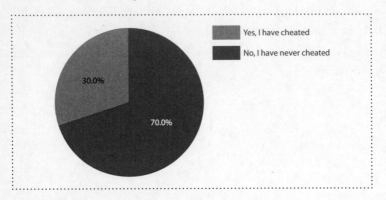

Yes, I have cheated
No, I have never cheated

30.0%

70.0%

What men are really saying

The reasons that men cheat vary, but when we asked men if they cheated, many men also provided reasons for why they did so. Either the guy was mad at the person he was dating, or he didn't really consider his relationship serious enough to call it cheating. Men told us:

"Yes, I was not married, and I was mad at her." —Mike, age 47

"Yes. I was just starting to date, and I wanted to get back with an ex-girlfriend and made a selfish mistake." —Stanley, age 38

The men who don't cheat just don't think it's worth destroying a relationship or that it's just better to break it off than hurt the other person.

"No. I don't get easily involved with women, and the few times that I have, it has been an emotional relationship in which I have never felt the need to look beyond for any need, be it emotional or physical." —Leonard, age 41

"No. I do not believe it is right to date or make moves on another woman when I am currently committed to someone. It is not fair to the person I am dating, and it is not something that I would want done to me." —Nathan, age 28

What to look out for: Assuming that your man will probably cheat because it's his nature.

Cheating is a touchy subject. Out of the men who were surveyed, more than two to one say they never cheated on the person they were dating. The men who did cheat either did so out of anger or believed their relationship wasn't serious enough. Most of those men also regretted doing so.

Why not leave, instead of cheating?

"I've been cheated on in the past two relationships. Both of them were relationships that I thought were on solid ground. The men were twenty-eight and thirty-seven years of age. In the last relationship, I actually thought he might be close to proposing before he cheated. And worst of all, I caught both men in the act as a nice little extra confirmation. Nice, huh? So, my question is simple: **why not leave the girl you're going to cheat on, instead of cheating?**"
—Samantha, age 21, single

What the men say

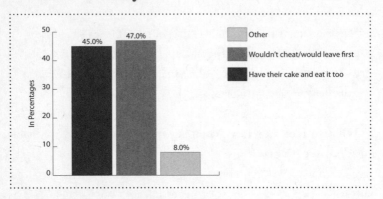

What men are really saying

Luckily for most women, 47 percent of men say they either wouldn't cheat or they would leave you before they moved on to someone else. The reason? Most men think it's pathetic to cheat and that leaving someone is the more respectable option.

"This is an excellent suggestion. I would say in some situations the woman you are in a relationship with is too clingy and that creates a difficult situation in order to break it off and move on."
—Tyrone, age 37

"I would not ever cheat on someone. But some men just like having many women in their life and like the thrill. It is a terrible thing to do. If you are not committed, then get out and avoid the additional hurt you will bring on the person." —Sebastian, age 26

"I totally agree. I do not know why either men or women do not do that. If you have no respect for your significant other, then you should break up. If you are looking for another girl, then break it off." —Matt, age 33

What about the ones who would cheat? What is their reasoning for cheating? Well, 45 percent of men say they want to have their cake and eat it too. Why ruin a perfectly good relationship if you just want to have a little fun?

"Well, cheating isn't something that is acceptable by most people in society, even though it obviously happens. The most compelling reason, for me, anyway, would be that I desire only a small change in my life, not one that changes my life completely. Leaving a girl you're dating is a complete change. Maybe I'd only be looking for a little excitement in my life, or I am getting little to no sex at home. I am not making an excuse for cheating, as it is not acceptable by most, but merely offering reasoning behind the behavior." —Paul, age 40

"The ones who cheat want the best of both worlds, or else they're too scared to go through that confrontation if they don't have to." —Bill, age 33

What to look out for: Assuming that if he's going to cheat, he'll use that as the reason to break up with you.

In Samantha's case, the men she picks seem to come from the 45 percent who want to have it all. It's unfortunate, for sure, but most men don't deliberately go out and cheat to get out of a relationship. There are usually other issues that we cover in this book. However, women like Samantha should have faith that not every man is a cheater.

What bothers men about being in a relationship?

"My last boyfriend and I had a good thing going. Most of our relationship was great. He had a good job. He respected me and cared for my family and friends. The sex was great. But in the last two to three months of the relationship, he seemed distant. I asked if it was anything I was doing or had done. He assured me it wasn't. Then one day, he asked to 'talk.' He wanted out of the relationship. He made the point that it was the relationship, and not me. So I'd like to find out **what irks men the most about being in a relationship?**"
—Ali, age 25, single

What the men say

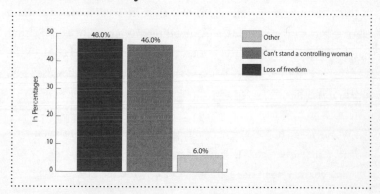

What men are really saying

There were two main factors that men said bothered them in a relationship. Forty-eight percent reported that they didn't like the loss of freedom. Men say once they are in a relationship they lose the ability to do the same things they used to and not have to report to anyone on what they are doing.

> "Not being able to do some of the things I enjoy when I want. For example, I like to let off steam by playing video games, but I have other responsibilities I have to put first. Being single means you can be more selfish." —Storm, age 40

> "Having less free time than I used to have. I find that life is so busy, and when you are in a relationship, you are even busier. Your free time is basically zero because if you say you want to be alone, that makes the other person upset." —Matt, age 33

Forty-six percent of men also said that they can't really stand a relationship where there is a controlling woman. They cited that they were "big boys," and they resented you deciding and controlling every aspect of their lives. You are their girlfriend or wife, they say, not their mother.

> "Women tend to become controlling when they are in a relationship. I am thirty-eight and have been in charge of my own life for many years. I don't need someone else to tell me how to live." —Bill, age 38

> "People who want to play games and try to control the relationship with those games. Long-term relationships are about two equal

people coming together. When you build a life together, it is not a ruler and servant; it is two equal people." —Wallis, age 28

What to look out for: Thinking men prefer that you control their lives.

While Ali got the old "It's not you..." line during the breakup, she can safely assume that her guy might have just become tired of not being single and having the freedom to do what he wanted in his life. Some men said they are selfish and think their needs should come first, even if that's not fair for all involved.

What signals you that it's time to break up?

"My girlfriends were discussing many topics related to men, but we all agreed that since men are visual in nature, women need to stay fit and keep up their appearance to keep men happy; otherwise, they're out. However, this was just our crazy theory. Since we have no real proof, once we found your website, we wanted to ask men this: **what is the main signal to you that it's time to break up with a woman?**"

—Julie, age 20, single

What the men say

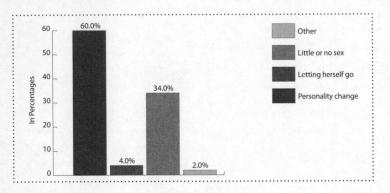

What men are really saying

We get a lot of questions on the website along this line about warning signs. Given that personality draws men to a woman, it should come as no surprise that it's an attitude or personality change that will cause them to break up with her. Sixty percent of men think as soon as their significant other's personality changes, it's time to call it quits.

"If a girl's personality has changed, it could mean a few different things. Most likely, they don't want to be with you anymore and are trying to show that without being jerks. Or it could just be that they don't care anymore about things, which is not something you want to be around in a relationship." —Mo, age 18

"The personality and attitude are the foundation of a relationship. Other things like sex will fall into place, but it is difficult to want to be with someone who was not like the person who you initially met. What really set the foundation is now gone." —Jürgen, age 37

We've already established that men are sexual creatures and women losing sexual interest or just pulling back sexually will also cause a man to end a relationship. Thirty-four percent of men agreed that little or no sex was grounds for breaking up.

"Because if she's not permitting much or any sex in a relationship, she's either become disinterested in me, or it means she may be cheating on me. Sex doesn't make the relationship, but it can certainly break it." —Paul, age 40

"I would say this is a major signal because most likely there is a reason there is no action in the bedroom, and that's because she may be cheating." —Maynerd, age 18

What to look out for: Believing that women need to keep up their looks if they want men to stick around.

Even though Julie and her friends assume looks play a part in the breakup, only 4 percent of men said that a woman letting herself go will cause them to break up with her. The main areas of concern for men were personality inconsistencies and loss of sexual interest or creativity.

Chapter 3

ROMANCE

We tackle the questions you have for men on the romance front in this chapter. The funny thing in reading what men have to say about romance is how many of them think (or like to think) that they're romantic.

Of course, what men think is romantic doesn't always match up with the woman's ideal. Some men are all about flowers, candy, cards, and notes tacked up on your mirror in the morning. Hell, some even call out of the blue to see how you're doing! Then again, some men think they're romantic because they invest two to three minutes in foreplay.

So let's dig a little deeper and find out what men have to say about being romantic, how they view romance, and what they find romantic. We think the answers will surprise you.

Is love at first sight possible?

"I'm not so sure, but I think that chivalry might indeed be dead, but I hope that romance or the notion of romance is not. **Do men believe in love at first sight?**" —Lisa, age 34, single

What the men say

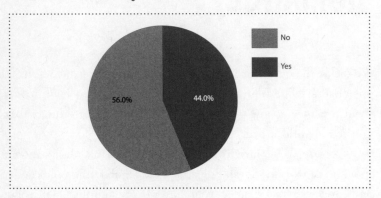

What men are really saying

Men can be hopeless romantics too. While not all have experienced love at first sight, some do believe it's possible.

"Yes, because it has happened to me…" —Jesse, age 36

"Yes, I do, because there is always that person out there who will hit you so hard when you first see her that it will feel like you know everything about her and love her already." —Craig, age 29

While 56 percent of men believe in lust at first sight, they believe real love grows over time.

"Love? Well, attraction at first sight, yes. Real love, no." —Alan, age 28

"No, I don't believe in love at first site. However, I do believe in attraction/chemistry at first sight. Love is something that develops over time with trust…" —Shawn, age 51

What to look out for: Assuming that he's a man and therefore doesn't believe in love at first sight.

Many men feel that it's possible. Some men disagree, but the big takeaway is that while whether a guy believes in love at first sight could be debated, a large portion still believe in instant attraction.

How does he know he's in love?

"I got divorced ten years ago. I just met a man while traveling in France. He is a banker in New York, and we hit it off immediately. Great travels, food, experiences, and the like followed for us over the last year and a half. But I'd like to know where he's at emotionally. We have fun. We have deep respect for each other. We care for each other. But he's yet to mention the *L* word, and I don't want to press. **How do you [men] know when you're in love?**"
—Marge, age 57, divorced

What the men say

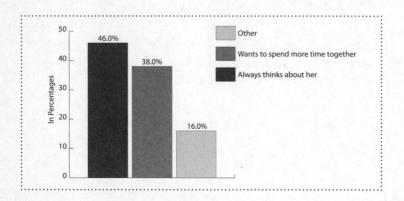

What men are really saying

This question can be asked a lot of different ways, but the basic premise was summed up in a question we got from Marge. And the answer? The biggest signal to most men on when they know they are in love is they always think about the woman. Forty-six percent of men say love to them is when a woman consumes their thoughts and that's all they think about.

"As far as I know, I've been in love one time. She was all I could ever think about. Literally anything going on, it somehow related to her. I put her feelings and her needs far before my own. I didn't care how I felt about anything; she was the only thing that mattered." —Brett, age 20

"I find that love is usually an emotion that distorts all others. What I mean by that is, it interrupts logical thinking and reasoning because the person you're in love with is all you can think about. I know if I'm already missing a woman the minute I'm away from her, I'm in love. It usually is accompanied by disruptions in sleep, eating, and daily functions. I don't say this in a bad way. It just has been my experience. If I can't imagine my life without the other person, I know I'm in love." —Paul, age 40

Another big signal is when they want to spend time with the other person. Thirty-eight percent of men say they knew they were in love when they wanted to spend as much time with their girlfriends as they could.

"You want to be with the other person more than anyone else. You see her as a young girl if she's old, and you see her as old if she is young. [You] can't imagine living without her. Your heart beats fast when you are around her." —Paul, age 41

"When you like to talk or hang out with the other person as much as anything else you do." —Devin, age 51

What to look out for: Believing that for men, love means sharing experiences.

Love is a four-letter word to most men, they say, and they have to be sure about how they feel before they say the words. In Marge's case, it could very well be love, but her man might not be ready to say it or is still hesitant. It doesn't mean he's not in love; he's just not ready to say it. Based on what men tell us, find out how often he's thinking about you and how much time he wants to spend with you, and you'll get closer to knowing how he really feels about you.

Are there any romantic men?

"Most of my past boyfriends have not been very romantic if at all. I can honestly say that I really don't think any guys I've dated are romantic. I hope I am wrong, but I have to ask: **is it that men just don't like being romantic, or is it just the ones I've been with?**"
—Mackenzie, age 21, single

What the men say

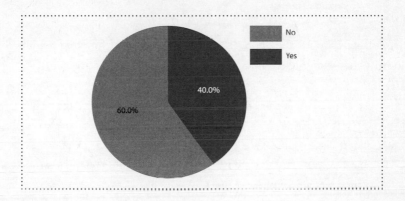

What men are really saying

Men who think of themselves as romantic took offense on this one. They almost universally cited that only young or immature men weren't romantic or didn't like to or know how to be.

> "Most young boys don't know how to be or don't want to be. Most men are fine with it." —Georgie, age 35

"A lot of men want to be romantic; you have to give them time to mature, though." —Clyde, age 55

"Well, I know that I love to be romantic, but then again I am forty-five years old. Assuming she dates young men near her age, I can understand where she may have a problem. I cannot relate to or understand a great deal of the younger generation, so she might want to consider dating older men, if she's not already doing so." —Benjamin, age 45

Interestingly, the younger men were the ones who cited reasons why they didn't like romance or didn't know how to be romantic.

"It's our DNA. We just don't know how to be." —Johnny, age 24

"Men like routines. We don't like having to try to go above and beyond every day. We like to get in a comfortable motion with a woman and keep it there. We do like to be romantic for special occasions like birthdays, Valentine's Day, anniversaries, etc. Most men won't try to be romantic on a regular basis though, at least not after the first six months to a year of dating." —Mitch, age 27

What to look out for: Thinking that men, no matter what their age, don't understand the concept of romance.

The data show that it's very much dependent upon age. Older men believe romance is important and embrace it, whereas younger men more often tend to shy away from romance. It appears as though, like wine, men and their romantic abilities, skills, and desires get better with age.

What do guys really think about cuddling?

"Women are more touchy-feely about romance and connection than men. I don't know a woman who doesn't feel that way. That said, it doesn't mean that men like to be intimate without sex, or more specifically, I want to know: **does it bother men that women like to cuddle?**" —Vicki, age 42, married

What the men say

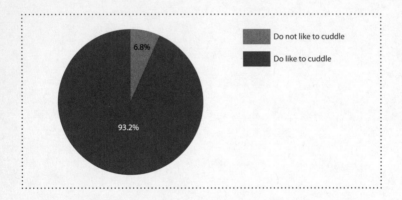

Do not like to cuddle
Do like to cuddle

6.8%

93.2%

What men are really saying

What big softies men are! They just love it. Such sweethearts. They love you so much, and they can't be apart from you. Well, it's not altogether true. Yes, the vast majority of men like to cuddle, but many of those same men do so because of what's in it for them or what they can get out of it.

"I love cuddling...that's the initiator. Women like that, and that gets me in." —Tony, age 28

"I am not in the slightest bit bothered by cuddling with a woman. Under the right circumstances of course. Those being that it gets me closer to sex or calms her down." —Joseph, age 22

"I [enjoy] being close to a woman at any time. If you cuddle after sex, it is always a pleasure to lie naked next to a woman. Sometimes, just lying next to a naked woman just after having sex will be enough of a turn-on to go for round two." —Rocky, age 31

"Cuddling is a great way to simply be near someone and enjoy the loving contact. Sex isn't the only way to be intimate and close to one another, but a lot [of] times cuddling before makes it easier to get sex going." —Aaron, age 26

Men in the vast minority also cited more selfish reasons for not doing so. (Shocker, we know.) But these excuses were more on the fringe. Here's a sampling:

"I can cuddle for a while, but prolonged cuddling gets annoying and makes it difficult to sleep. I need my sleep. No cuddling is worth missing that." —Rain, age 23

"It's just part of my OCD, and I also like to be comfortable." —John, age 25

What to look out for: Believing men are inherently not cuddlers.

Good news on the cuddle front: men like it. They enjoy it. They enjoy cuddling with you. Cuddle away. Just know that it's not all for the sake of cuddling. But hey, sometimes it's better to just enjoy it and not debate the "whys" of it all.

Dirty talk: romantic or vulgar?

"Do you consider it romantic or vulgar if she says to her boyfriend 'I want to fuck your brains out tonight' or 'how do you want it tonight?'" —Betty, age 34, single

What the men say

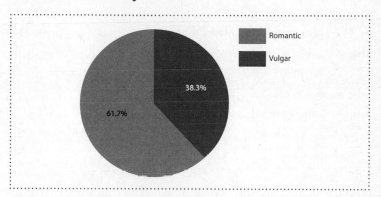

Romantic
Vulgar

38.3%

61.7%

What men are really saying

Most men consider this romantic. Yes, they have an issue here and there about the profanity (using the word *fuck* is a turn-on for some, but not for others), but mostly they're okay with it. So, yes, as the saying goes, men like a lady in public and a whore in the bedroom. Men who found it romantic summed it up this way:

"It shows that she really cares about him. She wants to please him as well as she can, so by asking him this question, she can do this. It is also good to communicate to him about how they can have sex, so that they can spice up their sex life and keep things interesting." —Eric, age 29

"Not so much romantic, but more like hot as hell. The only times I would find it vulgar is if you were to do it in public or in front of friends. Other than that, I would love it." —Mort, age 27

There were a bunch of men that even got into the semantics of what you say from a romantic perspective, as seen with this example:

"Saying 'I want to fuck your brains out tonight' is saying 'I want to do something special for you' and is romantic. If you said, 'I want you to fuck my brains out tonight,' it would be selfish and vulgar." —Phil, age 59

What to look out for: Assuming you'll be thought less of if you talk "dirty."

This isn't the case at all. So ladies, let your hair down and be forceful. There aren't many men who will oppose. Just be sure to keep it clean in public. (We know you will.)

Is sharing his interests romantic?

"At my age, dating is still fun and companionship is great. But when it gets to romance, I find myself wondering what men feel is romantic. For example, I'm a sports fan. Men like that, but **do men find it romantic that I actually like to watch sports, or is it 'just a plus'?**"
—Barbara, age 64, dating

What the men say

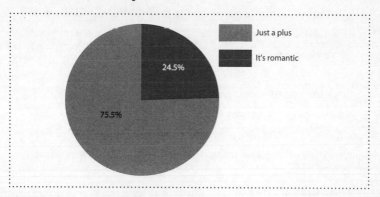

What men are really saying

This one was a little surprising. It's not that men didn't find something like watching sports romantic, but many of them thought it was barely a plus. In other words, many men found it obligatory that you women like what they like, watch what they watch, etc. A couple of examples illustrate the majority of men's opinion:

> "To me it is not even a plus, I do not have a preference whether you like sports or not. I liked it before I met you." —Mike, age 29

"I guess it's a plus, but barely. I'd categorize it as a plus because I've never met a women that I could watch sports with at all. Bottom line, there's no romantic adventure watching football."
—Damian, age 32

Even though there were some men who actually found it romantic, they too had reservations about even categorizing it as such.

"Well, it isn't really romantic… it is more like cool in a nag-free way. Like when a guy watches *Thelma and Louise* with you."
—Patrick, age 36

"Let's be honest: there is nothing romantic about watching sports. But it's nice to get our way once in a while, and we are more likely to go shopping without complaint if you watch sports with us once in a while, which might make it quasi-romantic." —Jason, age 36

What to look out for: Thinking that men view your interest in their hobbies as romantic.

Not really. Most men find it nice, but not anything romantic at all.

How do guys feel about PDA?

"I'm confused about whether men like to display their affections in public. Some think it's not romantic, and some are all about it, so I'd like to know: **do men find it romantic to show public displays of affection?**" —Destiny, age 19, single

What the men say

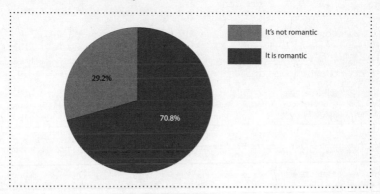

What men are really saying

Contrary to what manly men may think or say, many men like the PDA (public displays of affection). Most of the men said that they liked it, but the vast majority also added in some fashion that it be done tastefully.

"If you truly care about someone, it is fun to show affection in public. It tells a man that you are not afraid to be intimate with him and show it to others. Gross over-affection may be out of line, but simple displays show a man that you desire him no matter who is around." —Jerrod, age 31

"It is okay to show them, but only in moderation. It's not okay to dry hump your partner in public." —Austin, age 26

"If you love someone, then it doesn't matter where you show it. Obviously don't go too overboard, but showing your love for someone in public is fine." —Brian, age 35

For the men who didn't like it, most of them had issues with it not being private. It's the public part of PDA that bothers them most. Case in point:

"Affection is just best in private. I don't need the public display." —Kevin, age 39

"I believe that romance is something that doesn't have to be publicly displayed." —Joseph, age 22

What to look out for: Assuming that your man will frown on a public display of affection.

Based on the data, it's fair to assume that men by and large enjoy the PDA, so go for it in public. However, just be sure you know what he's comfortable with publicly. Otherwise, it could backfire in a big way. And that might affect you privately too.

What's his idea of a romantic getaway?

"My ex-husband was a terrible traveler. I think it was due to the fact that he traveled for business. As a result, he never really wanted to go anywhere with me. And forget about a romantic trip. But the romantic trip, I'm now very much looking forward to, but want to know: **if you were going to take me on a romantic getaway somewhere, where would it be, and what things would we do together to keep the romance going?**" —Marji, age 72, divorced

What the men say

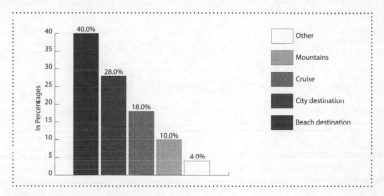

What men are really saying

Big romance at the beaches! Men overwhelmingly like to take you to beach destinations. Major beaches noted: Hawaiian islands, South America, Australia. Other men like the city and noted Paris as the top destination. Another common theme was that the destination was less important than the right person to go with. Most men could have a great time anywhere, but the woman and her attitude were key.

"Any place with sun and sand and the right woman is romantic to me. I love just relaxing and spending time together."
—Darnell, age 48

"If she's worthy, I would take her to the beach, and I would have a picnic set up. We would make love in the sand like wild animals."
—Justin, age 26

Some men don't leave much to chance and got really specific with their destination and the activities. Short of an actual itinerary, they had the event planned out in a very detail-oriented way.

"I would consider taking you to Uruguay. The reason being is that they have some of the most beautiful beaches there. There's even a place called Punta Del Este where you can see the ocean in all three directions of the street. Not sure what we would do, since I'm the type of guy who just plays it by ear." —Gilbert, age 29

What to look out for: Thinking that if he is a man, he won't know how to plan a romantic getaway.

We think the data here shows that's not true. We take this as good news. Men have you covered for a great getaway. Just be your pleasant selves, and men will largely take care of the rest. Will they ask for directions if they get lost on the way? We make no such guarantees.

Would he rather hang with me than the guys?

"I've noticed that my husband seems to have more fun being with his friends than he does with me. So I want to know: **do men prefer spending time dining and just hanging out with a woman, or is it just social pressure?**" —Kitty, age 51, married

What the men say

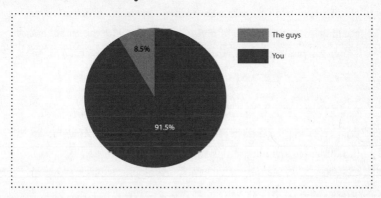

The guys
You

8.5%

91.5%

What men are really saying

This one was nearly unanimous in that men do enjoy the company of women. In fact, most of them said they did even if sex wasn't involved, planned, or remotely in the picture. It turns out the main criteria is being someone fun to hang out with.

"I love spending time with my long-time girlfriend dining and doing activities. That being said, if you put pressure on your man to make you happy during these things, then he will see it

as a job. If you are easygoing and treat it as just hanging out, he will too. Hey, ask yourself this: when you go out, are you doing things you want him to do with you, or are you doing things you both want to do? If you meet him halfway, he will enjoy your outings together much more and might even enjoy the ones where he takes you anywhere you want to go as well."
—Cyrus, age 28

"I definitely enjoy spending time with women. It's different from hanging out with a bunch of dudes, even if it's with a woman that I have no intention of being romantically involved with. Women are just different." —Tom, age 34

"Yes, I enjoy hanging out with anyone who is good company and fun to be with, regardless of whether there is a physical aspect to it. Men enjoy spending time with women who are engaging and exciting, so if a dinner and/or other social event is that, they are all for it." —Artur, age 31

That said, don't get us wrong: there is a subset of men who tell us that yes, they do like hanging out with women, but do so in hopes that sex comes into play later. Peter sums up the feeling of these men:

"I'm usually pretty hungry, and I like to let a woman think I am listening and interested in all her talking so I can get her in the sack later." —Peter, age 32

What to look out for: Feeling that he will always prefer to be with his friends to you for everything except sex.

This isn't the case. What you should know is that men like their friends as sounding boards and feedback, but they prefer being with you. So more good news for women: we like you. We truly like you.

Why does he forget important dates?

"I can remember every event my fiancé and I have together. His birthday, the first time we kissed, the day we met, his parents' birthdays and anniversaries, his friends' wives and kids' birthdays and anniversaries, etc. He can barely remember my birthday. I love him, but this drives me crazy! **Why do men forget birthdays, anniversaries, and other monumental dates and expect us to remember everything?**"
—Dominiq, age 24, engaged

What the men say

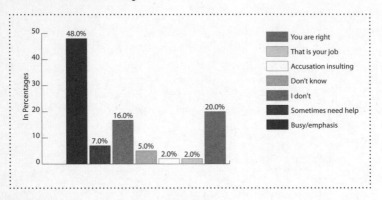

What men are really saying

This was an interesting question to research. The responses that men gave when asked this question could be categorized into one of three different areas: (1) Busy/emphasis, (2) I don't forget, or (3) You're right; I'm challenged with this.

A predominance of the men said that it really comes down to the importance that they (individual men) place on the date itself.

Instead, in many cases, it's that they are usually preoccupied with other day-to-day issues.

"'Monumental' is a pretty strong word. I think it has to do with the differences in what men and women consider are important. I remember the birthdays of the people closest to me, but more as a favor to them than because it's important to me." —David, age 45

"It really depends on the man. Some men are good at remembering monumental dates. Some are not. Personally, I'm somewhere in between myself, and for me, if I forget dates like that, it's because I'm busy with work or other concerns. On the whole, I think this is a stereotype left over from the days when the men worked and the women largely stayed at home. Since keeping track of these dates was seen as a more domestic responsibility, it fell to the wives to keep track and plan for these types of things, so the husband didn't have to. Nowadays the gender divide is much smaller (in the U.S. at least), and so the responsibility falls on both partners. However, men who grew up in a more old-fashioned household may consciously or unconsciously cling to the idea that it's the woman's job to maintain the calendar of special events, and so they make less of an effort to remember." —Wesley, age 29

"Men tend to lose the importance of these dates. While we understand they are important, we don't realize how important they are to others, so they do not become ingrained in our minds, and we tend to forget these dates." —Jameson, age 31

"Because we're too busy trying to contain all the lies we've told you to get you in bed. By now, there is no room for superfluous dates." —Josh, age 36

The men who said they didn't forget did also qualify it by saying they sometimes needed help. This meant they didn't necessarily remember the date themselves. They may have programmed the dates in their phones or were even reminded by someone else before they forgot. Funny, but in reading the comments from men regarding this subject, there were quite a few men who said they didn't forget these monumental dates, and while some were actually *very* insulted about the accusation, it seemed others were fine in justifying why "other men" might forget these dates.

"I actually don't forget birthdays, anniversaries, etc. The only dates that I personally forget are my wife's parents' birthdays. Perhaps I am the minority of men, but I actually remember all of these kinds of dates and do not expect my wife to remember everything. It would be a little bit of an overstatement to say that the roles are reversed from this question in our relationship, but if anything, that is the case." —Mike, age 32

"First of all, this is a question formed to a specific man or couple of men. It is very insulting to group all men in with this question. That's like saying 'Why do you talk to us while we're watching TV and expect us to drop everything to please you?' If you go into relationships expecting all men are like this, you will never be satisfied. All that being said, if a date is important to you, remind your man of it. Men see the year as a series of the same day, 365 days in a row. If he loves you on Monday and Tuesday, he doesn't necessarily see right away why Wednesday is so much more important because five years ago something or another happened. All that being said, if it is so important to you, remind him! And I don't mean drop subtle hints. Put it on the calendar. Say 'Hey, honey, it's our anniversary in two weeks. Are we going to do something?' He doesn't expect you to remember when the Super Bowl is; don't expect him to remember arbitrary celebrations like anniversaries without a little help. If you remind him, make plans, and then he flakes out at the last minute, maybe then you need a new man. But your question is just hostile!" —Lennard, age 28

"Most men nowadays just have a hard time remembering so many dates. That's why I put them all in my calendar on my phone. It's probably because these dates aren't that important to them." —Rollo, age 25

Lastly, there are the men who flat out admitted that they always forgot the dates, and they had no shame in it. In these examples below, men either admitted selfishness or inferiority to women in this area.

"Most men, including myself, are pretty selfish. It takes extra effort for men to remember such things. So if a man takes that extra effort, he really likes you." —Devon, age 21

"I've never expected any partner to remember anything; they simply always seem to. I have a horrible memory for dates and such, though I believe it actually has something to do with the way the average male and female brains work. It's simply harder for males to remember things like that." —Fred, age 42

What to look out for: Leaping to the conclusion that because he doesn't care about remembering key romantic dates, he doesn't care about you.

This isn't the case at all. Men might do it differently or with assistance in some way, but they do want to. Most of the men we interviewed felt very bad when they did miss a date. They care for their women deeply, but this isn't a major skill for most men. It's not deliberate and not against you. Play to each other's strengths, and you'll be much better off.

Dancing: does he like it or just tolerate it?

"When my boyfriend and I go out to the clubs, he will always avoid dancing. I've tried everything from bribing him to dragging him onto the dance floor, and his answer is always no. When I ask him why, he tells me, 'No men like to go dancing; we go because that's where the women are.' Is this true? **Do men like to go dancing with us, or are they just killing time?**" —Naska, age 24, single

What the men say

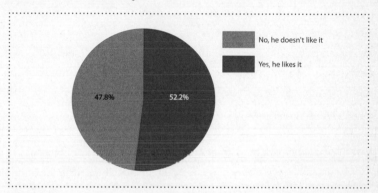

- No, he doesn't like it
- Yes, he likes it

47.8%   52.2%

What men are really saying

This one is pretty evenly split, but it's why it's split that makes it interesting. To a man, they don't mind doing something if they would do so anyway and/or enjoy it. But if they feel they *need* to do it for you, they don't like it at all. The men who like dancing feel that:

"I enjoy dancing and think it is a fun activity to share with someone. Besides, dancing can be sensual and lead to a wonderful night together. The closeness and everything associated with it can lead to great sex." —Phoenix, age 31

"I love dancing. It's a great way to meet girls, and since most men don't do it, it is a great way to get head and shoulders above other men." —Alfie, age 25

"I enjoy going dancing with my fiancée, because I know it makes her happy. Plus, in general men typically don't object to women dancing around close to us in the first place." —Kenneth, age 26

When men talk about not liking it, many of them said that men only dance "as a way to get sex." This may or may not be true, but the non-dancing man often sounds just as passionate about *not* dancing as the dancing man sounds about dancing.

"I don't care much for dancing. I would rather do anything else. Even non-sexually. I would even rather sit at a table, order a few drinks, and talk." —Jonathan, age 27

"Dancing is embarrassing and a waste of time. We could be doing other things. Going for a ride in the country. Watching a movie. Having a romantic dinner." —Wiley, age 37

"I hate dancing. I would rather watch *Titanic* three times in a row than go dancing." —Quinn, age 32

What to look out for: Believing that men only dance because they're being forced into dancing.

Not the case at all. You have to know where your man stands on this before you do it. Don't assume that all men hate dancing, but just as important, be sure that your man likes to dance before you drag him out on that dance floor.

Do men appreciate the women they are with?

"I recently had a relationship go bad. Long story short, I felt that I wasn't being appreciated. It wasn't that he was a cheater, was bad to me or with me, but I felt like he almost took advantage of all that I brought to the table. I'm not asking for constant praise, but I didn't think that his silence spoke to the value of what I offered him. What I'd like to know from men is, in your heart of hearts, **do you really appreciate the one you're with?**" —Sally, age 41, divorced

What the men say

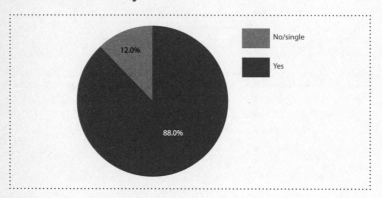

What men are really saying

While to most women this might come as a big surprise, the vast majority of men, 88 percent, really do appreciate what their wife or girlfriend does for them.

"Yes, because she is my best friend and helps me whenever I need it. She is my main source of support and makes a wonderful mother to our daughter. She is my soul mate and challenges me to become a better man." —Matt, age 33

"She is my everything. No matter what walls I come across, she is always there to help me out. She keeps me going every day. They say you should do things for you and no one else. Well, she is my everything; I do everything for her; making her happy is for me. Example: when I needed help with bills one month, she didn't waste any time grabbing my bills and helping me out so I could make a payment for school. So I very much appreciate the one I'm with." —Devin, age 26

What about that 12 percent who actually said no? It's a simple answer, really; they're either single or the woman they are with are nags and they are not happy.

"Being single, I am with nobody, so I thought 'no' would be the best answer." —Harvey, age 24

"She's always yelling at me and telling me I don't do things right." —Daniel, age 49

What to look out for: Thinking that men tend to take women for granted.

Even though they don't always say it and do forget to say "thank you" occasionally, men do appreciate everything you do for them. If you feel you need to have your efforts noticed more, talk to your man (nicely) about how he can show you he appreciates you. Communication is key when something is bothering you. If men tell us anything repeatedly, it's that they are definitely not mind readers.

Can I call him Schmoopy?

"I made the mistake of calling my boyfriend a pet name that I thought would be cute and our little inside joke. I called him 'Bear,' because he's a big guy, loves to give me hugs where he lifts me off my feet. When I did, he looked at me with a straight face and said, 'Don't ever call me that again.' What gives? **Do you like it if we have pet names for you?"**
—Shanko, age 18, single

What the men say

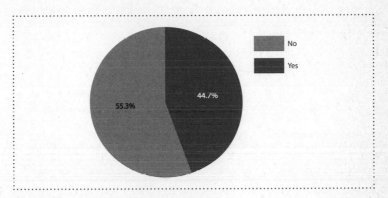

No
Yes

55.3% 44.7%

What men are really saying

This one we could have guessed and gotten right. The vast majority of men don't like to be called "Snookums," "Babycakes," or similar. Many of them feel embarrassed by it, even if it's just between themselves and their significant other. Most men summed it up this way:

"No! Be playful, by all means, but leave the name alone."
—Ira, age 33

"I do not have a pet name, but I think men are not fans of pet names because they would be embarrassing to us in front of other men. I think most men would cringe at being called by a pet name in front of others." —Lyn, age 31

"Snuggle wuggle or cuddly bear type names sound like something you'd name your cat, not me. Not cool." —Patrick, age 36

Some men don't mind it, however. Some find it very endearing to have something that's akin to an inside joke between themselves and their loved one.

"Pookie is my pet name. I like pet names because they make me feel like I have a special inside joke. It makes me feel more connected because it's a name that only the two of us know and use." —Jonathan, age 27

"Yes, I think it's cute as long as it's sweet, only used in private, and not just a generic." —Marc, age 21

"Every pet name I've ever had was cute and fun, and my girlfriends were great about not using them at embarrassing times. I do not currently have one, but the most memorable one came out of a spat I had with a past girlfriend, where I randomly started making up ridiculous names. She threw them back. Pufflekins stuck from that moment on." —Edmund, age 26

What to look out for: Thinking he will love your pet name for him because he sees it as a term of endearment.

Before you start calling your man by that cute little name you like so much, be sure that he isn't recoiling in horror every time you utter it. And keep it just between you two. For all of our sakes.

What's the hottest lingerie?

"I just got out of a long-term relationship with an abusive boyfriend. After breaking up, I am trying to switch things up. I bought a thong before a date with a guy I met about two and a half weeks ago. When I put it on, I couldn't help but think that I looked ridiculous. I thought to myself: 'Am I a forty-two-year-old woman trying to recapture my youth?' So I took it off and used my regular underwear (boy shorts.) While on the date, I found myself both wondering and justifying my decision, thinking he would probably think the same thing: 'That looks odd.' So help me with this: **what lingerie do men think is the most romantic?**" —Ann, age 42, single

What the men say

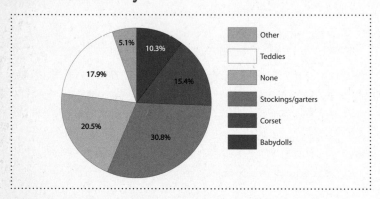

- Other
- Teddies
- None
- Stockings/garters
- Corset
- Babydolls

5.1% 10.3%

17.9% 15.4%

20.5% 30.8%

What men are really saying

Short of you being naked, which came in second, men like you ladies in stockings and garters. It's certainly a look that never goes out of style. Yes, garters may not be something you wear every day, and frankly, you have to make an effort to put it together, but the payoff for men is big.

> "It makes a woman look very sexy and look like a bad girl, which turns me on." —Rick, age 48

> "Stockings and garters seem to accentuate the sexiness of a woman's legs and a woman's butt." —Paul, age 53

> "There is something really sexy about garter belts and thigh highs. You can wear them with anything." —Patrick, age 36

> "The tall stockings are a huge turn-on for me personally, and it feels adventurous." —Michael, age 20

A lot of men gave additional feedback on this question in the form of advice for women. Mostly it was along the lines of: let men choose your lingerie; it's for them, after all. Here's a sample that goes to the core of what men told us:

> "Preference for lingerie is a very personal choice. Instead of spending a lot of money on lingerie that your partner may or may not like, I would suggest having your partner help you surf the web for lingerie, because when they say, 'You would look good in that,' it is a clear indication of their taste. Once you have picked a style, make sure that you wear it. Be confident. Forget how you think you look in it; to a man, it's going to be great." —Phil, age 57

What to look out for: Believing that he will think you look silly in lingerie or sexy outfits.

Oh, how wrong you are!

You can't put enough emphasis on lingerie. Men are specific about what they like and don't like. The key is finding out what your man likes. By purchasing and wearing it, it not only helps him, but it also helps you, too, by increasing the intimacy.

What's the most romantic thing he's done?

"I've been married for almost twenty years. We have a regular date night, which includes dinner and some drinks. Next month is our twentieth anniversary, so I asked him if he had anything planned for the big night. He didn't really have an answer, so I think that it's going to be just 'business as usual' in the romantic planning department. I wonder if all men are like this? **What's the most romantic thing you've ever done?**" —Maria, age 44, married

What the men say

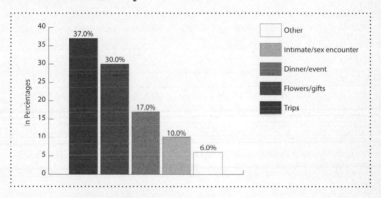

What men are really saying

Eighty-four percent of men place their romantic efforts in three key areas: taking you on trips, buying flowers and gifts, and planning a dinner or event out. This might appear boring, but what we found interesting is that men (a) like doing this for the most part and (b)

put a large degree of thought into making you happy in the romance department. Here's a sampling:

"I took my girlfriend to New York City; it was her first time there. It was around Christmas and so I decided to take her to the big tree. When we got there, I had her looking at the tree when I noticed that the light show was going to start in the building behind us, so I whispered in her ear to turn around. Once that was over, I whispered for her to turn around again, and she got to view a man proposing to a woman in the middle of the ice. It was the first time I ever saw her cry, and she said they were happy tears because of how emotionally overwhelming everything was."
—Gustavo, age 27

"I took my girlfriend to San Francisco for a weekend. Went to Fisherman's Wharf, the Golden Gate Bridge, the Walt Disney Museum, had dinner at the Spinnaker in Sausalito, and even a baseball game in Oakland (she's a sports fan). It was spur-of-the-moment, and I planned everything out on the fly. I think it was the most romantic because of the setting and how much she meant and in many ways still means to me." —Clarence, age 31

"I took my girlfriend out on a mystery date once. She knew I was taking her out, but didn't know where. I took her to a museum she always wanted to go to, a restaurant she always wanted to go to, then I took her to Madison Square Garden to see Ringling Bros. Circus. She loved every second of it." —Rashaun, age 28

"I backed up to the beach in my van with my wife. We had good music, wine, and strawberries. It turned out great because the dolphins just happened to be swimming around a few yards from us." —Michael, age 20

What to look out for: Focusing only on the outcome and not on the efforts in his attempts to be romantic.

Men can and will think through a romantic adventure for their wives or girlfriends. Let your man plan away, his way. It might not be very off the beaten path, but most men aim to please, so enjoy your romantic trip, gift, or event!

Attractive, sexy, or erotic?

"I've gone to lunch a few times with some of my guy friends, and it never fails that when they see a good-looking woman, they will call attention to the girl. Sometimes they will make a comment about her being sexy or attractive. I can't seem to distinguish between what they see as attractive versus sexy versus even erotic. **Is there a difference between attractive and sexy? Sexy and erotic?**"
—Sue, age 24, single

What the men say

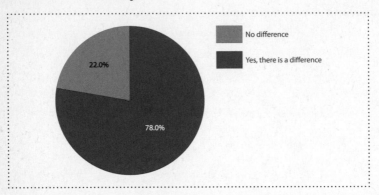

- No difference
- Yes, there is a difference

22.0%

78.0%

What men are really saying

Much to our surprise, men were fairly definitive on this one. We thought this was so subjective that the answers would be all over the place. Some of the answers varied, but overall, they could easily compartmentalize among the three. We'll let the men speak for themselves here. Most comments from men fell along these lines:

"Oh, that's a tough one, mainly because those words [are] both subjective and dependent on context. In my humble opinion, attractive is the sum of the whole of the woman. Face, body, personality, smile, eyes, all of these contribute to attractiveness. Also, attractiveness doesn't really change depending on the situation; an attractive woman will usually always remain attractive, no matter the situation or style of dress or whatnot. Sexy, on the other hand, is more specific and usually situational. 'You look sexy in those heels' or 'That was a sexy look you just gave me.' Thoughts are more focused on, well, sex, but as a whole, sexiness is usually more playful and less hot and heavy. It's similar to erotic, but while sexy is more of a public idea, erotic is more private. If you're in erotic mode, sex is front-and-center in your brain. You're trying to turn someone on, and there's a very good chance that sexual activities will ensue. You can be sexy in public, but being erotic in public is usually frowned upon (by the authorities)."
—Chris, age 29

"I think the difference between attractive and sexy is cuteness. A girl can be attractive because she's cute, and if a girl is sexy, she just looks hot. Sexy is more like looking hot, and erotic is more like acting dirty." —Sherman, age 28

"Attractive is based on a person's natural features. Sexy is determined by clothing or actions the person wears. Erotic is some action by a person that causes their mate to become sexually aroused." —Matt, age 21

"Attractive is a woman wearing a beautiful smile. Sexy is a woman wearing a beautiful smile and a short skirt. Erotic is a woman wearing a beautiful smile and nothing else." —Rudyard, age 28

"Attractive refers mainly to visual appeal; that is, a first-glance approximation. Attractive could also, I suppose, refer to personality characteristics. Regardless, if I say a woman is attractive, that merely indicates a mild interest, enough to want to know more about her, not necessarily sexually, but certainly socially and personally. Sexy, for me, is more a matter of confidence and self-assurance. A sexy woman may or may not be considered a classical beauty. I find confidence to be a woman's sexiest trait, and confidence is more a function of accomplishment than anything else. This means that for me a sexy woman is typically someone who has had time to establish herself in some way and experience enough of life to know herself well and be comfortable with herself. That is sexy. Erotic is more problematic to define, but in general I consider some element of danger or uncertainty to be a key element of eroticism. That is, a woman frankly interested in sex can be erotically stimulating, mainly because it raises the uncertainty of will she or won't she, or more personally, is she interested in me or just showing off? Eroticism is not necessarily a show-all and tell-all thing; there must be something hidden to further tempt the imagination. A woman wrapped in a towel stepping from a shower is frankly more erotic than most unimaginative porn pics, which leave nothing to the imagination."
—Drew, age 48

What to look out for: Thinking men find all tight-fitting or revealing clothes to be sexy.

Men have definite ideas about what is attractive, sexy, and erotic. What women need to understand is how men see sexy can be drastically different from how women would prefer to see sexy. Case in point are cougars. Older women who date younger men might think that dressing like a nineteen-year-old in age-inappropriate clothing, sporting big fake boobs, and getting other "work" done, such as collagen injections or even spray tans, is sexy and would therefore be attractive to men. Most men, however, think that it's nothing close to sexy, attractive, or erotic. (See other question on cougars, page 145.)

Is it romantic if I make the first move?

"I've always thought that romance was a prelude to a strong relationship and even sex. I've found myself at times turned on by a man who took charge. Now I'm interested in a guy who hasn't made a move yet. I would love to start something with him, but really need to know if men have the same view of romance as I do. **Do men find it attractive or romantic if a woman makes the first move?**"
—Lillian, age 28, single

What the men say

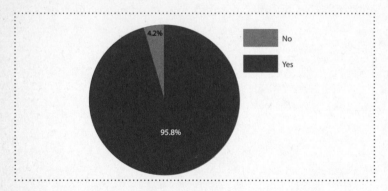

What men are really saying

Your move, ladies. Literally. Men had no qualms whatsoever about you making the first move. The data from men came from all walks of life, regions, ages, etc. Men are completely okay with it as they find your confidence attractive while taking some of the pressure off of them at the same time. Many men described it this way:

"If a woman makes the first move, it certainly shows her interest, and that is always attractive to a man. Men like it when we feel like we are someone they can't wait to make a move on. It also takes off some of the pressure on us, and we appreciate that."
—Criss, age 31

"I like a take-charge kind of girl." —Herschel, age 35

"I am not as interested in women who cannot express themselves openly and act on what they want, so a woman making the first move says she is able to do that." —Brian, age 26

"I love confidence in a woman. If the woman makes the first move, then she is confident, and it is a major, major turn-on."
—Brad, age 25

Of the small minority who didn't want you making the first move, most of them cited tradition or it being a male responsibility. In the minority, this was a common concern:

"I am more a traditional guy, so I don't like women who make the first move; it's the man's job, and we should." —Marcus, age 28

What to look out for: Thinking that men have to be the ones who make the first move.

We think it's clear that you're able to make the first move without any hesitation. Men won't find it offensive, nor will they think any less of you. In fact, it's just the opposite; men will respect your confidence in choosing them and hold you in higher esteem for doing so.

More romantic: massage or oral?

"I'm perplexed because I planned a romantic evening with my husband. I sent the kids to my mom's house, I made him dinner and even laughed at all the jokes I've heard before. The night ended with me giving him what I thought was a sensual blow job. While he enjoyed it (a lot) I got the impression that he missed the fact that the blow job was intended to be romantic. It was almost like he thought, 'Cool, I just got a blow job.' So my question is **what would have been more romantic for a man: a full-body massage (no sex) or a hand/blow job?**" —Debbie, age 27, married

What the men say

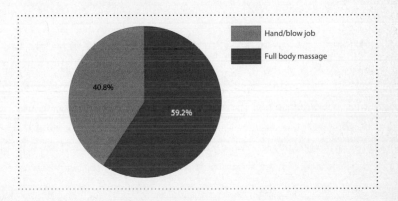

What men are really saying

At first glance, looking at the graph, you might think we are crazy, but it is important to understand that we took Debbie's question literally. We asked men to tell us which they believed was the more romantic (not what they preferred) of the two options, and two-thirds said that blow jobs were not.

> "There isn't anything really romantic about a blow job; that's more instant gratification and easy. The other is hard and requires thought." —Marc, age 28

> "Don't get me wrong, hand/blow jobs are very fun! However I do believe that full-body massage is more romantic. It spends so much time building up toward the sexual action. Gotta love anticipation." —Joseph, age 22

> "A blow job is very sexy but not romantic at all." —Marshall, age 23

Men who said that hand/blow jobs were the more romantic of the two tended to infer that things were always more romantic when a woman was touching their penis. As a matter of fact, they tended to tie both the intimacy and release to romanticism because in their eyes, they could always get a massage from the masseuse around the corner, whereas they wouldn't let just anyone touch them. Also, they said that the sexual act would let them know they were appreciated by their significant other.

> "A full-body massage would put me to sleep, whereas a hand/blow job makes me feel like my significant other wants to do something that she knows I'll enjoy and that doesn't happen all the time." —Erik, age 26

"Technically my answer would be both. Massages are great if followed by sex or oral sex. Men are wired so that if things get touchy or physical, it has to end in sex. Once we think we are going to get sex, you can't stop short, not if you want to maintain the relationship. If a woman is touching us and giving us a massage, we expect that it will lead to other things and end in us having an orgasm. Physical touch leads us to sexual tension, and we're only happy if it ends in getting off." —Mitchell, age 27

"I know it said to answer which I thought was more romantic and not which I would prefer. BUT…the reason I think it is more romantic is because it's what I want. So when a woman does such a thing, it shows that she has my wants and needs at heart…and she is willing to do things to keep me happy and interested…so that's why I think it's romantic." —George, age 31

What to look out for: Assuming that nothing is more sought after by a man than oral sex.

Not exactly because men see romance as romance and sex as sex. What women can do is make sure they differentiate between the two as well, so they don't feel any disappointment if men react differently to two things you see as equal.

What does he want for Valentine's Day?

"I never know what to get my boyfriend on Valentine's Day. He's always getting me things and planning something, and I want to give him something really cool this year. I'm just not sure what might have the biggest impact. So, help me out: **what's the best gift to get for a man on Valentine's Day?**" —Ikeisha, age 23, single

What the men say

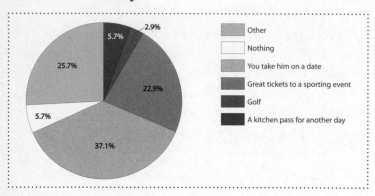

Legend:
- Other
- Nothing
- You take him on a date
- Great tickets to a sporting event
- Golf
- A kitchen pass for another day

Pie chart values: 2.9%, 5.7%, 22.9%, 25.7%, 5.7%, 37.1%

What men are really saying

If you're going to get a man a present for Valentine's Day, most men like a Valentine's gift where you take them on a date for a change. They like this for a variety of reasons.

"I don't want anything wrapped. I prefer experiences. Surprise me with a night out somewhere." —Tommy, age 40

"Valentine's Day is especially for a couple. As a gift, a date would be the most precious. I suggest that." —Larry, age 24

"Men usually take her out on a date…it's a nice change for her to take him out." —Tom, age 34

"Take him somewhere he wants to go. This will ensure he enjoys the gift." —John, age 37

Sporting event tickets were also cited as a great gift. It might seem obvious, but a lot of men think it's something that you'd like to be a part of with him.

"This shows that a woman wants her man to take part in fun 'guy' stuff. Women tend to dislike sports, and when they show they want a man to take part in such things, it shows their willingness to accept a big part of what he wants." —Quincy, age 31

What to look out for: Assuming that you can get him anything for Valentine's Day and he'll be happy.

Actually, men do have preferences, but they're pretty simple gifts, and there are many ways to provide that impact that you're looking for in your quest to give your man a memorable Valentine's Day gift.

Authors' note: We also would be remiss if we didn't point out that 38 percent of the men who chose the number-one choice for men (taking a man out for Valentine's Day) also appended it in some fashion with the date ending in sex (with the term *blow jobs* being provided most often).

New Year's Eve: what's best?

"My husband likes for us to stay home on New Year's Eve, and we wind up watching others going out on television. I'm up for going out or staying home, but since he always wants to stay home, I'd like to know if all men prefer this or just my man. **So, how do you men like to spend New Year's Eve?**" —Summer, age 27, married

What the men say

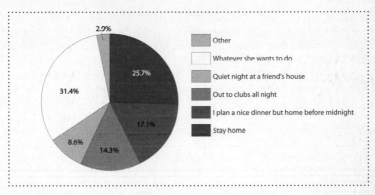

What men are really saying

They are up for what you want to do on New Year's. Many men see it as a day for you and your choice of whatever you want to do.

"Usually, I've been in a relationship during that time of year. I believe that it's not what you do, it's the company you keep. If she wants to party all night, why not? It's New Year's. If she wants to stay home, that's cool. I don't have to start the New Year with a hangover. The main thing for me with New Year's isn't what you do, it's planning. If you're gonna go downtown, make sure you know how you're getting there, and more importantly, how you're getting your drunk-ass home. This goes for most other events on New Year's, except for staying home. Getting drunk on New Year's is fun. Spending an hour looking for parking because you didn't leave early enough is not." —Tyson, age 29

"Usually it isn't bad what she chooses, but letting her choose starts the year off on a good note, so she doesn't start mad at me for a new year." —Julian, age 26

"She is usually pretty good at selecting the festivities for the night. She has a lot of friends, and finding the hot spot on important nights isn't a problem." —Michael, age 44

A big section of men would just prefer to stay home with you. They enjoy being with you, and going out for New Year's isn't preferable in their minds, as its cheaper, safer, and more intimate.

"It is safer and better to be home with family!" —Ariel, age 35

"I love being home and not going out, so this is best for me. It is more comfortable and convenient." —Otto, age 25

"I would rather stay home with my girl and just chill. It's too much trouble to go out and worry about drunk drivers." —Harmon, age 32

What to look out for: Believing that he doesn't want to go out on New Year's Eve.

Actually, you're in good with your man if you want to go out on New Year's and direct what's going to happen. Most men are just fine with it. If you're undecided, the safe bet is to plan something at home together and enjoy that new year in a closer, safer, and more intimate fashion.

Chapter 4

SEX

We're willing to bet that over half of the people who bought this book headed right to this chapter! It's okay if you're in that group. One of the interesting things about running www.wtfarementhinking.com is that we get an inside look at what women think about based on the questions they send us to ask men.

And our data shows that women think about and have a lot of questions about men's attitudes toward sex.

More than we thought, actually. And that's a good thing! The more information women have about sex, the better off men are. (Men have told us this fact, as you'll soon see.) We'd argue that you'll be better off as well.

Most of the questions were not surprising, but many of the answers were. In fact, after reading this chapter, we'll probably get more questions from you now than ever before on the topic.

And that's just fine by us.

So let's get going. A quick caveat: yes, there are some risqué questions and feedback in this chapter, so if you're a little on the shy side when it comes to sex, you may flip through this quickly.

But based on the frequency and depth of the sex questions women ask us, we seriously doubt it.

Who initiates?

"I've been married to my husband for six years. Lately I've really been wondering whether he's cheating on me because he doesn't often initiate sex, but when I initiate it, he gets really turned on. Is it something I'm doing (or not doing), or could there be a mistress in the picture? I'd like to know: **in terms of sex, do men like to be the aggressor or the one being pursued?**"
—Jeannie, age 30, married

What the men say

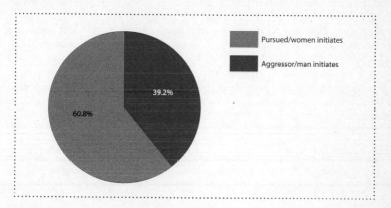

Pursued/women initiates

Aggressor/man initiates

39.2%

60.8%

What men are really saying

Most women will probably be surprised to hear that 61 percent of men want to be pursued sexually.

"I think most men are ready and willing to have sex at any time. I think when a woman actively engages in pursuing sex, it shows the man he is not the only one interested in sexual relations and makes him feel wanted. Not to mention it is extremely sexy for a woman to pursue a man sexually." —Marc, age 31

"Aggressor is the normal role for a guy. A girl who pursues and initiates sex is so incredibly sexy and turns me on like no other. Men are always ready for sex, but being jumped is especially fulfilling." —Wilkie, age 28

The 39 percent of men who admitted they like to be the aggressor said it was because they like to be in control. There is nothing more satisfying than the hunt and getting a woman to submit to them.

"Men need the chase. We have to hunt. Now, ideally the ratio should be about 80/20 in favor of the man being the aggressor. Neither man nor woman should be the aggressor all the time." —Spencer, age 52

"I see myself as an aggressive person. I like to be in control of situations." —Mark, age 22

What to look out for: Believing that men always want to be in complete control when it comes to sex.

Men like to feel wanted. There's nothing more erotic than a woman wanting a guy so much she just takes him. In Jeannie's case, her husband might just be unsure if she is in the mood before he pursues her, but he really enjoys when she knows what she wants. If it bothers her that much, she should talk to her husband and discuss both of them being both aggressor and the pursued.

What turns men on?

"Over the past thirty years, I've been having sex the same way with my husband. As I get older, I'm becoming more concerned with my age and if I'll still turn my husband on. I assume that the biggest turn-on for men is being with a younger woman. So I guess my question is: **what are men's biggest turn-ons?**" —Victoria, age 50, married

What the men say

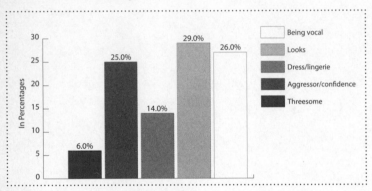

Legend:
- Being vocal
- Looks
- Dress/lingerie
- Aggressor/confidence
- Threesome

In Percentages

6.0%, 25.0%, 14.0%, 29.0%, 26.0%

What men are really saying

What turns men on the most? The men we asked varied a lot in their responses, but the majority agreed that a woman being aggressive about what she wants really does it for them. Nothing is hotter to a man than a woman knowing what she wants.

"When a woman is aggressive, not shy at all, completely into it, very passionate, tries just as hard to please, mutual effort. Dirty talking, confidence." —Shane, age 20

"A woman who knows what to do and is willing to do what the man likes. For example, a woman who knows that men love receiving oral and will do it without being asked or told and at least pretend like she enjoys it." —Cody, age 22

Next on the list was a vocal woman. Men love the sounds a woman makes during sex. From soft moans to screams to just telling a guy what feels good and what she wants.

"It really turns me on when the woman I am having sex with is enjoying it as much as I am and completely lets go until climax with sexy moaning." —Archie, age 35

"I am turned on most when my girlfriend gives good feedback, but is not faking it. I also love being complimented. These two things are good to do during sex because they make the guy feel like he is doing a good job. It makes us feel better about ourselves." —Dave, age 19

What to look out for: Thinking that youth beats attitude when it comes to turning him on.

There were many other answers men gave to what turns them on, but none of the answers were a younger woman. Some did say looks mattered, which included various body parts on a woman, but most of men's answers revolved around your attitude and mindset as the thing that turned them on the most.

Do men really enjoy foreplay?

"Based on my husband's approach to sex, I think that men just don't like foreplay. His approach is about five minutes long, and then he jumps right into it. I'd like to know: **do men really enjoy foreplay?**"
—Debi, age 42, married

What the men say

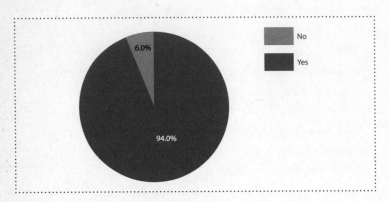

What men are really saying

The overwhelming majority of men, 94 percent, do enjoy foreplay. To men it sets the mood for sex and it makes it more enjoyable.

> "Foreplay allows you time to get aroused and ready. It sets the tone for sex. You can be tender and gentle or you can be rough and active." —Shane, age 34

"We really do because it is fun to play around and touch each other and really develop a connection with each other. Obviously sex is more fun, but foreplay makes sex even more intense."
—Sven, age 33

As for the 6 percent of men who say they don't enjoy it, the main reason they give is that they just want to get to the point! Foreplay takes too long.

"Well some men have different preferences. I like getting down to business, and that's sex." —Zach, age 22

"I answered yes, but some men don't enjoy it. I would guess that some men don't enjoy foreplay when it is dragged out and lasts too long." —Wyatt, age 24

What to look out for: Assuming that foreplay is just a prelude to sex.

If your guy doesn't like foreplay, try something new. Maybe it's not that he doesn't like it, but he's bored with starting off the same way. Add a little spice to the bedroom and see what happens.

Foreplay versus sex

"I'm getting back into dating again and notice that most men jump right into sex without much foreplay, so my question is simple: **do men believe that foreplay is just as important as the actual act?**" —Cathy, age 40, divorced

What the men say

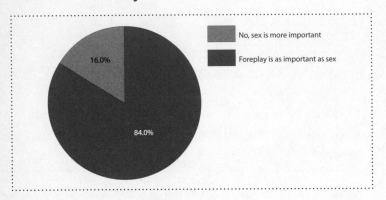

- No, sex is more important
- Foreplay is as important as sex

16.0%

84.0%

What men are really saying

Eighty-four percent of men agree that foreplay is as important as actually having sex for one specific reason: it gets the woman in the mood. Most men, however, also feel that if both parties are ready to go, then just jumping into having sex is fine.

> "Some people call this pleasure delaying. When you know that sex is inevitable, foreplay extends the time each person is aroused and heightens the intensity of the eventual act. The longer you hold out, the more you will want it." —Bill, age 30

"I find foreplay extremely important. Just jumping into sex is fine and dandy when both partners are raring to go, but very often, the pleasure of sex is intensified by a long, tortuous session of foreplay." —Reagan, age 24

Even though the other 16 percent say that foreplay is important (sort of), they think it's just not as important. Many men think that if time is an issue, then a quickie will do, and foreplay is the first to go.

"This is a difficult question to answer. For most men, there is no real difference between foreplay and the act. For example, most men would consider lightly masturbating you as a sex act. They would also consider stimulating your breasts part of the act because they are being just as stimulated as you are. In fact, many men don't really care about sexual intercourse because mutual masturbation or oral sex are just as good. They would consider those forms of stimulation to be 'the act.'" —Paulie, age 50

"Foreplay is for people who have time to screw around. If you are short on time, a quickie is a must, so it isn't as important." —Dimitri, age 26

What to look out for: Assuming men prefer sex to foreplay.

The vast majority of men prefer foreplay even to sex because of one major consideration: it helps you get into the mood to have sex with them. If there is anything in a man's world that is a win-win, it's this. Men understand that foreplay leads to a better sexual experience for everyone.

What positions does he prefer?

"I know that men love to have oral sex performed on them. Based upon what I've experienced, what men have told me, and what I've read, I think it's probably true. What I'd like to know is: **what are men's favorite sexual positions?**" —Araceli, age 21, single

What the men say

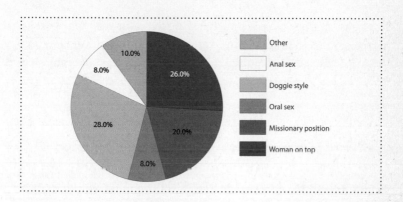

Other	
Anal sex	
Doggie style	
Oral sex	
Missionary position	
Woman on top	

What men are really saying

The results are in, and men's favorite sex position is doggie style. Twenty-eight percent of men agree that it's the best, and they feel that way because it borders on naughty and because they think the view for men is amazing. Some men added that it gives them the opportunity to get creative with their hands.

"The position seems to touch different nerves than more traditional positions. In addition, there is something about the image of a woman's back that is visually more attractive during the act of sex to me." —Nate, age 27

"I love doggie style because it feels almost dirty when you are having sex. I really love being able to see my girlfriend's butt and back. It's so hot. Also, it never hurts to smack her butt and gently pull her hair :) !" —Weston, age 24

Coming in at a close second is having the woman on top. Twenty-six percent of men love having a woman in this position because it puts the woman in complete control and hopefully that will lead to better sex for her. Other reasons include (selfishly) that they love the view.

"Having the woman on top is incredibly sexy. I love for her to be on top and direct the flow of sex, but sometimes I like to give her a chance to show me her wild side. I think I am able to have a stronger orgasm when I can see her writhing on top of me, watching her breasts sway with the motion. I also love being able to grab her butt as she bounces, as I find that to be very sexy." —Adam, age 29

"Her controlling how she reaches orgasm is a large turn-on for me. Also I seem to resist reaching an orgasm for a pro-longed time. Seeing a full body view of her is very nice also." —Andrew, age 18

What to look out for: Believing that he prefers oral sex above all else.

Surprisingly oral sex did not top men's preferences; in fact, it came in fifth and tied for last place with anal sex. While it is true that oral sex is commonly mentioned throughout many of the areas covered in this book as being popular for men, it's not described here in the same way. This is partially due to the fact that most men don't think of oral sex as a position.

What is so appealing about anal sex?

"I find it odd that my husband always tries to bring up the subject of anal sex and wants to know if I'm curious to try it out. I want to know: **what is it about anal sex that is so appealing to men?**"
—Alicia, age 23, married

What the men say

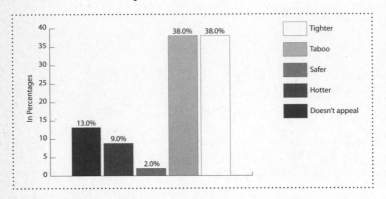

What men are really saying

Surprisingly it's a tie for why the majority of men like anal sex. Thirty-eight percent of men say they like anal because it's taboo and thirty-eight percent because it feels better. For men, doing an act that most people don't talk about doing increases the excitement.

"I love anal sex :) First off, it is appealing because it is exciting! There are a couple odd reasons I like anal sex that make it exciting: (1) The taboo nature of anal sex makes it exciting. (2) I am in a very loving relationship with a woman who has had a few sex

partners before me; however, I am the first partner she has had anal sex with (that I know about). The 'virgin territory' makes anal sex exciting. (3) I enjoy anal play too—be it a strap-on or butt plug. I would imagine the pleasure is similar between a man and a woman. Being able to share the experience is exciting."
—Drew, age 28

"From my opinion, it is something that is naughty and unaccepted on some levels. It is also a different feeling than vaginal intercourse. Some women actually really enjoy this." —Clark, age 37

Along with the excitement about doing something so naughty, men love the way it feels. It's tighter and just more pleasurable for men.

"Anal sex does not appeal to me, but for men, the reason I can come up with is the tight feeling that happens for the penis entering the anus." —Cal, age 23

"For me, it's almost as if anal is a far more intimate sharing than vaginal intercourse. You have to take time to work your way into it, and once you have started, you have to be gentle and deliberate. The level of trust between partners that the act entails is much higher than regular sex." —Carson, age 39

What to look out for: Assuming that he isn't even interested in anal sex.

Actually, while some women like Alicia do not find the act appealing, there are those who are willing to try new stuff with their man to enhance the fun in the bedroom. Most men do like anal sex for various reasons, and when they feel comfortable enough with a woman to broach the subject, they will do so.

Will he care if I am experienced?

"I'm a youngish woman with little sexual experience. Not because no man will have me; I've had my suitors, but because I haven't had an overwhelming desire for sex. I realize that I'm not getting any younger, but will my lack of experience hurt me in getting a man? **Does it matter to men if your future wife is sexually experienced or not?**" —Deborah, age 38, single

What the men say

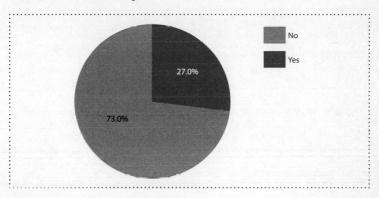

No
Yes
27.0%
73.0%

What men are really saying

Does your experience matter in your relationship to men? Seventy-three percent of our men say no. Either way, they see it as a plus. If you know a lot, great! They'll have fun finding out what you know, and if you don't, they are more than willing to help you learn.

"No! Why would it matter if you are sexually experienced when we have a whole lifetime to experience everything together? It is definitely not a deal breaker." —Mike, age 22

"Not particularly. While it would be nice if she knew a few things that I didn't, it can be fun to experiment with someone who is inexperienced. Just so long as she's open to trying new things to keep the sexual experience fresh, it shouldn't matter if she's experienced." —Michael, age 24

What about the men who care? Twenty-seven percent of the men who care would prefer it if their partner was more experienced.

"Double-edged question. In the end, yes, [I] would want [my] future wife to have some sexual experience. It would somewhat ensure a healthy sex life, and it would be a bit more comforting to know that she chose to settle down with me after previous experiences." —DeShawn, age 32

"Yes, it honestly does. I don't want to have to waste time guiding a woman into her sexuality. I'm not looking for a freak, but I want someone who's comfortable with who she is sexually." —Wendel, age 31

What to look out for: Thinking that you need to be sexually experienced by a certain age.

You don't have much to worry about the experience question because three-quarters of men don't care either way.

Do all men like to experiment?

"I am a very happily married woman, and by anyone's assessment have a great life and have nothing to complain about really, but I do have a question. I'd like to know why my husband doesn't ever seem to be content with our sex life. He always wants to do new things. Sometimes it's fun, but I'm totally content with the missionary position and maybe one or two others. I think I'm fairly aggressive, and on those 'special occasions,' I'll go the oral route. Look, I know he's happy and gets everything he needs, but **do all men like to experiment during sex?**" —Dana, age 35, married

What the men say

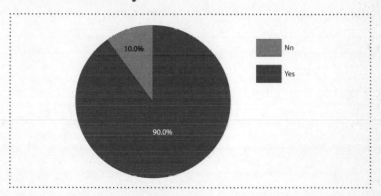

What men are really saying

Men are sexual creatures, so it should come as no surprise that a whopping 90 percent say they do like to experiment during sex.

"I think it's important to experiment during sex so you can know what your partner will and will not like. Sex can get boring if you do the same things over and over. Plus, your experimenting may help you discover something you can make routine."
—Gary, age 19

"The same acts and positions tend to get boring, even when in a loving relationship. Some variety tends to keep the intimate relationship more interesting, especially with all of the demands and stresses in our lives." —Hammond, age 44

What about those men who do just love "plain vanilla" and don't need to try new flavors in the bedroom? While most just like to keep things simple and just share the loving experience, others just haven't found the right person to experiment with.

"I am not very adventurous during sex. I think that my sex life is improving, but not because myself and my partner are doing new things. There are things we both like to do, and we do them almost every time we engage in sexual activity. I am not into anything too kinky. Just being able to love the lady I am with and express my feelings about her in that way is enough. I don't need extra props or to learn new positions to enjoy sexual activity."
—Armand, age 34

"Never found a partner with whom I'm comfortable enough. Maybe if I did, my answer would be different." —Maddox, age 32

What to look out for: Believing your sex skills are just fine and your man is completely satisfied sexually.

If you are like Dana and are concerned about why your man is asking you to experiment, the honest truth is: be happy he is asking you and not looking elsewhere. Men get bored easily. If you keep giving them the same thing over and over and are not willing to try anything new to spice things up, he may start straying. If you aren't comfortable trying new things, men say to start small with sexy outfits and work your way up to new positions and toys. What you need to remember is not to be complacent. Most women think they're "taking care of" their man, and yet man after man tells us he wishes his girlfriend or wife would be more adventurous sexually. There seems to be a disconnect there, but the good news is that you can control that.

Do men ever not want sex?

"My boyfriend and I have had a pretty regular sex life since we've been together. Over the past couple of months, the frequency has really dropped off. I mean, we went from twice a week to maybe once or twice a month. I'm concerned that maybe he's found someone else or perhaps he's going through a phase? I want to know: **do men go through times when they really don't want to have sex?**"
—Alicia, age 28, single

What the men say

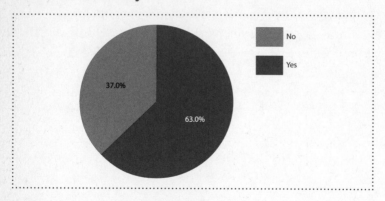

What men are really saying

Indeed they do. Often, sex is the motivating factor in why men do what they do, act the way they act, and say what they say. But not having sex happens, too, and in many situations, it has little to do with you. What men cite the most are stress, work, and depression.

"Well, stress is a huge factor in my libido, that's for sure. If I'm under a lot of pressure for work, or family issues, or anything like that, I can go days without wanting any sex—with my partner or myself." —Jonathan, age 28

"It is rare, but there are times when we just don't feel like it. We get tired, stressed, irritated, and so on, just like you do." —Benton, age 33

"There are many reasons a man can not want sex. The reasons I would not could be something like stress at work or worry over bills. If I've had a particularly hard day, I'm not always in the mood. Everyone's method may vary, but it's not odd to see a guy who just doesn't want to have sex all the time." —Zach, age 29

It's not always a fact that the periods of no sex have nothing to do with you. Some men discussed boredom in the bedroom or with their partner as reasons.

"The guy probably just might not be that into the girl, or he just might not be in the mood sometimes to have sex." —Asher, age 25

"If the relationship is not fluid, it can make a guy shut down sexually." —Frank, age 40

"Sometimes, like women, men shut down sexually when the sex gets old." —Lee, age 40

What to look out for: Believing that you're the reason you're not having sex.

Rest assured that men go through periods of not wanting sex. It happens. Mostly it has nothing to do with you but just life in general. However, be on the lookout for anything stale or boring in the bedroom that could lead to his disinterest.

What does he think
about performance issues?

"Every now and then my husband has had performance issues in the sex department. Nothing I would define as being impotent, but my husband takes it that way. He feels demoralized after. Sometimes I think maybe it's me? Am I just not arousing him anymore? He says no, but I'd like the male perspective. **How do men really feel about impotence?**"
—Candace, age 39, married

What the men say

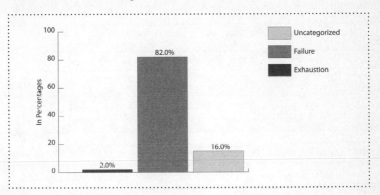

What men are really saying

An overwhelming amount of men, 82 percent, see impotence as a sign of failure. To men it lowers their self-esteem, and they see it as a reflection of their manhood.

"Men are very competitive and that makes them results oriented. No man wants to 'fail' at doing something, especially when it comes to providing and receiving sexual pleasure. Impotence, I imagine, can make a man feel completely worthless because he's failed at something that is inherent in all men. I feel as though women are fairly understanding of the situation, but I can't imagine them wanting to be with a man who couldn't sexually satisfy them." —Thad, 24

"A man would probably feel ashamed, feeling stripped of his manhood. The most masculine thing is to be able to have sex, and to be impotent shoots that possibility down. A woman probably does not see it as much of a roadblock, as they tend to look at the whole package of the man, rather than just that one attribute. I am sure for a lot [of men] it is very difficult, as being impotent has far-reaching implications." —Barry, age 37

The rest of the things men think about impotence range from exhaustion to saying they've never experienced it to some men not even knowing what the term means. There are some men who say it can happen to any guy, and it's something they can overcome.

"It can mean anything. I have not been able to get an erection for every reason from being exhausted to not thinking my partner was attractive in the morning. It is not fair to assume that it is a woman's fault that a man cannot maintain an erection. If it is just tiredness, oral sex can overcome fatigue." —McLean, age 21

"She may see it as her fault or because of her, especially if the woman thinks the man perceives her as unattractive."
—Ryan, age 23

What to look out for: Thinking that you are the main cause for his performance problems in the bedroom.

For men, not being able to perform is a sign of weakness, and that is something men have trouble coping with. If it happens to your man, show him it's okay and help him overcome the feeling. Remember, this has nothing to do with you. It's about helping him get through that while not obsessing about it. If he's tired, try other tactics. Who knows, you might find a new thing to try out in the bedroom.

What's he staring at during sex?

"I like to think that I have a decent body. I mean, I could lose some fat around my hips and thighs, but overall I think I look pretty good. My problem is that when I'm having sex, I know that my hips and thighs take center stage, and I hope to God that it's not a turnoff in any way. I'd like to know: **what part of the woman's body do men stare at during sex?**"
—Jessica, age 25, single

What the men say

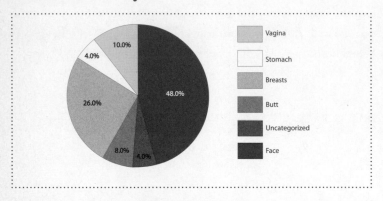

- Vagina
- Stomach
- Breasts
- Butt
- Uncategorized
- Face

What men are really saying

The majority of men, 46 percent, like to look at a woman's face during sex. Why? Men enjoy seeing the look of pleasure on a woman's face.

> "Every part of a woman's body is enjoyable to look at, but the only part of a woman's body that explicitly tells you how she feels is her face, so I find myself staring into my partner's eyes when we make love." —Eugene, age 24

"Specifically her eyes. You can tell so much about how she is feeling just from her eyes alone. The intense pleasure that I see is seen best by looking deeply into her eyes, and it is a huge turn-on also." —Matt, age 33

In a slightly distant second with 26 percent are breasts. The reasons vary, from if it's just a hookup and she's not the most attractive woman, he'll look at her breasts for the simple pleasure of watching them move around during sex…to the typical obsession men have had since they were young boys.

"I like to look at breasts because I love to see them be perky. I also love to see them bounce up and down." —Conor, age 27

"Staring into her eyes or around her face can get awkward. Also, if you're hooking up with a not-so-hot girl, you don't want to look at her face. If a chick has a nice rack, it keeps me going." —Joe, age 21

What to look out for: Thinking he is going to focus on your physical flaws during sex.

Women shouldn't worry too much about being a turn-off to men during sex. First of all, they wanted to have sex with you, so they're attracted to you. Second, most men like watching a woman's sexual expressions. And finally, if there's a part of your body they don't like, they'll look at something that they do. You want to be confident sexually as this is the most attractive thing of all for men.

Ask men your question at www.wtfarementhinking.com

How often does he want it?

"I date pretty regularly, and I think I have a great sex life. That said, I find that men I've dated recently are content with having sex once or twice a week. I'm not sure if it's just me, but I would prefer to have sex more often. **How many times a week do men like to have sex?**" —Diane, age 57, single

What the men say

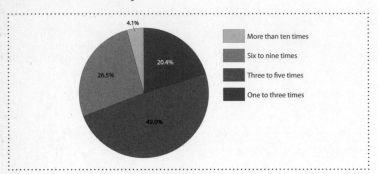

- 4.1% More than ten times
- 26.5% Six to nine times
- 20.4% Three to five times
- 49.0% One to three times

What men are really saying

Men make no secret about the fact that they love sex. The majority of men, 49 percent, say that they like to have sex three to five times a week. Men indicate that this is easy to accomplish, no matter what is going on.

> "I want to have a healthy sexual relationship with my partner, but I do not want to have so much sex that it ruins the original intention of it. After a stressful day, having sex is truly the best kind of relief. Sex is a beautiful thing, and it must be experienced as often as possible." —Zak, age 19

"Due to work/life schedules, this would probably be the right amount of sex, without sacrificing the quality of the interaction."
—Jake, age 32

Coming in second with 27 percent is six to nine times a week. These men say that sex every day of the week shouldn't be unreasonable; they just like sex!

"Sex every single day of the week at least once would be very nice because sex can be such a solution to every problem, even stress." —Rudy, age 23

"Honestly, I'd do it as often as possible given the choice, but more than nine times is stretching the amount of time in the day."
—Emory, age 31

What to look out for: Thinking that his having sex once or so a week is definitely enough for him.

Twenty percent of men fall into the category of one or two times a week, and those men say they work hard and are tired at the end of the day, often choosing sleep over sex. Other factors, including kids, time, and just their age, make them want to have sex less. However, the majority of men said they want sex more often than that, which is good for Diane. We think she's just been unlucky with the men she's been dating recently.

Does he fake it?

"I recently broke up with my boyfriend. In our very last argument, I told him that I often faked orgasms, but he said that he did too. I don't think that's possible. **Do men ever fake orgasms?**" —Ashley, age 23, single

What the men say

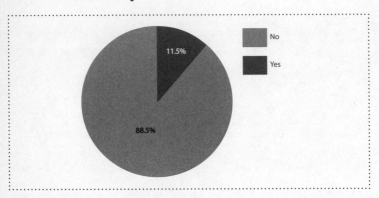

What men are really saying

The vast majority of men, 89 percent, say they wouldn't fake an orgasm. While it is possible for men to fake it, the majority didn't see the point. Simply put, it's a waste of effort.

> "No, I don't fake it because when you are a man and you ejaculate, there is no faking it. If she's good, there is no faking it. If she's bad, there's no ejaculation." —Ty, age 23

"I also believe a woman can tell if a man is faking it. A woman would be able to feel the pulsation as well as the ejaculation of sperm by the man." —Ed, age 51

The 11 percent that said they have faked an orgasm say they have because if they can't reach orgasm, it's easier on the woman to make them think they did. Sound familiar?

"Occasionally I simply cannot achieve an orgasm. I've found many women to get extremely distressed over this, which in turn makes it even more difficult for me. So, I fake it." —Mickey, age 26

"Sometimes it's easier, no explanations. Unusual, however." —Hugh, age 52

What to look out for: Assuming that there is no way he can fake an orgasm.

While it is rare for men to even want to fake an orgasm, it can be done. A lot of it does have to do with not hurting a woman's feelings, the men say, and that's why they have faked it. But the majority say it's just a waste of energy to fake it. Women can usually tell when they do.

Can he tell if I fake it?

"I'll admit that my sex life is not that great. I rarely have an orgasm. I can give myself one, but not with the men I date. Because of that, I believe that it's the men and not me. However, to keep the peace, I fake orgasm almost every time. What I'd like to know is, **can men really tell when a woman is faking an orgasm?**" —Lyndsie, age 25, single

What the men say

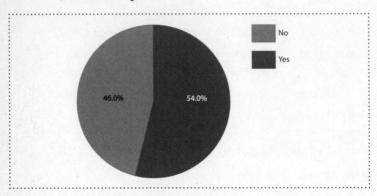

No

Yes

46.0%   54.0%

What men are really saying

Straight from the mouths of men: 54 percent said absolutely they can tell.

> "I answered yes because I think it's certainly possible to recognize if a woman is faking an orgasm, since there are certain physical reactions associated with an orgasm that can't easily be faked." —Lance, age 32

"There is such a thing as overacting, but more than that, it's that little bit of extra wetness that happens when a woman reaches orgasm. Not only that, but her womanhood tightens, and of course there are the moments when she would lose control of her body movements or not be as aware, and this would result in her gripping onto the man's shoulders or her body tightening overall. For the most part, yes, I can tell when a woman is faking an orgasm, but I am not her, so I can never be one hundred percent sure." —William, age 20

Forty-six percent of men have a hard time telling if a woman is faking it. While some admit they are too self-absorbed to pay enough attention, others say that women don't orgasm enough to be able to compare to see which are real.

"While having intercourse, a woman can do a lot of things to make a man believe she's having an orgasm. The way she moves, acts, and sounds she makes can be easily faked so that the man thinks she is having one." —Chandler, age 36

"Frankly [I'm] probably too self-oriented to notice. Also, while I have been able to tell a few times, orgasms have been infrequent, so it's hard tell what the real clues are." —Evan, age 53

What to look out for: Assuming that you can successfully fake an orgasm without him knowing about it.

The men split the vote closely on this question: it's nearly fifty-fifty as to whether they can tell if you're faking it. In Lyndsie's case, she might want to think of what could stimulate her enough during sex to actually achieve orgasm, or maybe it's quite possible that she just hasn't met the right man yet.

What are his fantasies?

"I want to spice up my sex life with my husband. I'm thinking through it, and I'm getting bogged down on what I should do. I'd like to fulfill my husband's sexual fantasies, but he's not very specific about them. What I'd like to know is: **what are the top sex fantasies for men, and how detailed do I need to get when making a sex fantasy happen?**"
—Carey, age 42, married

What the men say

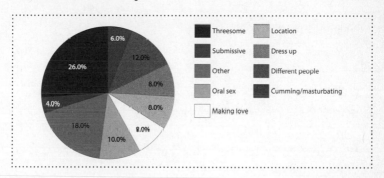

■ Threesome	■ Location
■ Submissive	■ Dress up
■ Other	■ Different people
■ Oral sex	■ Cumming/masturbating
□ Making love	

What men are really saying

The ultimate fantasy for the majority of men is having a threesome (or more, in some cases). In fact 26 percent of men agreed that a threesome was their ultimate fantasy.

> "My number-one fantasy is a threesome with my girlfriend and another girl that I find very attractive. I would like to be able to experience them both and see them enjoying each other." —Ethan, age 20

"Obviously I would love to have a three-way with my girlfriend and another girl, but I doubt that she'd be as into it as I would be. Why? I think that's every man's fantasy." —Jim, age 21

And the others? Well, that's just it: men were all over the place about their fantasies and could only be classified as "other." From extremes like water sports to just trying to have sex standing or up against a wall or on a kitchen table, the men we surveyed varied in what they really want.

"Number-one fantasy, role playing. It adds a lot of spice to the bedroom." —Jeff, age 26

"I'd like her to have sex with me in a public place, on a plane (mile-high club), or while I'm driving." —Ely, age 37

What to look out for: Believing that he needs you to pay attention to every detail of his fantasy.

While men's fantasies vary, if you are like Carey and are looking to try something new, don't worry about what your guy's fantasy is. Men love the element of surprise and will enjoy anything new you are willing to try in the bedroom (or on the kitchen table).

Can fantasies be deal breakers?

"I've been dating a man who, frankly, I want to end the relationship with. I care for him but really just want it over. I know I'm being passive-aggressive about this, but my thought was to not perform any of his fantasies as a way to break up with him. I want to know: **if you had a fantasy that your partner refused to participate in, would that end the relationship?**" —Anna, age 25, single

What the men say

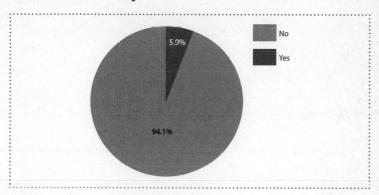

What men are really saying

You can call men many things, but they just aren't that shallow. In fact, 94 percent of men say they wouldn't end a relationship over a fantasy. However, some did say it would hinder what they would be willing to do sexually in return.

> "Because if you love somebody, something as meaningless as that would not be cause for ending a relationship. However, depending

on if you are serious or not with your partner, it may be grounds for breaking up when you are in it mainly for sex." —Mike, age 25

"Mostly because my relationship is not dependent upon whether my sexual fantasies are fulfilled, I would much rather talk with my wife-to-be about why she did not want to do it and then maybe find something that was more suitable for fulfilling both of our fantasies." —David, age 22

Six percent said that this was a deal breaker, and of those, the consensus was that the relationship should be a two-way street, as summed by these responses:

"I would want my partner to participate. That is what makes a relationship." —Jon, age 23

"I would wonder why my girlfriend would be unwilling to fulfill my fantasy. It tells me that she isn't willing to do something that makes me happy. It's not like I'm asking her to have sex in a church or her grandmother's bed." —Stan, age 39

What to look out for: Thinking that men absolutely need every fantasy fulfilled by you.

In Anna's case, she's much better off just ending the relationship than trying to figure out ways to get her man to break up with her. Men may be sexual, but they aren't going to ruin a relationship over one fantasy.

Ask men your question at www.wtfarementhinking.com

Does he fantasize about two women?

"I'm married to a man I love. Recently, I've been attracted to another woman. I think that it would spice up the relationship with my husband, in addition to adding to my sexual experiences. I'm thinking of discussing it with my husband, but before I do, I'd like to know: **do men ever fantasize about their girlfriends or wives being with another woman?**" —Grace, age 50, married

What the men say

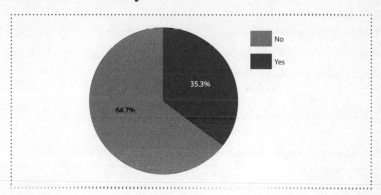

- No
- Yes

35.3%

64.7%

What men are really saying

Most women will be surprised to hear that 65 percent of men do not fantasize about two women in bed together. The reasons are rather logical and vary from being jealous of the other woman to not being able to satisfy two women at once to just really wanting to be intimate with the one they love.

"It may be a fantasy for most, but the reality for an experienced man is that one-on-one is the best. If I were a woman, I would never consent to a ménage à trois." —Spencer, age 42

"I really think my girlfriend is plenty for me. I know a lot of men do fantasize about that, but I'm also kind of a jealous person. She is more than enough for me in the bedroom :) !" —Matt, age 24

Thirty-five percent of men say they fantasize about woman-on-woman and threesomes in general, but a lot of those that do say it's just that, a fantasy. There are men who have done and love it and those who haven't yet had it and want it. But all men realize, however, that it is primarily just a fantasy.

"It's not a regular fantasy, and I'm not certain it's one I would like to come true, but it is something I have thought about. Two naked women is exciting." —Jacques, age 40

"The reason I answered yes is because in my experience, two booties are better than one. I have had numerous threesomes. The best part is watching one girl go down on the other while you hit it from the back." —Sky, age 25

What to look out for: Assuming that he wants a threesome. Even the men who said they didn't want to participate in a threesome did say they've fantasized about it. In reality they're not sure a threesome is what they would want. Grace should talk to her husband and see if that's a fantasy he would want to fulfill with her. His response could surprise her.

Do all men look at porn?

"I got married recently. My boyfriend before my current husband was in a band. He was into lots of weird stuff, and watching porn was one of them. I assumed it was something he was into and left it at that. My husband, a very conservative tax lawyer, recently admitted to me that he, too, had some porn movies that he watches every now and then. So, I'd like to know: **do all men look at porn?**"
—Amanda, age 30, married

What the men say

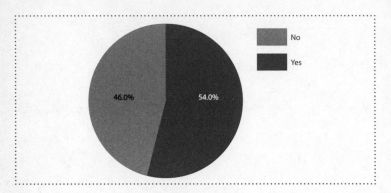

What men are really saying

While many women believe that watching porn is weird, men don't. In fact, 54 percent of men admit to watching porn. Why? Read on.

> "If women had to carry around testosterone, they would watch more porn also. It's not the people in the movie. It's the act and the fantasy." —Billy, age 39, TN

"Simple: I've never met a guy [who's] never looked at porn. In fact, I've never even met a guy ashamed of admitting he looks at porn. I think it's in our nature to crave things sexual in nature."
—Drew, age 18

"The question should be 'Do all normal men look at porn?' I'm sure that some religious fanatics do not, but they do not fall into the 'normal' category. Unlike women, men are stimulated by images, not emotions. We clearly can't have sex with every woman we meet, but to us, viewing porn and imagining having sex with the performers is virtually as good as the real thing. It does not mean we are cheating; in fact, it probably prevents us from looking for other women for sex." —Barry, age 50

What about the 46 percent who say they don't watch porn? Their answers vary from being religious to claiming that porn doesn't stimulate them.

"Many men look at porn, but some men get nothing from it. Porn can be visually stimulating, but some men simply find it boring. Depends on the man." —Stu, age 56

"I said no because there are some men who don't look at it. They are either not interested or are inclined by religious/moral proclivities to avoid it." —William, age 27

What to look out for: Assuming that while you and he are in a relationship, he has no need for porn.

Women may think that men watching porn is unnecessary, but it's a natural thing for most men. Don't forget that many men provided feedback that it actually keeps them from cheating.

But will he look at porn if he's got me?

"So I've got to ask a porn question. All men I've known have been into porn, mostly just movie watching, to varying degrees. I don't really care one way or the other, but it does make me think about how it could affect relationships. **Would men still view porn, even if they were in a committed relationship with a woman?**" —Dora, age 57, dating.

What the men say

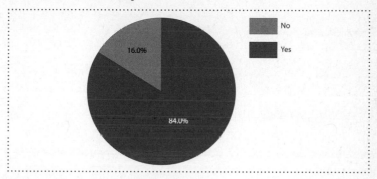

What men are really saying

Men watch porn. They're going to keep watching porn, even if they are in a serious relationship. The reasons why men still watch porn varies.

> "Yes, I think that porn would provide me with an outlet for my sexual desires while still maintaining the integrity of the committed relationship." —Nicholas, age 41

"Yes, it's normal, I believe. My past girlfriends even watched porn with me or by themselves. So yes, I watch porn." —Roy, age 37

"Yes, I would watch for fantasy. I will also ask my wife to accompany and try those positions with me." —Benjamin, age 55

"Yes, to change things up from time to time." —Bruce, age 44

"Yes, I do. :) There's nothing wrong with porn. Love goes beyond physical attractiveness; so porn only adds to the fun." —Brandon, age 31

"Yes. It is every guy's right to view porn if he wants to, it's completely natural, and it's vastly preferable to cheating." —Adam, age 26

While most men watch porn, some will stop once they are in a serious relationship.

"No. I think my partner might be offended if I did. At the very least, it might make her feel insecure." —Dave, age 32

"No real need to watch porn for knowing what I already know how to do." —Fred, age 31

"No. It would probably hurt her feelings and make her feel inadequate." —Wayne, age 40

What to look out for: Believing that because he is satisfied with his sex life, he won't have a desire to watch porn.

You could be having sex with him every day of the week, and it's possible he's going to still keep a small stash of porn somewhere for his viewing pleasure. Nearly every man told us that no amount of sex will stop that. This is mostly due to the fact that men are visually stimulated and that you're not always around. But this isn't worth being offended over. The majority of men think of this fun on top of, not in place of, sex with you.

Are condoms uncomfortable?

"Most of the men I've been dating have been my age or a little older. I want them to use condoms, but I hear every objection in the book why they don't want to. Number one on that list is that 'it's uncomfortable.' I'd like to know: **are condoms really that uncomfortable?** I always thought they enhanced sex." —Cindy, age 50, divorced

What the men say

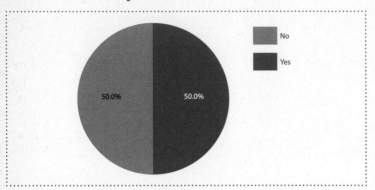

No

Yes

50.0%   50.0%

What men are really saying

This was an interesting question because the results came in at a fifty-fifty split. Let's start with the men who said they are uncomfortable.

"Condoms themselves are not uncomfortable, but they change the whole feeling of having sex. Everything about the sensation is different and makes sex seem more of a chore than an enjoyable experience. It is also harder to please a woman with a condom because sensitivity for both parties is reduced." —Matt, age 33

"Condoms can be very uncomfortable. The biggest problem is condoms are not one size fits all, though they claim to be. There are large condoms, condoms that are only large at one end, slim condoms, small condoms, thin condoms. Every man is different in size, shape, and texture preference. For me, I found condoms to be uncomfortable until I found out, through some Internet research, that I needed a large-size condom. Even then, I disliked the way the condom felt (really, I disliked the fact that I couldn't actually feel my girlfriend through it) and had to find a large-sized condom that was thin. In the end, it's all about finding the right one. Of course, nothing beats not having to use a condom."
—Dusty, age 24

The men who said they are not uncomfortable did admit they aren't the greatest thing to wear, but the security of knowing you are having safe sex is worth it.

"Because they tend to irritate the skin and often pinch. They may also be painful to put on, due to them pulling at the skin. Still, I would rather have that than an STD." —Deiter, age 28

"Condoms are in fact very uncomfortable because they constrict a man's member. For me at least, this is true because mine is wider than the condom, so it pinches it in a very painful way. Not only that but it takes away from the feeling much so that I can hardly feel anything. It sucks, but it's better than catching a disease." —Jamal, age 30

"I wouldn't say that condoms are uncomfortable. I'm pretty fine with wearing them, at least the ones that I've been using. The only hassle about them is the time you waste putting them on."
—Oscar, age 30

"No, condoms are not that uncomfortable at all. They do decrease the sensitivity of intercourse and are less enjoyable to use, but in no way are they uncomfortable." —David, age 29

What to look out for: Thinking that sex feels the same with or without a condom.

While men are split on whether condoms are uncomfortable, the majority of men agree that wearing a condom takes away from the sensation of sex.

Tightness: does it matter?

"I had a child a year ago. I've always been under the assumption that men want their woman's vagina to feel tight. I think that after my baby was born, I'm not as tight as I once was. I'd like to know: **does a girl's tightness make a difference during sex for men?**" —Madeline, age 23, committed relationship

What the men say

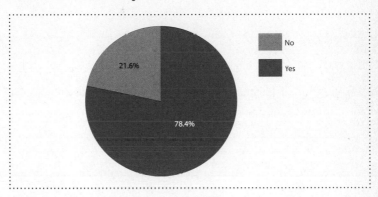

No
Yes
21.6%
78.4%

What men are really saying

Seventy-eight percent of men say yes, tightness during sex does make a difference. For some it means a girl has been "used" more, and they question what she's been doing. For most men, however, it's just a matter of pleasure: the tighter the woman, the better the sex.

"For men, the main stimulation during intercourse is, of course, friction. When a lover isn't tight, men get less friction, and thus it takes longer, although not much longer, to achieve orgasm. Plus, the feeling of a penis being squeezed during orgasm tends to make said orgasm better." —Preston, age 24

"Whether the guy is inserting a finger or a penis, tightness definitely makes a difference. A tight vagina signals to the male brain that he is truly penetrating the girl; she is feeling his actions. A loose vagina signals that the area is used and no longer responsive to his actions. You can definitely feel the tightness of different girls; all it takes is how many fingers he can get in before it becomes snug." —Jens, age 50

For the 22 percent who didn't seem to care about the tightness, some said tighter is actually more uncomfortable. Other men said they just didn't really pay attention to how tight a woman really is.

"Because for me, it is the motion of sex that I like more than the tightness/feel. I can tell a little, but it is really not that noticeable. I'd rate it about the same, though given the choice, I would prefer tight." —Shane, age 34

"I dated a girl for a while in high school, and she lost her virginity to me. The first couple times weren't that enjoyable because we were really limited in what we could do. I wasn't a big fan of the almost 'pinching' feeling I felt. You can usually tell the extremes if a girl is very tight or very loose. I think it's almost more pleasurable to have sex with a girl with a slightly loose vagina. You can turn and twist into different positions!" —Matt, age 24

What to look out for: Thinking that it doesn't matter how tight you are, that he'll be just as satisfied.

While most men do prefer a woman that is tighter, it is not necessarily a deal breaker. The only difference between feeling tight versus loose, according to the men we asked, is the length of time it takes for a man to have an orgasm.

Can my weight push him away from sex?

"I got married eight years ago, and I've gained some weight (twenty-five pounds) over those years. My ex-husband denies that it was a factor in our divorce. I believe that love is blind and that most men don't care about if a woman is a little heavy. But I am curious to find out: **does a woman's weight really bother men enough to keep them from having sex with her?**" —Jessica, age 28, divorced

What the men say

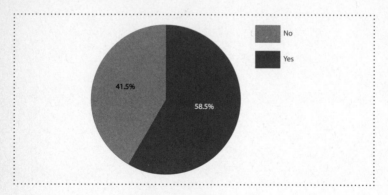

No
Yes

41.5%
58.5%

What men are really saying

Though the results are close, almost 60 percent of men say that a woman's weight would bother them enough to keep them from having sex. Now, before any woman goes and gets outraged at men's superficiality, the men who did say it would stop them said it would only if a woman became obese.

"To a point, it doesn't matter to me. If my girlfriend gained a few pounds, I would be okay with it. I mean, I eat a lot, and I'm lucky, I have a high metabolism; my girlfriend should be able to enjoy herself. But if she gained one hundred pounds, I would probably be disgusted by her." —Harry, age 19

"Neither men nor women want to have sex with a severely obese partner (unless they're into 'plumpers'); however, there's nothing wrong with not being the size of a model. A woman with some meat on her bones tends to look delicious…" —Grant, age 24

Forty percent of men who said weight doesn't matter also mentioned if they are in a committed relationship, there are more important things to consider than weight.

"This is dependent upon preference. Some men prefer thin women, while others prefer fuller-figured women. If you are in a loving and caring relationship, then weight should not be a factor." —Alphonzo, age 37

"In a committed relationship, love is more important than weight. In a casual situation, the sex is more important than weight." —Phil, age 67

What to look out for: Believing that if he loves you, he'll have sex with you no matter what you weigh.

Generally speaking, weight isn't a huge factor in a man deciding to cease sexual activity. Most men can appreciate a few curves on a woman and it won't turn them off. However, almost all men agree that they will get concerned when it actually hinders being able to perform the act and affects a woman's health.

How important is oral sex?

"I'm in a disagreement with my girlfriends. I think that it is all hype that men 'need' to have oral sex, but my friends say that it's mandatory in a relationship with a man. So, can you tell me what men think? **How important is it for you to give/receive oral sex in a relationship?**" —Nichole, age 25, single

What the men say

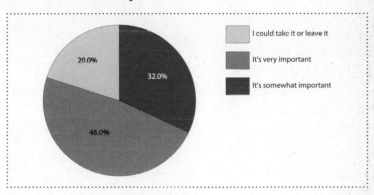

■	I could take it or leave it
■	It's very important
■	It's somewhat important

20.0%

32.0%

48.0%

What men are really saying

Men were pretty clear on how they feel about oral sex: 80 percent of them said it's important in a relationship. Oral sex, to men, is something special that tends to take the relationship to a deeper, more meaningful experience.

The misconception might be that men like to receive more than give, but to men, it's an equal opportunity type of situation.

"I find oral sex in a relationship to be important because I enjoy oral sex. I can't say that every man agrees, but I know that more than a few share this opinion. There are some very deep psychological desires that make men want oral sex, and each person has a different reason for why, but all men who enjoy receiving (and giving) agree that it feels amazing (most of that is a mixture of the sensations: wet, smooth, the feeling of an oscillating tongue, not to mention a well-placed, very gentle, scrape along the teeth)."
—Natt, age 24

"If you give, then you shall receive. Giving tastes good, is a complete turn-on, and is great for a man's self-confidence in the bedroom (if done right). Receiving can sometimes be better than penetration." —Drey, age 40

"Because we both enjoy receiving oral sex and it is kind of a gift that we give to each other and show how much we love each other. It is the one time when you are completely giving."
—Matt, age 33

"You don't constantly need the oral sex in a relationship, but some along the way is important because it slowly makes the relationship closer. The key to relationships is doing it slow and at a nice pace." —Denton, age 23

What to look out for: Thinking that because you have vaginal sex, oral sex is not important.

While men don't necessarily need oral sex, they do say it's at least somewhat important in any relationship. It's a very intimate act where one partner really focuses on the other.

Why doesn't he perform oral sex for very long?

"I'll admit, I love to perform oral sex. My experience is that I'm doing it 'forever' but I don't think I get the same attention in return. So my question is: **why is it that most men say they love performing oral sex, but when it comes down to it, they only perform it for a couple of minutes?**" —Debbie, age 42, married

What the men say

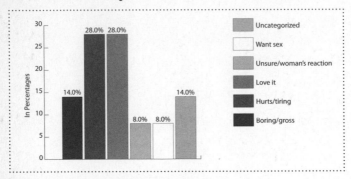

What men are really saying

The majority of men (58 percent) love giving oral sex. In fact, the majority of men said that saying they don't enjoy it or don't like to perform it for long is just plain wrong.

> "I myself love to taste a woman when I am having sex. Her juices and wetness are an indication of how much pleasure she is experiencing. Even for a few minutes, the oral will turn her on significantly. The wetter, the better, I say." —George, age 42

"If my partner enjoys me performing oral sex on her, I will continue until she reaches orgasm or asks for something different. I enjoy this because it pleases my partner." —Loyd, age 37

Even though the majority of men enjoy it, 28 percent said that giving women oral sex was tiring. Men don't have the stamina in most cases or the strength in their mouth and jaw to perform oral sex for an extended period of time.

"I would have to say I like to go down on a woman; however, my tongue just isn't as strong of a muscle as I'd like it to be. Try wagging your tongue for five minutes straight. It's much more tiring than you'd think." —Mike, age 25

"Sometimes it just gets hard to breath down there. Takes some work and commitment." —Nate, age 22

What to look out for: Thinking that "forever" and "a couple of minutes" mean the same thing.

Considering most men don't mind giving oral sex, maybe women like Debbie shouldn't focus so much on the time spent performing the act. If you are looking at a clock and are distracted thinking of how long a guy will spend giving you oral sex, then you aren't really into it, and he can tell. What man wants to do it if you aren't enjoying it?

Does he like a screamer?

"I've seen some porn movies, and the women are always screaming when they have sex. I'm not a screamer by any means. **Some of my girlfriends say that men like when women scream during sex as it's a big turn-on for them. Is it?**"—Jasmine, age 30, single

What the men say

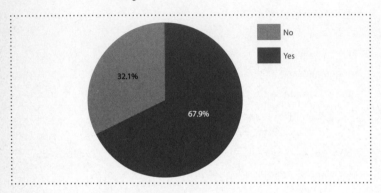

No
Yes

32.1%

67.9%

What men are really saying

Men love a vocal woman; in fact, 68 percent say they love it when they can make their partner scream.

> "It makes them feel 'manly,' like they are driving them to a point where they can't control themselves and are experiencing pure pleasure that he is providing." —Angel, age 61

> "I love when my girlfriend gets vocal during sex. There aren't many things that turn me on more than knowing that my girlfriend

is enjoying herself. Of course, there is such a thing as being too loud. I like my eardrums, thank you very much." —Cletus, age 24

Some men just don't like a loud woman in the bedroom. Men are turned on by different things, and some say soft moans are enough for them to know their partner is enjoying herself.

"I prefer things to be quiet and soft. It creates a more sensual atmosphere and is more fun when you have to try and suppress urges such as yelling." —Kolbe, age 19

"I love to hear my wife moan passionately like she's enjoying it and it feels really good, but I feel like if a woman was screaming, it would be for two reasons. Either she's faking it and the sex really isn't any good, or she's just way too loud and wild in the bedroom for me." —Robert, age 20

What to look out for: Assuming that all screaming is appreciated. While most men love a vocal woman in bed, keep in mind that there is a limit to how loud they want her. Women screaming is a major turn-on to men, and it means the women are enjoying it to the point of losing control. However, fake screaming or even being too loud can be a turn-off.

Sensual or rough?

"My sex life is fine. My husband is very loving and caring and romantic when we have sex. However, I'd like a little more spice. Maybe it sounds bad, but I'd like some hair pulling, some spanking, and the like, as it's a turn-on. But I don't think men (in particular, my husband) would really want to do that. **Can you tell me if most men like sensual sex or rough sex?**" —Margaret, age 43, married

What the men say

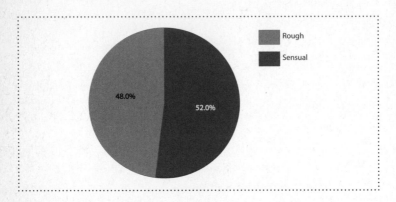

48.0% Rough
52.0% Sensual

What men are really saying

Percentagewise, most men say they prefer sensual sex, although it was a very close vote, with 52 percent clocking in on the sensual side. But those who answered this way said that while they enjoyed it, they admitted that they like it both sensual and rough.

"Sensual sex is more loving for two people. Rough sex is fun every once in awhile, but sensual sex is more active in engaging the two people romantically and sexually." —Isidore, age 31

"I prefer sensual sex because it is more fulfilling sexually. It makes me feel more connected. Not only does it feel good for the body but it works on the soul of the person also, making one feel better overall." —Ron, age 40

There's something primal about rough sex, letting your inhibitions loose, and having some fun. Again, while men say they like it rough, they also enjoy sensual as well.

"I don't like it rough per se, but I think that rough sex can be more fun. It's more animal and you get a more raw sense of the person. I feel that when actively trying to be sensual, you have to hold back in a way that's not natural for sex." —Raghnall, age 22

"Rough sex is the most fun because it turns a woman on so much more when you take control and use her like she only has one purpose. Sensual sex is reserved for a woman you love, not a woman you wanna have sex with." —Brandon, age 24

What to look out for: Assuming that men like sex only the way they typically do it.

There seems to be no preference, really, between sensual and rough sex. Why should men pick one or the other when both are equally acceptable? The type of sex is really based on the mood they are in that day. If you are like Margaret and think your husband won't accept it, just talk about it. The answer may surprise you.

Shaving: yes or no?

"I used to shave all my bikini area. I like the clean look. But recently I stopped doing so because of all the maintenance, and I just got lazy and let it grow out more than usual. I ran into an old boyfriend, one thing led to another, and we had sex. It was totally unplanned. But he noticed right away that I didn't shave. He didn't say anything about it, but I read it on his face that he was taken aback. So, my question is: **do men want women to shave their vaginas?**" —Jennifer, age 30, single

What the men say

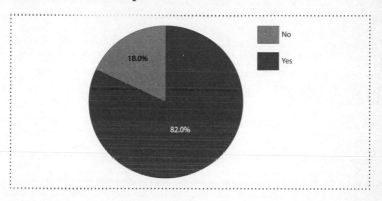

What men are really saying

(*Authors' note: We are aware that technically and physiologically speaking, the vagina is not what is shaved. However, many men are not aware of this. When we originally asked this question about shaving, we used the terms "bikini area," "vulva," or "pubic hair/area," and we got some confusion. When we used the term "vagina," they all understood what we meant by that naming convention. So this is how we refer to it here.*)

Most men, 82 percent, say they love it when a woman shaves or at least trims. When we asked men this question, we anticipated that you would probably want to know why they answered either yes or no, and there are many reasons why men answered yes to this question, ranging from it makes oral sex more pleasing to it means a woman takes care of herself and is clean.

"Seeing a shaved vagina is a turn-on, because to me, I can see everything. When I see a vagina with hair, I'm turned off. Also during sex, hair scratches the skin, and the feeling is not very pleasant. I'll say it again, I prefer the shaved vagina." —Mikkyl, age 27

"A shaved vagina shows that a woman is neat and clean and takes pride in her womanhood. It is also a lot sexier and tastes much better during oral, plus no pubic hairs in teeth :)" —Avi, age 35

Even though most men prefer shaving, there are 18 percent of men who like it hairy and all natural. From enjoying the look, smell, or feel of it, some men just think it's sexier.

"It's creepy looking. It would be like looking at a pre-pubescent girl. I would rather be with a woman who looked like a woman." —Elsdon, age 53

"I like the bush. It attracts more smell and looks so much better. It feels good against your face. Shaved looks too childlike, and I'm not sure why any man would find that attractive." —Issac, age 40

What to look out for: Thinking that he won't care about how you're groomed as long as you're having sex with him.

Many men like the look of a shaved vagina. You may not want to take it all off, given that some men and even women told us that they get turned off by the pre-pubescent look, but at the very least you'll be safe in the knowledge that most men prefer a close trim.

What can I do to make sex better for him?

"I got married two years ago and recently had a baby. Since the baby, I haven't lost the baby weight, and I feel insecure about it. I want to know how I could make the sex better for my husband. I know it might sound weird, but in my mind, this would make me feel better. **So can men tell me what one simple thing could women do to make sex better for you?**" —Samantha, age 20, married

What the men say

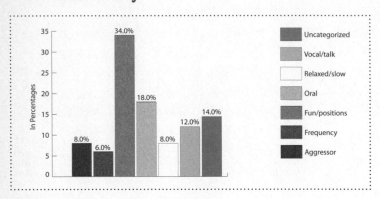

What men are really saying

The majority of men want you to have fun in the bedroom. If you are physically able to do various sex acts, then go for it. Men want women to let loose, try new things, from sharing fantasies to trying new positions.

"I enjoy my wife; we have a special bond. We have a very active sex life. She is willing to try and be open in our sex life. I do not think after all these years together I would be interested in other women." —Edward, age 55

"I think the best thing to do to make sex better is to mix it up. Once sex gets routine, it is less fun for men. Mixing it up changes that problem." —Conner, age 31

Outside of trying new positions and letting loose, a surefire way to spice things up based on what men told us was more oral sex. As we've mentioned before, men find oral sex very erotic and very stimulating.

"Trying different positions and oral activities, and if a woman really wants to impress her man, she can try by seductively sucking all of the semen out of the man's penis after sex." —Sonny, age 35

"They could be more giving. Blow jobs are hard to get out of a woman once you start pleasuring her." —William, age 18

What to look out for: Thinking that what you know about sex is plenty to keep him happy.

We hear all the time from women that "my man is taken care of" or "he's got nothing to complain about in the sex department" and other statements of bravado. But what men tell us is that they want more variety and fun in the bedroom. Not much is worse for men than keeping things the same when it comes to sex. In Samantha's case, she should just have fun. Don't worry about the baby weight and/or the insecurities, just let loose and enjoy the moment. Switch it up, try new positions or oral techniques, and you will certainly blow your guy's mind.

Chapter 5

MARRIAGE

Love and marriage might go together like a horse and carriage (as the song goes), but men's attitude about marriage, and how they decide to go about getting married, who they want to marry, and why they find it tough don't always fit together so easily.

Many women have told us that they think about (or have thought about) getting married since they were young. The romance of it all, finding their prince charming, and being swept off of their feet are very common fantasies for many women. (The movies *Pretty Woman* and *Dirty Dancing* aren't exactly popular because of the great acting.)

So if you're wondering what men think and feel about marriage and how they approach it, you'll find this chapter very interesting. And if you're already married and know how it is being married to your man, you'll find out why he thinks the way he does. You might actually understand him a little better.

We didn't say you'd agree. We're only saying you'll understand him better.

When does he think about marriage?

"I live with my boyfriend and have done so for about a year and a half. We have a great time together, but I will from time to time ask if he ever thinks about settling down. He does a pretty good job of avoiding the question. I'm still wondering if he'll ever decide to ask me to marry him. My question for men is: **how long would you date someone before you start thinking about marriage?**" —Lori, age 35, single

What the men say

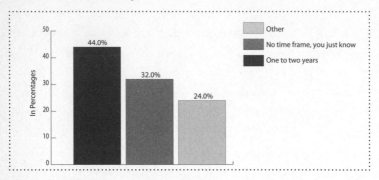

What men are really saying

So when do men start thinking about whether or not she is "the one"? The slight majority, 44 percent, say they start thinking about whether she is marriage material after a year to two into the relationship.

"I would want to date someone for at least a year before I thought about asking her to marry me, which would give us both plenty of time to really get to know one another and to see whether we would be compatible with one another. Sometimes it takes time to see another side to a person that you do not notice in the beginning, when you first start going out." —Patrick, age 42

"I would date someone for at least two years before considering marriage and at least five years together before tying the knot."
—Paul, age 31

Coming in a close second is the 32 percent of men who believe time doesn't tell you when it's right; you just know.

"Don't worry about a calendar…date them till you know who they are. I only dated about four months before my ex and I decided."
—Dave, age 56

"I dated my wife for seven years, but there is no magic number. You can't change someone, so as long as you really know and accept the person, you are ready." —David, age 36

What to look out for: Thinking you can decide the timeline for when to get married.

There is no magic number that you can depend on for when your guy will be ready, but around the year to year-and-a-half mark is when most men mentioned that they start seriously considering it. When they are ready, they'll ask, and only then.

What is the best age to get married?

"My boyfriend of two years has been strategically bringing up the fact that we are too young to get married. **So, do men have an idea as to the best age to get married? If so, what is it?**" —Debbie, age 22, single

What the men say

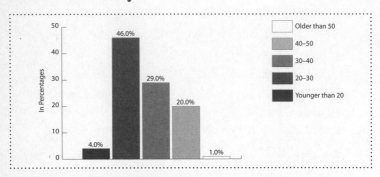

What men are really saying

Not surprisingly, the answer for this one was all over the place. While the average was twenty-nine, most men agreed that the best age to get married was anywhere from your midtwenties to your early thirties. The reason was simple: most couples will have finished school and are on a career path, and their partying ways will be out of their systems.

> "I would say the best age to get married is after twenty-five, but probably closer to thirty. It all depends when you are mentally and even fiscally ready." —Mike, age 24

"I feel that everyone should finish school, get a career, and then be financially stable then get married. So I would probably say anything over twenty-five." —Hartley, age 44

Even though the majority leans to the mid-twenties to late thirties, 12 percent responded that it's not about age, but about maturity. When you feel ready to get married, age doesn't matter.

"No specific age per se, but you should feel that you are a mature and confident person who is ready to take on responsibility and are comfortable with the decisions that you make. If you haven't grown up yourself and are still immature and irresponsible, it'll be a difficult ride." —Spyros, age 42

"I think it's whatever age you know you truly want to be with that person for the rest of your life. Once you're confident that you know that person will stick with you through thick and thin, you can get married." —Adam, age 19

What to look out for: Assuming that men want to stay single as long as possible.

Is there really a "perfect" age to get married? Many men reasoned that getting married in their late twenties was best. However, it's really up to you and your significant other's maturity and readiness level to truly answer that question.

Does he see marriage as a trap?

"My fiancé and I have decided to get married but haven't set a date yet. Call it cold feet or just hesitation, but I'm worried that I pushed him into marrying me before he is ready. The last thing I need is for him to think that I've pressured him or trapped him into marriage. **Do men perceive marriage as a trap?**" —Juanita, age 21, engaged

What the men say

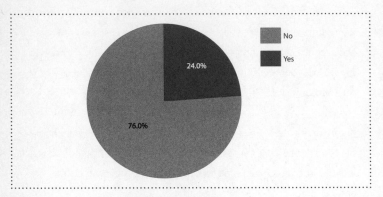

What men are really saying

The majority of men, 76 percent, agree that marriage is not a trap. Marriage to most men is a rewarding commitment in which two people share their lives together and support each other.

"I certainly don't think of it as a trap. I was the one doing the proposing, and I went into it with my eyes wide open. In many ways, marriage has made my life easier—we can afford a bet- ter quality of life with two incomes, we enjoy spending time to-

gether, we will have a more stable environment when we start
to have kids, etc." —James, age 31

"Definitely not. I honestly don't know what I would do without my
wife. She is always helping me with remembering things and how
to do things properly and orderly. Sure, there are moments when
you have your ups and downs, but you learn to work things out."
—Matt, age 21

The more jaded ones, 24 percent, say marriage is in fact a trap. The
reasons why varied from being tied down, to women changing soon
after the wedding, to getting married for the wrong reasons like money.

"In many cases, marriage can certainly be perceived as a kind of
trap, particularly if the marriage were to progress in an increasingly negative direction, and escaping such circumstances can be
fraught with numerous disadvantages." —Jakob, age 31

"I believe marriage is a trap, because it is usually something very
hard to get out of. Legal, moral, and even religious restrictions
make it difficult to get out of a marriage." —Robert, age 39

"Yes, it is a trap because it limits you to only one person to bump
uglies with. You can cheat, but that is dangerous." —Ryan, age 29

What to look out for: Believing that men almost always feel
trapped into getting married.

Even though there are some bitter men in the group, for the majority of men, marriage is not a trap. In fact, since they are doing the asking, they believe it's up to them whether or not to get married in the first place, and they have the choice.

What's he scared of?

"My boyfriend and I got into a fight about marriage. You see, I feel that he simply wouldn't commit to me. I didn't think I was asking for everything, just the commitment that we'd start talking about the next step. He wouldn't do it. As a matter of fact, things got ugly. Really ugly. It got to the point that we decided to break it off for a while. I think that he feels that something will change after we get married and we'll have to get a divorce. Is this what goes through men's heads when thinking about getting married? **What are the biggest fears men have regarding getting married?**" —Lynn, age 33, single

What the men say

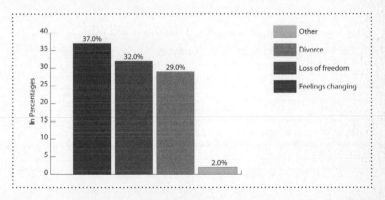

What men are really saying

Men have a few concerns when considering entering into marriage. The top concern, which 37 percent of men share, is the fear of feelings changing over time.

"I think my biggest fear regarding entering into marriage is that people often change over time, resulting in the possible failure and dissolution of the marriage and then the subsequent nightmare of the process of divorce." —Fyfe, age 31

"My biggest fear entering into marriage is boredom. I'm concerned that ten to twenty years down the road, my wife will become bored with me and be sick of seeing me every single day. To me, a spouse who is bored will often be likely to stray and cheat, and that will lead to all kinds of infidelity and ultimately divorce." —Stephen, age 33

The second biggest fear, with 32 percent of men chiming in, is loss of freedom. Marriage is a serious decision, and while it's not a jail sentence, men fear that they won't be able to do anything, and it is a very final decision.

"It feels like you have no freedom anymore. Everything is set in stone now, and you can't get out of it." —Cody, age 18

"The fear of not being able to do what I want to do when I want to do it." —Lester, age 28

Not surprisingly, divorce comes in at 29 percent. Marriage is a lifelong commitment, and men are afraid it won't end up that way.

"That it wouldn't last and there would be an expensive divorce. Huge suck of money and time and stress. People do change when they get married. Some people 'stop trying' and gain weight, etc."
—Chris, age 38

"That I may not be entering into a relationship that lasts forever. I want it to, but the potential for disaster is evident in the number of divorces in this country. That is the scariest fear for me."
—Dave, age 40

What to look out for: Thinking that men are afraid of divorce.

Marriage is a great responsibility and should not be entered lightly. The majority of men, nearly three-quarters, don't fear divorce as a reason why they wouldn't get married. Instead, they mainly cite feelings changing and loss of their freedom. All couples should evaluate all their concerns and discuss them before vowing to be there for one another for the rest of their lives.

Living together: yes or no?

"I'm forty-five years old and never had a boyfriend serious enough to live together until now. I'm seeing a man who seems to understand me and who I am, and the great thing is I feel the same way about him. He's asked me to move in with him as a step toward marriage. I'm not sure that I want to do this because I just don't think it's right. **Do men think it's a good idea to live together before getting married?**"
—Dorothy, age 45, single

What the men say

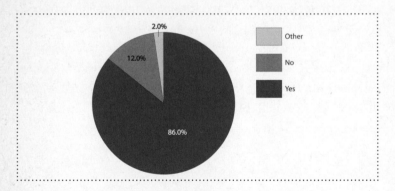

What men are really saying

Does she leave dirty laundry all over her place? Does he let the dirty dishes pile up? Do you know your significant other's annoying habits, and should you know them before you get married? Our men say yes. An overwhelming 86 percent say that couples should live together before tying the knot.

"It is good to live together before [getting] married, because you will have an idea of what it is like to live with the other person prior to the commitment." —Jimmy, age 21

"Yes, living together can be a trial run of marriage. If you learn that you cannot live together when you are dating, then how are you going to live together when you're married? You will learn what you like about your partner and what you dislike about your partner." —Jacob, age 19

While the purists of the group are small in number, 12 percent of men say you should not live together before getting married.

"Absolutely not. If you live together before you are married, what do you gain from that? Statistics show that you are more likely to break up if you live together before you are married, anyway." —David, age 35

"I don't think it's a good idea to cohabitate before marriage. Multiple studies have shown that the odds of a marriage succeeding increase if the couple doesn't live together until after getting married." —Vic, age 30

What to look out for: Assuming that he believes you'll "learn" to live with him after marriage.

Though some studies show that not living together increases the chance that your marriage will succeed, men believe the best move is to find out all of those weird habits that may drive you (or him) crazy for the years to come before you make it official. Men believe that couples need to see each other in their best and worst light before they can truly decide to walk down that aisle.

How would he pop the question?

"I've thought about my wedding since I was a girl. But for me, even more important than the wedding or the day was how my future husband decided to propose. Maybe simply or maybe an elaborate plan, but how do men go about it? I want to know from men: **How do you plan to propose? (Of course, if you've already proposed, how did you do so?)**" —Avril, age 23, single

What the men say

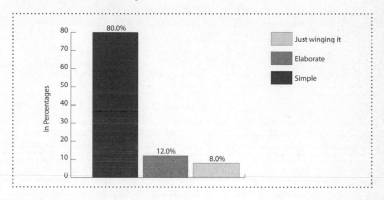

What men are really saying

Most men do think about proposing and how they plan on doing it. That said, most of them want something very simple and intimate and not very elaborate.

"I proposed to my wife while on a secluded camping trip. While sitting at the campfire, I pulled out a bottle of champagne, started to open it, but stopped and told her we needed something to

celebrate. I then took the ring from my pocket and proposed."
—Tom, age 34

"I took my wonderful girlfriend to her favorite restaurant on Valentine's Day. After she ordered her favorite meal, I popped the question on one knee. Not very fancy, but I proposed to her like this because it was one of the best ways I could think of."
—Christopher, age 31

"I plan on doing it in a very low-key way. Nothing too fancy for me." —Jon, age 25

Sometimes, even the best laid plans go awry but end nicely enough.

"Sadly my 'official' proposal was pretty pathetic, as my fiancée and I had already looked at rings together. I was going to show up at her work and have our son (one year old) walk around the corner to her desk with a balloon holding the ring and a note, but when I was buying the ring, I had to ask a question about it, and she figured out what was happening. Since she had an idea that it was coming from previous talks, I managed a small candlelit dinner at home with our little guy throwing his food in my face while I knelt and asked her." —Avery, age 36

What to look out for: Believing that men really don't think about getting married and put no effort into the proposals.

What we found interesting in reading the responses from men is that most men, whether they liked to plan something elaborate or simple, all had a pretty good idea of how they wanted to do this. This was true no matter what age they were or if they were married or had proposed. The vast majority of men thought this one through.

So while women make plans for the wedding and the ceremony, men plan their proposals.

Do men want to help plan the wedding?

"While planning my wedding, I find myself stressed. It seems that I've been making all of the decisions. I really don't think my fiancé has any interest in planning our wedding. I'd like to know: **do men actually care about having input in the wedding planning process?**"
—April, age 23, engaged

What the men say

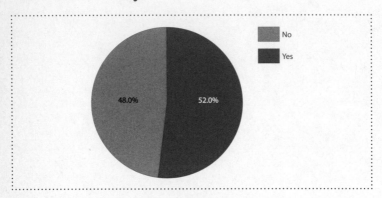

What men are really saying

Stereotypically "the special day" is all about the bride. Movies highlight that, TV shows, books, etc., but is it really just about what the bride wants, or do the grooms have a say too? Fifty-two percent of the men we surveyed said they do want to help plan their weddings.

"Yes, ultimately it is the bride's day that she has been dreaming about since she has been a little girl. However, I have a vested interest in making sure that I am marrying the girl of my dreams, so I better have a vested interest in helping with the wedding planning." —Jeff, age 32

"Sure, depending on what it is. If we could get a sweet band to play at the wedding, then yeah, get me in on that. But if it's about what kind of forks we use, I'd rather shoot myself in the face than have that debate." —Adam, age 21

The close second at 48 percent are the men who don't want to help, and other than really being concerned with paying for the event, they agree it's the bride's big day.

"In the sense that I'm potentially expected to act as some sort of prop in her childhood fantasy (and often to pay for it these days), I'd like to be comfortable with the arrangements. Do I care about the color scheme or other minutia? No." —Fred, age 50

"No, it is her day, and I do not care about what happens, I just hope it isn't too expensive; that would probably be my only say." —Mike, age 24

What to look out for: Believing that he could care less if he's involved in the wedding planning process.

If you are planning a wedding or hope to be in the near future, ask your man if he wants to be involved. It's a near fifty-fifty split on whether he'll want to play a part, but even if he does, don't worry; men don't want to plan your colors, just be part of the process.

Ask men your question at www.wtfarementhinking.com

Does he believe marriage is forever?

"My husband and I were talking about marriage recently, and he actually said 'I'm very happy being married to you,' but he followed it up with 'right now.' This scared me quite a bit. **Do men believe marriage is forever?**" —Rosalyn, age 29, married

What the men say

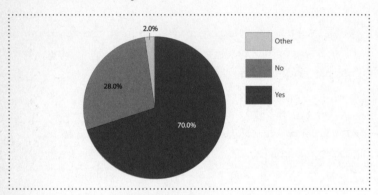

What men are really saying

Happily ever after sounds nice in the fairy tales, but is it reality? Surprisingly, 70 percent of men say that marriage is forever, as long as both people work at it and they end up marrying "the one."

> "If you have a true marriage, it is a commitment that will last forever, or at least until one person of the two is deceased. A true marriage means that you will fight through ups and downs, good and bad, and work to improve each other through your marriage. If you don't believe in improving yourself, your partner, your life

experience, and your relationship, then it's not a commitment to make just yet." —Michael, age 31

"I believe that the concept of marriage being 'forever,' or more appropriately termed as lifelong, is actually the ideal to which married couples should strive." —Jakob, age 42

So what makes the other 28 percent so jaded? The reasons vary from marriage being a fad, to getting married for the wrong reasons, to just growing tired of each other.

"No, I believe that either you will be with someone forever or not, regardless of marriage. I have even seen people get divorced, take a break, and get back together. Happily unmarried." —Paul, age 31

"No, I don't believe so. I am beginning to think that people are put together for a time and a season to help each other out when they need help or to learn a lesson about life and then be moved on to someone else." —David, age 18

What to look out for: Assuming he thinks that marriage isn't forever.

The majority of men still believe in the happily ever after and the fairy-tale ending. There are some realists in the group who believe it's just not possible anymore, but if you're working at it together, it stands to reason that you'll have a better chance for success.

Are men happy being married?

"I've been dating a guy now for two years and have been think-ing about marriage. While I think he is the one, I've seen friends' 'perfect' marriages fall apart and even my own parents' marriage fall apart. **Are most men happy being married?**" —Beth, age 32, dating

What the men say

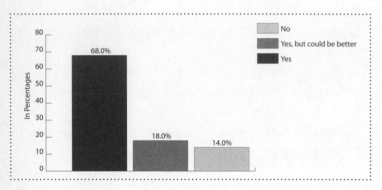

What men are really saying

Most married men are happy in their marriage. In fact, a whopping 68 percent said they are.

> "More than ever. What more can I want in life than someone who will care for me and love me for the rest of my life and I, her?"
> —Matt, age 21

> "I suspect that happiness in marriages is a bit like enjoying one's job. You've got to have good working relationships with your busi-

ness partners, whether they're coworkers or spouses. I am responsible for my own happiness at the end of the day." —Paul, age 26

While an additional 18 percent said they were happy being married, they did sense that things could always be better.

"I am usually happy in my marriage. I wish my wife was more passionate and sexually driven. She seems very passive, which creates self-doubt in my own mind. However, she is loyal and faithful to a fault and continues to do household chores and work two jobs, even though I am disabled and feel I cannot give my full contribution to the household. (I work full time as well, but I cannot do physically intensive things like cleaning or carrying groceries.) So I am happy with the woman I married, but it often seems like she is not attracted to me or at least passionate about me." —Hillel, age 31

What about the 14 percent who said no? These men gave several reasons for why married life wasn't for them.

"No, we never were able to reach out and accommodate each other; we spent more time protecting ourselves instead of nurturing the other person." —Bud, age 61

"No, life has been so much worse since I have taken this marriage thing on, dealing with cheating and finding my wife with all my friends. So now no wife and no friends…" —William, age 27

What to look out for: Thinking finding the right guy is all it takes.

Marriage is part work and part finding the right person. While you can marry the perfect person, if you don't work on your marriage and make sure both of your needs are taken care of, things can fall apart. Conversely, even if you work hard on making your marriage work, you can't fake chemistry.

Should the man be the spiritual leader?

"I've been married for six months and I would consider my husband to be fairly religious. He hasn't taken much of a lead in spiritually guiding our new union. **I always thought that men would be the spiritual leader in the household: is this true or not?**"
—Christine, age 28, married

What the men say

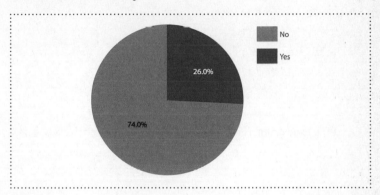

No
Yes
26.0%
74.0%

What men are really saying

Seventy-four percent of men do not consider themselves to be the spiritual leader of the household. When asked why, 32 percent believe it is a shared experience, and there should be coleaders, while 19 percent say there should be a leader, but that it's not gender-based.

> "I think that particular title should fall on whoever deserves it more. There are some men who are more capable of it than women and vice versa. Ultimately, though, I don't see why

there should be a 'leader' of any kind. Perhaps more 'spiritual partners.'" —David, age 26

"No. I think that anyone, regardless of gender or age, can be the spiritual leader of their household through strong spiritual leadership and example." —Jose, age 24

"No. Everyone needs to be their own spiritual leader. Anything less is the worst sort of irresponsibility." —Bill, age 33

What about the 26 percent of hardcore traditionalists who believe it is a man's role in the household?

"According to Ephesians Chapter 5, a husband is the spiritual leader of the household. This is the famous 'wives submit yourselves' portion, but don't forget the next part, which is 'Husbands, love your wife as Christ loved the church.' If you believe the Bible, yes, the man is the spiritual leader." —Spencer, age 41

"I am a man and you follow my religion." —Joe, age 18

What to look out for: Thinking that he will expect you to follow him in all facets of the marriage, including religion.

While most men are becoming more open-minded regarding religion and head of household, there is still that small percentage of conformists who believe the man should rule the religious roost. Seventy-four percent, however, don't share that view.

Will he expect me to work?

"I've been dating a guy for about four months, and as we talk about life and love and potentially marriage, I'll never forget that he once said that 'a woman's place is in the home.' At first, I thought he was kidding, but now I think he might be serious. In this day and age, could he be serious? I'd like to know: **do men expect their wives to work?**" —Maria, age 34, single

What the men say

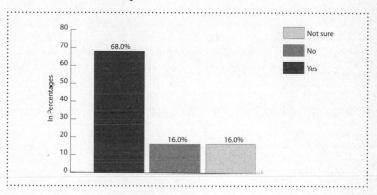

What men are really saying

Times have changed. When asked if they expected their wives to work, 68 percent of men said yes.

> "I do expect my wife to work when I get married. It's a new world, and women have just as much right to go out and make a living as do men. Also it would help with the finances if two incomes were coming into the home instead of just one." —Mike, age 24

"Of course I expect my wife to work. If the relationship is an equal partnership, then we both need to contribute to it. I have no intention of putting food in your mouth if you're capable of doing it yourself." —Vic, age 30

The other 32 percent of men varied on what they expected, but 16 percent of those did not expect their wives to work.

"No. Taking care of family and home are a job. But I wouldn't stop her if she wanted to work." —William, age 41

"If I were married, I would not expect my wife to work. She would do enough at home to justify not working." —Anthony, age 21

What to look out for: Believing that he secretly wants you to stay home.

The days of June Cleaver are gone, and the pressures of today's economy and the need to be financially secure have taken over. Marriage is now an equal partnership in the eyes of most men.

Will he feel insecure if I earn more than him?

"I just got a promotion at work that has really caused stress in our relationship. Along with my promotion came a raise that really separates our income range. I don't know if my new financial status intimidates him, but I think it does. **Would other men feel insecure if their wives earn more than them?**" —Jessica, age 37, married

What the men say

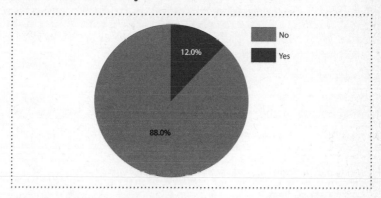

What men are really saying

Gone are the days when men feel they have to be the main breadwinner to feel like a man. In fact, 88 percent say that it's more than okay for their wife to make more, but they understand why other men would not be okay with that fact.

"Yes, what backwards idiot would answer no to this question? Look at the society we live in today; this is old news. A man should support and be happy for his wife, no matter what. If you're with a man who answered no to this question, you should not marry him in the first place." —Frazier, age 33

"Personally, it doesn't bother me if my wife earns more than me. It doesn't bother me because in a marriage, it's about both the man and the wife. There will be times where the husband is making more and times where the wife is making more. It will probably bother some men because of their own ego, and it gives off a perception that a woman is supporting a man, when it should be the other way around. But when you are in a marriage, both of you are supporting each other." —Stephen, age 33

Does making less money make a man feel inadequate? Twelve percent say it does make them feel weird and less manly, and others say they simply do not want to lose the position of power in the household.

"No, it puts the woman in a more powerful position which they cannot handle using pure emotions. Men use more logic." —Montgomery, age 32

"No, it makes me feel like I am not doing enough to support my family. I do not want my wife to have to worry about earning money for our family." —Matt, age 33

What to look out for: Presupposing that men's egos make it impossible for them to accept their wives earning more money than they do.

We think it's safe to say that the caveman days are finally over, and men appreciate women earning more and being recognized for their talent and hard work. While there are a few barbarians who are straggling behind, more and more men respect women and their accomplishments.

What role am I expected to play?

"My ex-husband used to frustrate me because whenever our house was messy, he never seemed to want to lift a finger to help me clean up. Maybe 'never' is a strong word, but trust me, it was seldom. When I confronted him about it, he would just blow it off as woman's work. My current boyfriend is showing some of the same traits. Is this common among men? **What role do men expect their wives to have in the marriage?**" —Annie, age 31, single

What the men say

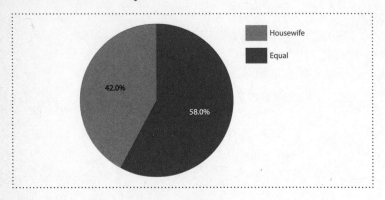

What men are really saying

Good news, ladies: while the margin is slight at 58 percent, the majority of men say their wife's role in the marriage is as an equal.

"I expect my wife to have an equal role as myself, whether that be working to earn money for the family or staying home and raising the children. My wife should not feel pressured to do anything extra for me or assume the 'traditional role' of a woman. She should simply do what she feels best, and it is my judgment to find a wife who can do that for herself." —Michael, age 18

"I would expect my wife to have essentially an equal, although in certain respects different, role in my marriage. The appropriate term here would be partnership." —Vlad, age 31

What about the traditionalists? Forty-two percent of men still wish they were married to June Cleaver.

"Just a basic housewife. Keep things clean and cook. I have a high-paying job, so she doesn't ever need to work." —Brett, age 29

"I expect my wife to play a secondary role in our [future] marriage. She will of course be entitled to her freedoms, but will primarily follow my overall lead. She will assist with household chores and possibly with bills and also take care of me sexually (I have a large sexual appetite) and can expect the same in return." —Mike, age 23

What to look out for: Assuming that men still want to have women in "traditional" roles in marriage.

Most men see their wife's role as an equal partner in marriage. However, as progressive as we sound in the media, 42 percent of men still expect traditional roles of a housewife. While no men used the terms "barefoot and pregnant," those beliefs, in the minds of more than a third of men, still exist.

Will he do some chores?

"My sister's new husband is a pretty nice guy, but I think it's strange that when I visit their house, she seems to be the one who picks up the place, etc. He seems to keep the yard and outdoors clean. I would never embarrass my sister by asking her this, but I'd like to know **if men are willing to share in the housework?**" —Megan, age 27, single

What the men say

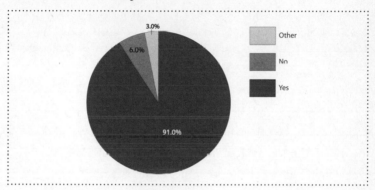

- Other
- No
- Yes

3.0%
6.0%
91.0%

What men are really saying

Is housework "women's work," or have times changed enough for household chores to be a team effort? An overwhelming 91 percent of men have no problem pitching in, ranging from just helping out with the chores to doing a lot of them.

> "Very willing...No offense, but the best meals I have had in my life were cooked by men. The cleanest places I have been were cleaned by men. Men naturally have more 'elbow grease,' so they

make better cleaners. I personally like a clean house, and I get things cleaner than my girlfriend. The cooking thing, I have no clue...I think it's because men know how to cook meat better." —Carl, age 33

"I'm reasonably willing to share housework. I vacuum as much as she does, and I often start the laundry (she does the folding afterwards). I make sure all the household bills are paid and the finances are in balance. She does most of the cooking and grocery shopping. I clean, maintain, insure, and repair the vehicles and do any maintenance on the house. I deal with creepy-crawlies in the house." —Dick, age 38

A caveman gene still affects 6 percent of our men, who are adamant in the fact that they will not help out with the housework. These men think that they work hard enough outside of the house and shouldn't have to help when they come home.

"I'm lazy when it comes to housework. She does most of the housework, and I work long hours, including overtime, so we can live in a nice house and take nice vacations, etc." —Rob, age 45

"I really don't like to. She doesn't share in the outside work (which is my job)." —Rick, age 47

What to look out for: Concluding that men still see household chores as women's work.

Barbaric tendencies are a thing of the past. The overwhelming majority of men do not think they are king of their castle and the "little lady" should wait on them hand and foot. Housework, like paid work, is a shared responsibility, and the majority of men are happy to help.

Why are men so messy?

"I come from a family of three brothers and no sisters. I'm currently married and have one child, a boy. Throughout my life I've noticed that the men I've lived with have a real difficult time keeping their living areas tidy. This spans from childhood to my current husband, and now my own son is leaving a mess everywhere. I've got to know: **are all men messy, or just the men in my world? If it's all men, why are they so messy?**" —Lanea, age 24, married

What the men say

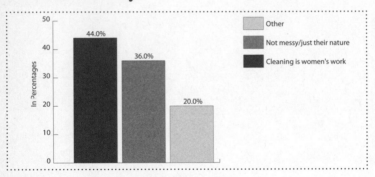

What men are really saying

Some men were coddled as children and never had to pick up a thing in their lives, while others were brought up in a traditional household where cleaning and taking care of the house was a "woman's job." So it should come as no surprise that 44 percent of men think that cleaning should be taken care of by their wife or girlfriend.

"Men are messy at home because we are generally not brought up to tend to the cleaning of the home. When I was growing up, my mother was the one who did all the cleaning. She didn't expect her children to keep the house clean. She felt it was the job of the parent(s) to make certain the household was clean. I think more women are taught to maintain the household and make certain it is clean and tidy." —Alfred, age 34

"They are brought up in a culture where they see women as sub-servient and bound to home care. Their job is to hunt (bring in income), not clean up." —Monte, age 61

In second place is a tie at 36 percent. These men say it is either in their nature to be messy or others feel they are not, in fact, messy at all!

"Men are messy because we don't see the need for everything to be spotless. Why spend all day cleaning when there are balls to hit at the driving range?" —Brice, age 29

"We are not all messy at home. Maybe the man you are referring to is lazy? My wife and I are both neat freaks, so I can't say why I am messy. Men who are messy just do not care about their personal belongings and are being lazy." —Matt, age 33

What to look out for: Thinking that all men are slobs. While Lanea has just had the misfortune of living with messy men, it's an unfair generalization to assume all men are messy. It's the equivalent of saying all women nag. In some cases it was how the men were brought up, and some think it's just natural, but there are those who are clean to the point of being neat freaks. That said, there is a significant segment of men who just think that cleaning is not their job. Maybe it's time to set expectations with the men in your life about what work is to be shared.

Do men feel an obligation to make wives happy?

"My husband goes out of his way to be sure I'm taken care of. For example, when he gets up to get something, he'll always ask if I need anything. He'll bring me flowers, and a couple of times a week will make dinner. When I hear my friends talk about how their husbands don't do these things, I wonder if my husband is the odd one? **Do men feel it is their responsibility to make sure their wife is happy?**"
—Terri, age 29, married

What the men say

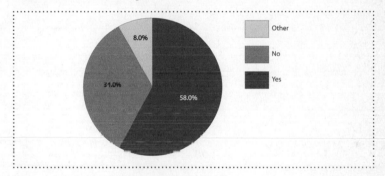

What men are really saying

Fortunately for you ladies, the majority of men, 58 percent, think it is their responsibility to ensure you are happy.

"Yes, it is my responsibility. If she becomes discontented and unhappy, life will become nothing but hell for me. If the discontent and unhappiness prevail, she will find another man. The pervasive fear of loneliness keeps us tied, even when we are unhappy with the person or the relationship." —Mark, age 47

"Yes, she's your wife, dammit!" —Jon, age 33

Even though the majority of men think it is their responsibility, 34 percent said no, it's not the man's role. The reasons why included that it's up to her to be happy or that happiness is a shared responsibility.

"I feel as though my wife would have to be happy on her own and that my actions toward her would add to it. You can't force someone to be happy if they are not." —Sam, 45

"No, it is not my responsibility to make sure my wife is happy. A marriage is a team and takes work from both parties to work. While I do try to contribute to her happiness it is not totally up to me." —Dan, age 35

What to look out for: Thinking he doesn't feel some responsibility for you.

Most men will work to keep you happy, but they also think that your happiness is your own responsibility to a large degree. That said, do not depend on or expect them to be the answer every time you are down. Nice goes a long way, but ultimately you will decide what mood to be in, which can influence not only your husband, but also your marriage.

Do men think their wives are less attractive with age?

"Over the last couple of years, I've watched my husband as he notices younger women on TV, at the store, etc. I can't help but think that he in some way wishes I was young again. Is it me? Because I really don't like this insecure feeling I have. **Do men think their wives will become less attractive as they age?**" —Sarah, age 39, married

What the men say

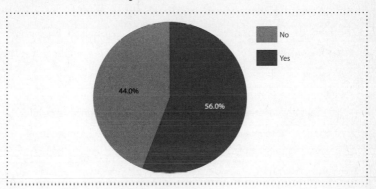

No
Yes

44.0%   56.0%

What men are really saying

With age comes beauty? Or with age comes crow's feet and softness? The slight majority (56 percent) say with age comes wrinkles, and they think their wives will just not be as attractive as they age. On a positive note, however, they also think their perception of what is attractive will change with time as well.

"I do believe she would, but my perception of attractiveness would also change." —Raphael, age 27

"Yes, everybody becomes less attractive as they age. Wrinkly, loose skin, less muscle tone, skin blemishes increase. But beauty is not everything. People who have spent their whole lives together can still see the younger person their spouse used to be."
—Kevin, age 49

What about those noble men who think they will be attracted to their wives throughout the years? Those 44 percent report that the wrinkles and gray hairs will add character and are signs of a life well lived.

"No, I find my wife attractive as ever. Men have the uncanny ability to fixate on the most sexually attractive area of a woman; if that area changes, their fixation will change, but not the level of attraction." —Makari, age 31

"No, I have been married for twenty years and still find my wife as attractive today as I did twenty years ago. Beauty is within the eyes of the beholder (no pun intended). As we age, we age slowly and do it subtly. So therefore as we age, these qualities stay the same over a slow period of time." —Chris, age 44

What to look out for: Assuming that he thinks you are less attractive every passing day.

While we grow older and our looks fade, most men will find you beautiful for your personality and will love how you age.

Does love change in a marriage?

"I've been married for twenty-five years. I can confidently say that the love I have for my husband hasn't changed. But he tells me otherwise. We seem to argue more than we used to, but we have sex more than we used to as well. Is it possible that his love for me has changed? **Do men think that love changes in marriage?**" —Elizabeth, age 49, married

What the men say

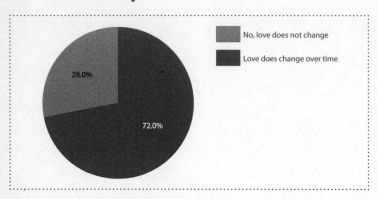

No, love does not change

Love does change over time

28.0%

72.0%

What men are really saying

Does love grow and increase with time? Does it diminish and fade over the years? Or is it a constant, never-changing feeling? Seventy-two percent of the men we asked say love does change after time, and 42 percent of those say it changes for the better.

> "I am divorced, and love definitely changes in a marriage. If you get along well in a marriage, your love will grow stronger for your spouse. If you are in a bad marriage, your love will decrease, as

was the case with me. The amount of love in a marriage basically comes down to how good the couple is for each other and to each other." —Richard, age 31

"Yes. The initial wham of it dulls, and it becomes as routine as putting on underwear." —Glenn, age 46

The 28 percent of men who say love doesn't change with time indicate that they love their wives as much as they did the day they got married.

"No, I love my wife as much as I did when we got married eight years ago, and I can't see it changing." —Alasdair, age 31

"I don't think so, for me. I think marriage will make the [love] more intense. I mean it will become stronger. Those couples who fail in their marriage are those who didn't know the real meaning of love. Who easily give up whenever they have problems. So no matter what the problem, you should face it together for the relationship to last. Trust, respect, and love are the main ingredients." —Richard, age 27

What to look out for: Presuming that men think love never varies. Men believe that love changes, but most see it maturing in a positive way versus fading with time. Love changing, from a man's perspective, isn't always bad, but rather that it's just human nature. Couples grow stronger or distant, people mature, and things will change that will reflect how you feel about the other person. It is up to you as a couple to make sure it grows stronger and doesn't fade with time.

Does he think about his exes?

"My boyfriend called me by his ex-girlfriend's name last month while we were having sex. It still bothers me. When he did it, he immediately dismissed it by saying that he must have heard the name earlier on the news. Not buying it, I let it go, but I can't let it go completely. So what I'd like to know is: **do men reminisce about past lovers?**"
—Carolyn, age 20, single

What the men say

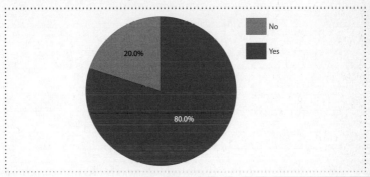

No
Yes

20.0%

80.0%

What men are really saying

Reminiscing about what could have been or dodging a major relationship bullet is just built into everyone's DNA. It came as no surprise that the majority of men, 80 percent, admitted to thinking about a former lover, ranging from once in a while to all the time.

> "I do about once or twice a week, I just think about what could have been and how good the lovemaking was. I think this is just

because I get bored with how my lovemaking is now, or sometimes it's fun just to look back." —Mike, age 24

"Once or twice a month; it's usually when I am masturbating."
—Cristian, age 33

The 20 percent who do not think about former lovers say they are happy in their current relationship and have no reason to think about the past.

"I do not reminisce about past loves; they remain in the past. If they were meant to be present, they would be here." —Sam, age 45

"Never. All my past lovers were terrible disappointments compared to my wife. I don't know why, but I dated losers before I met my wife." —Jo, age 36

What to look out for: Assuming he never thinks about the past. A few men may think what happened with past relationships should stay in the past, memories included. But the majority of men still think about what happened back then. Some are thinking about the one who got away, but others are thinking about how lucky they are now compared to way back when.

Children: yes or no?

"My boyfriend is pretty career-minded. He's been married once before, and when we talk about being together, one thing he always mentions is that he doesn't want to have kids. Okay, he doesn't want to have kids, but is that because he wants an 'easier out' or fewer strings attached? Or, he doesn't want to pay child support if we separate? Is this common? **Do most men want to have children?**"
—Sheila, age 33, single

What the men say

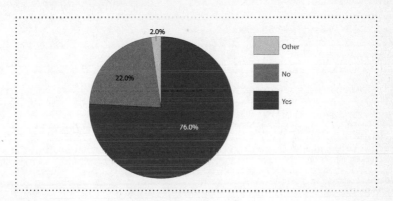

What men are really saying

Should the family name live on? Seventy-six percent of men say yes. Most men, when asked, do want to have children someday and believe roughly 2.6 children would be ideal—even though we're not sure how a 0.6 is achievable.

"Someday when I have a solid foundation on which to build my future, I would like to have children, but only when I know that my wife and I are strong and solid in ourselves." —Truman, age 19

"Yes, but only when I know that the women I am with will be with me forever." —Trent, age 25

While 22 percent of men said no, most were an adamant no, and there really was no reasoning behind why they felt that way or felt so strongly about it.

"No. Never." —Jalen, age 28

"Not anymore. It has its rewards, but you give up an awful lot that you can never really get back." —Wilfred, age 50

What to look out for: Presuming that the reason he doesn't want kids is because it's easier to get out of a relationship without them.

Most men want a family when the time is right. This is something you should talk about with your man to see if you both are on the same page and figure out the *when* and *how many*.

Would he cheat if he could get away with it?

"Whenever my husband and I talk about his work, he always seems to bring up the same woman's name. At first I thought nothing of it. I don't even think he notices it. But it seems to be happening more frequently. Is he thinking about or would he start something with this woman? So I'd like to ask men, **would you cheat on your wife if you know you could get away with it?**" —Diane, age 35, married

What the men say

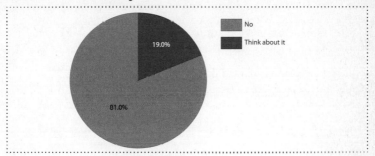

No

Think about it

19.0%

81.0%

What men are really saying

You can rest easy, ladies, because most men, 81 percent to be exact, claim that they would never think about cheating, even if they could get away with it. The main reason behind why, you ask? They just would feel too guilty and bad to live with it.

"No, I wouldn't be able to live with myself if I wasn't being honest with my wife." —Matt, age 33

"No, I would never cheat on my wife and risk losing my family, besides the fact that I love my wife more than any other woman on this earth. More importantly than that, I vowed before my friends and family and also before God that I would always remain faithful." —Brad, age 30

What about that 19 percent who says they think about it? While they do think about it—because let's face it, it's just a guy thing to think about other women sexually—the majority said they would never act on it.

"Just to be clear, you are asking if I think about it, not if I would actually commit the act of cheating? That being said, my answer is yes, because I imagine doing sexual acts with every woman that I think is attractive." —Paul, age 23

"Think, yes. Would I actually? No. Some men may act that out. Not me; think it every so often." —James, age 25

What to look out for: Thinking that if he can get away with cheating, he will cheat.

The good news is that most men won't cheat, even if they thought they wouldn't get caught, because they wouldn't be able to live with themselves. Of the men who think about it, that's all it is, just thinking about it.

What would he consider unforgivable?

"I'm a thirty-one-year-old woman born and raised in Texas. Recently I saw a show on TV about the divorce rate in the U.S. My parents always found a way to work things out in their marriage, and it made me wonder: what could be so unforgivable as a committed married couple that you couldn't work it out? **Do men consider anything unforgivable in marriage?**" —Mary Jane, age 31, married

What the men say

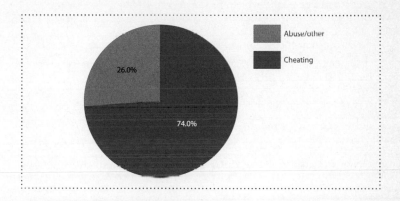

Abuse/other

Cheating

26.0%

74.0%

What men are really saying

Of the thousands of men we asked, the most unforgivable act is adultery. In fact, out of all the various reasons given, 74 percent agreed that cheating was the worst thing you can do in a relationship.

> "It's a cliché answer, but cheating is unforgivable. Unless you enter a marriage where polygamy is the norm, having sex with

another person is a huge violation of trust. Once a cheater, always a cheater. You just cannot change that." —Kyle, age 32

"When I am in love with someone, they're all I need. I would never cheat. If I fall out of love with someone, I communicate with them—not hurt them and screw someone else." —Neil, age 27

"I consider cheating unforgivable—either physical or emotional cheating. Even if there is no physical contact involved, it is possible for cheating to take place on an emotional level. That type of connection should only exist between you and your spouse. I have not done this myself. It is too sacred for me to mess with." —David, age 25

The other 26 percent vary on what they find unforgivable. Coming in second was a tie between abuse of all types and the opinion that there is ultimately nothing that is completely unforgivable.

"To me, an unforgivable act is physical violence. It is unforgivable because once someone assaults another person, the cycle will never end. If there are kids involved, it will cause permanent damage in the marriage. I have never been involved nor have I ever put my hands on a woman. I would never want to have a reputation of being a wife beater. There is no real excuse for ever putting your hands on a woman." —Stephen, age 33

"I am no angel by any means, but I truly believe that anything can be forgiven if the couple truly wish to stay together…forgiveness without resentment is the key." —Jeff, age 44

What to look out for: Presuming that all things can be forgiven in marriage.

Short of adultery, almost everything else is forgivable. With adultery, trust is lost, and that is something that men cite as hard to regain, if it's even possible. Men believe that the constant wondering and uncertainty will almost always lead to the end of a relationship.

Why do men cheat?

Authors' note: Of all the questions we've received on www. wtfaremen thinking.com, we get this question the most by far, in various forms, with varying stories, and from women of various backgrounds, ages, experiences, and values. So instead of using one specific woman's question, we asked 1,000 men bluntly what women all seem to want to know: **Why do you cheat?**

What the men say

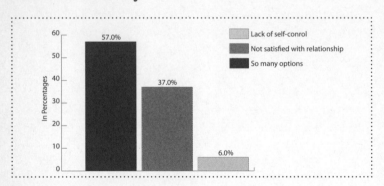

What men are really saying

Men cheat for a variety of reasons, and each man has his own justification, reasoning, or excuse as to why they have or would. Nevertheless, we could accurately categorize them into three core areas:

Because there are so many options available to them

Because their existing relationship is not satisfying

Because they lack self-control and discipline

Some of the comments from men really helped to sum up their reasoning. While you may not agree, how they rationalize their feelings are as follows. For the "options" reason, 57 percent of the men think this way:

"Before I got married, I used to cheat on my girlfriends. I was immature. I wanted constant attention, women were always around me, and I didn't have a real reason to say no. When I got married, I thought it would be different. It's not. There are so many opportunities for men that it's difficult to pass up. What women will never understand is that while they look at being in a committed relationship or marriage as the pinnacle of their life, most men, if they're honest, look at it as a sacrifice. Sacrifices are hard to maintain. I know that doesn't sound good, but it's the truth. It's like dieting. If you only eat steak and eggs, you can survive. It fills you up. It tastes good. But there are so many other foods and tastes to try. While you can limit yourself to one type of meal and survive nicely, it's not realistic to maintain that diet for the long term. One woman? Could I live with just one forever? Sure, but there are so many other tastes around me to try, it takes a lot of self-discipline to stick to the same thing, as good as it may be, every single day. It is a sacrifice. And it's not about love. I love my wife. I'll always be there for her, but every now and then, a new taste is important too. This is my opinion." —Daniel, age 33

"Why do men cheat? Because most of us can, and alternative women are always available. I don't mean that to be flip or cal-

lous. It's just how life is. I'll put it this way: if I have a pool in my backyard, I can enjoy it all year round. It gets me wet, I can swim laps, it cools me off on a hot day. I love my pool. It doesn't mean that when I go to the ocean I'm going to pass on jumping in simply because I have a wonderful pool. What a waste of experiencing life. I can be back at my pool and enjoy it again. I'm taking nothing away from my pool by swimming in the ocean every now and then. I know this might be an odd analogy and women will hate it, and it's not how I'm justifying it. I'm just trying to explain a very complicated topic in a way that might be understood."
—Anthony, age 48

Coming in at a close second is how their current relationship is going. Thirty-seven percent of men say they would or have cheated if they are unhappy or unsatisfied in their relationship.

"They are not getting what they want from their wives. All men I know look at porn. If I watch a video of a hot sexy girl giving a man awesome sexual acts, I want those same acts from my girlfriend (or wife). Most women will not do these acts, so a man goes out to get them elsewhere. Simply, I am not physically attracted to her anymore, so I go out to cheat (this does not mean I don't love her anymore). It's funny how I hear women say that they take care of their man and their man gets everything he wants and needs at home. We've all heard this. And yet, ask any man, and he'll tell you that he's not getting everything he wants at home. No man does. But all women think they're great at sex, that they fulfill all their man's fantasies. And yet, men cheat all the time with women who aren't better looking than their wife, smarter, or better personalities. So what gives? Why did Tiger Woods do it? Lack of a beautiful, sexy wife and mother at home? No, he just wasn't completely happy at home. Women need to get their heads out of the sand or the clouds and realize that they're always competing for their man's affections, attention, and devotion. There are too many options for men for women not to." —Milton, 33

"Usually because the women deny the man sex, or push them away by their lack of affection…Sadly women, once married to men, seem to lose their sex drive, and as a result a man will look elsewhere to satisfy his sexual needs." —Jeremy, age 24

A small segment of men just said that it was their lack of self-control that leads to their infidelity.

"Men often cheat for rather uncomplicated reasons like simply being extremely horny in combination with having a certain lack of self-control. Sometimes, cheating can be influenced by being mistreated at home and not having enough sex. Some men simply must have a variety of women in order to be sexually satisfied, regardless of their marital status. However, some men just simply lack the self-discipline of saying no when it's offered. It takes a lot of willpower to do it and it's why so many men fail." —Lorrin, age 31

What to look out for: Believing he won't cheat on you because you give him everything he wants in every way.

We believe that we've uncovered enough data to say with a great degree of certainty why men cheat. It really comes down to three main reasons we cite here. We think that there is some degree of nature that can't be overcome and some degree of nurture that you can. The key it would appear is to find out what truly makes your man happy, what he really wants from you as his wife, girlfriend, mother of his kids, etc., and deliver that to him. Even with all of that, it's still a gamble, but at least you can rest assured knowing that you did all that you could, and ultimately the choice and fate was in his hands.

WORK

Another key area of focus that women ask us about is how to relate to the men they work with.

It's an interesting dynamic, as women are now the majority of the work force, glass ceilings are being shattered, and the pay scales are becoming even.

Do men embrace this, or is there some resentment? Have the "good-old-boys" clubs in the boardroom and in the executive suite become a thing of the past? Do men admire their female executives for their accomplishments, or is there a thought that it's not based solely on merits alone?

Even subtleties are explored, like what men think about how you dress at work. Think it's not an issue or shouldn't be made an issue? Think again. Men have a lot to say about this and much more about working with you, and they've answered your questions directly.

Read on to find out what they're thinking about working with you.

Can he take a boss seriously if she dresses provocatively?

"I'm in sales, and I have a question about how my male coworkers might perceive my boss. She isn't in the field dealing with accounts, but she dresses a little provocatively. I ask because I'm on the path to having my own team, and I don't want to obstruct my career path due to my choice in dress. So my question is: **can you take a boss seriously if she is in a management role and dresses provocatively?**"
—Amy, age 29, married

What the men say

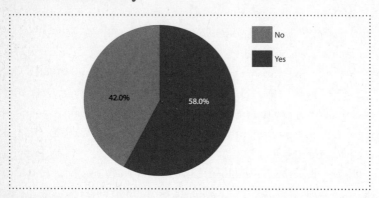

What men are really saying

Dress isn't everything in the workplace, and 58 percent of men agree. Men believe that if their boss happens to be a woman and she dresses provocatively, they will still listen to her and respect her, if she acts professionally.

"If she presents herself in a professional manner, then I would have to take her seriously, regardless of my personal thoughts of her." —Irvin, age 37

"This is simply a matter of professionalism. I can take Amy seriously because I am simply a professional at what I do. Also, you better take her seriously, because she has the power to say good-bye to your job." —Chris, age 34

The 42 percent of men who don't think it's acceptable say that dress and appearance are part of professionalism. The more provocative the dress, the less respect is warranted.

"A female boss should set a good example for her subordinates. It would be hard to take such a manager seriously if she is flaunting her body or provoking lust or desire in the workplace. This is a distraction to people who want to focus on their work." —Scott, age 33

"There is no need to dress provocatively in a business setting— unless business is of such kind that it would require her to dress so. Bosses (female) should be decently dressed in a workplace and before their prospective clients" —Mark, age 28

What to look out for: Assuming that men are distracted by well-dressed women at work.

While the majority of men still work with and respect women at work no matter how they're dressed, it's a fine line for women and how they dress in the workplace, especially in a position of power. Women still sometimes struggle to be taken seriously in these roles, no matter their dress, and men tell us that women should err on the side of caution when dressing for that role.

What does he think about appropriate dress?

"I went shopping to update my wardrobe and found myself actually debating whether or not I wanted to go with a more feminine/sexy look or keep my conservative pants-and-a-nice-top look. Does it make a difference in how I'd be perceived? **Is it better for a woman to dress in a more feminine or masculine fashion at work?**"
—Barbara, age 29, married

What the men say

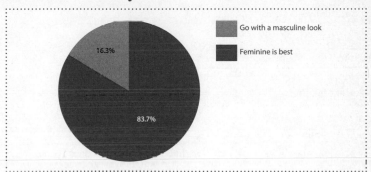

16.3%

83.7%

Go with a masculine look

Feminine is best

What men are really saying

The majority of men, 84 percent, indicate that a woman should dress the way she feels comfortable and not try to fit in. They expect women to be dressed feminine since they are, after all, women.

> "We understand we work with women and expect them to act feminine. When a woman tries to act like a man, she is basically

showing her fears and acting out of character. Acting natural is what men will respect." —Carter, age 31

"Men like women to look like women. So long as it is acceptable and professional, there is nothing wrong with dressing femininely at work. Masculine attire is trying too hard to fit in, almost, and can appear threatening." —Eli, age 40

The other 16 percent of men say that dressing more masculine is a way to play in the big leagues and warrant more respect. Plus, for some, it's less distracting.

"In business, professional appearance counts. You have to prove that you can play with the big boys and assert yourself. So men's wear is optimal." —Melvyn, age 30

"Depending on the workplace, women usually look classier in a more masculine look. This includes suits, pants, jacket, etc." —Luther, age 19

What to look out for: Assuming that men prefer that you're dressed more masculine at all times in a professional context.

There are ways in this day and age for a woman to be professional in a nice suit or in very business-casual attire and still show her femininity, and men say that they appreciate that quite a bit. Women's clothing companies are tailoring suits and business-casual clothing to show off curves and complement a woman's figure but still cover everything so as not to be perceived as provocative.

What does he think about office hookups?

"I met a man at work who is a little older than me. We recently started the innuendo type of flirting at work, and I think that he'd be willing to go out on a date. I'm unsure, however, if he thinks that flirting is all we're doing. Maybe he wants to keep things professional. I've never actually gone out with anyone from work before and don't know if it's a good idea to pursue this. **Do men think office relationships are appropriate or professional?**" —Sheri, age 25, single

What the men say

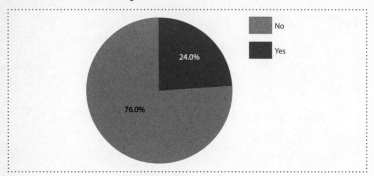

No
Yes

24.0%

76.0%

What men are really saying

The majority of men, 76 percent, think that having a relationship at work is a bad idea. The biggest problem is the aftermath when the relationship goes south.

"Office relationships are complicated. If either one breaks the relationship up, the quality of work could be affected, and

work could go from a peaceful environment to a hostile one."
—Zac, age 19

"Unprofessional in the context of the word. Relationships should
not occur in the office. If you do have a relationship with someone you work with, keep it outside the work environment."
—Ash, age 23

The 24 percent of men who feel it's acceptable say that you can't
really control where you meet the one you are supposed to be with. If
you don't let it affect your work, why risk missing out on the relationship of a lifetime?

"It's a great place to meet someone: you see them for long periods of time, and you get to know someone even before you date
them." —William, age 53

"The one is the one, and it doesn't matter where you meet them.
Just make sure to be professional about it." —Kipling, age 25

What to look out for: Presuming that men like interoffice
romance.

There's the saying "don't get your honey where you get your money,"
and most men tell us that women should abide by that policy. Yes, there
are workplace relationships that happen all of the time. That said, office
relationships that end badly can become a major issue at work for both
your career and the work environment.

Ask men your question at www.wtfaREmenthinking.com

Can you cry at work?

"I'm thirty-two-years-old, but I feel that I'm a little more mature than my age. I work with a woman who is living with her boyfriend, and I hear about every detail of their relationship. If he's nice to her, I hear it. If he's rude to her, I hear it. Sometimes she'll even cry at her desk. I'm a little distracted by her behavior, and I consider her my friend. The issue is that I think she does it for attention from men. How do men respond to this? **Do men resent women who become overly emotional in the office?**" —Jen, age 32, married

What the men say

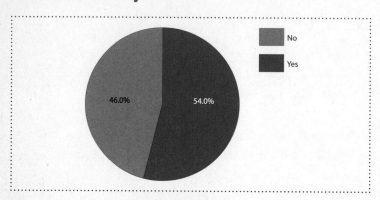

What men are really saying

The slight majority of men, 54 percent, are in fact bothered by women who get too emotional at work. It's a distraction and shows their weakness, and men just don't care for it.

"This just creates more stress to our day at work. Not only are we having to deal with work-related stress, but now we have a woman with issues to deal with or work around." —Harry, age 37

"Yes, I think other workers are extremely annoyed by this. Especially if the person ends up getting some benefit out of being overly emotional." —Branden, age 28

Forty-six percent of men think it's a bit extreme to resent a woman for being overly emotional at work; however, while "resent" may be extreme, they did say that they still have an issue with the behavior.

"No, but an overly emotional woman in a professional setting can be quite annoying." —Borys, age 35

"I just think it would be silly to resent women for being overly emotional at the office or any place, for that matter." —Eddie, age 45

What to look out for: Believing he can and will overlook emotional outbursts at work.

A professional work environment is no place for tears or other extreme emotions, men tell us. Women should keep their emotions in check and try to remain professional, and they will avoid generating ill feelings from other coworkers, especially the men.

Can I be too opinionated?

"How do men feel about women who are overly opinionated? My husband is a pretty laid-back guy and tells me about the people he works with. There is a woman who works there who comes off as kind of bitchy. I even told him so, but he seemed to not be affected by her attitude. Is this because he's easygoing, or am I just oversensitive to how women act at work because I'm one of them? I guess I'd like to know **if men find women who have strong opinions in the workplace annoying?**" —Leigh, age 32, married

What the men say

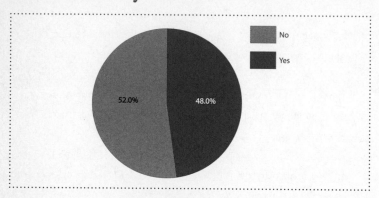

What men are really saying

The slight majority of men, 52 percent, don't consider an opinionated woman annoying at work. If the opinion is thought out and well explained, they actually see it as a strength.

"Having a strong opinion is not annoying. The fact that it comes from a woman should not matter. Annoyance comes when the person voicing the strong opinion is inflexible or unable to see an issue from other perspectives. Folks need to be willing to analyze, rather than dictate." —Stern, age 45

"Men (and women) find people who have strong opinions that are based on incorrect assumptions or baseless claims annoying. A well-informed strong opinion can be refreshing." —Jonathan, age 26

The 48 percent of men who find it annoying seem to have had experience with women who have strong opinions about the wrong thing.

"It has been my experience that the strongly opinionated woman at work is a nuisance and has a big mouth." —Rick, age 47

"Yes, I sometimes am annoyed with women with strong opinions in the workplace. A couple of my female coworkers have complained that their boss is treating them unfairly. I get tired of hearing about it, especially since I think that they are supposed to submit to authority and just do their jobs. I get along better with women with positive attitudes." —Scott, age 33

What to look out for: Assuming that men find opinionated women annoying.

Men are fine with you being opinionated. They are. They only suggest that you think before you speak and make sure whatever you are arguing about or standing your ground on is warranted and appropriate for the workplace.

Am I professional or cold?

"When I went through my last merit review with my boss, a topic covered was my demeanor. It was explained to me it is an area I need to focus on: how I come across in the workplace. Apparently I come across as impersonal. I think this is bullshit. How many times do you hear men say, 'I get paid to work, not to make friends?' Is there a double standard here? **Do men respect women who are unemotional and professional in the workplace?**" —Amelia, age 32, married

What the men say

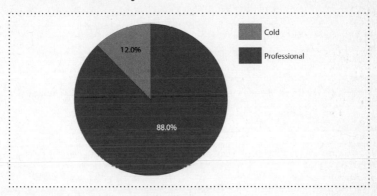

Cold
Professional

12.0%

88.0%

What men are really saying

Most men respect women who can keep a professional attitude in the workplace. Eighty-eight percent of men say that a woman who is unemotional means she is working and focusing on her job, and he can't fault her with that.

"Not showing emotions at work shows a high degree of professional attitude. Personally, I feel if you aren't showing emotions at work, then you are concentrating more on work than your emotions." —Jeff, age 40

"Yes, with reservations. Yes, I would respect a woman who is totally unemotional and professional, but only if it didn't come across uncaring and cold. If I don't think you have my back, I won't have yours." —Thomas, age 33

The rest of the 12 percent think there should be a balance between being emotional and professional. A woman shouldn't be completely devoid of emotion because she can just come across as a bitch.

"I believe there should be a little bit of both. Strictly unemotional and professional will not work for most men." —Mark, age 28

"Being unemotional and professional in the workplace doesn't guarantee that they will be respected. I had a female section leader in marching band who was unemotional and professional with her position, but in being professional, she was demeaning and incredibly insulting, so I never gave her the time of day." —William, age 27

What to look out for: Thinking that restraining your emotions at work will make you seem cold.

If the intention is to move up in the workplace, men believe that women should stay professional and show their worth in order to be taken seriously. One thing men mentioned quite a bit was for women to stay slightly less emotional and more professional at work. Don't worry; most men won't view this as you being mean, rude, or condescending.

Can you be too friendly?

"Next month I'll be starting a new job. Fortunately it's a position I've wanted for a while, but it's in a new city. The problem is new city plus new job equals not knowing anyone. I know that eventually I'll meet people, but the majority of my opportunity to meet people will be at work. How personal should I allow myself to get once I start in the new position? **Would it bother men if a female coworker is behaving too personally toward you instead of professionally?**" —Rose, age 25, single

What the men say

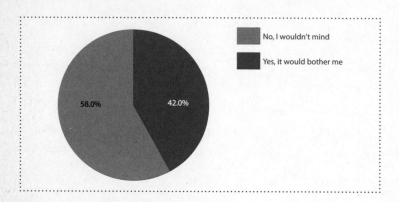

- No, I wouldn't mind
- Yes, it would bother me

58.0% 42.0%

What men are really saying

Becoming friends at work is completely natural and happens in most work environments, so it shouldn't come as a surprise that 58 percent of men don't mind a woman being chummy with them.

"Most of my coworkers are friends, and we work together better as friends. Being personal (in a good way, not just overly nosy or adding advice all the time when it's not welcome) can lead to a better working relationship." —Thomas, age 33

"Behaving too personally would never bother me in any context. I don't see why the workplace would be any different." —Rob, age 31

The other 42 percent indicate that the workplace is just that, a place to work, and they think that a woman getting too personal with them is inappropriate and would distract from the job.

"It would bother me if any coworker was behaving too personally and it was impairing our ability to be professional—I wouldn't want to jeopardize my job performance." —Matt, age 20

"In today's economy, I don't want to participate in any behavior that would put my job at risk. I don't want some woman to get too personal with me at work. Work is a place where a professional environment is expected. A woman who is too personal with me (regardless of her feelings toward me) would make me feel uncomfortable and would tend to make me want to avoid her." —Scott, age 33

What to look out for: Believing that men want a stoic and professional demeanor from women at all times.

There are various levels of "personal" in the workplace. Friendships tend to develop over time, and any woman who can roll with the punches and hang with the men in a professional and casual setting is almost universally accepted by the majority of men. However, it all depends on the man you are trying to get friendly with. In time, it will be obvious whether that man is just there to work or knows how to have fun at work too.

Can I be too strong?

"What is it about having a strong woman in the workplace that is so intimidating to a man? **Men are stereotypically strong at work, so why does meeting up with a strong female scare them so much?**"
—Marcia, age 53, single

What the men say

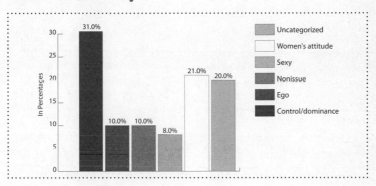

What men are really saying

Interestingly, when it comes to perceptions of strong women, 31 percent of men can be intimidated by a strong woman because to them it's a matter of control or loss of control. They believe that pay, opportunity, and advancement are equal, but they still see men as the ones who should assume more control and don't do well when a woman appears to take on the controlling role.

"Men feel threatened by powerful women. Men still think of themselves as dominant over women, so when they are confronted with this it threatens their masculinity. It is merely a defense mechanism over who is in control." —Harrison, age 31

"Some men feel that women should take orders and be supervised by men at work. Interaction with a strong hard-working woman in the workplace may be scary to them. They feel that a woman shouldn't be their peer when it comes to work." —Brian, age 21

Thirty-nine percent of men say they don't necessarily feel intimidated by a successful woman, but instead dislike the shift in attitude toward being in power.

"It is not the fact that a strong woman in the workplace is intimidating to a man; it is more that some strong women seem to have something to prove. They have to be mean and intimidating, just so they can feel above the male work force. A strong woman who is an equal is great, but not one who is intimidating with something to prove." —David, age 59

"We always assume that strong women are faking it to make it and just trying to overly assert themselves because if they're in a position where they can, they will." —Reggie, age 45

What to look out for: Thinking that men view strong women in the workplace the same as they view strong men.

Not all men find a strong woman intimidating, and some just don't see it as an issue at all. The majority of men only have the issue when it's a sense of control. Men don't like to feel like they're controlled at home or at work.

What is the best way to be assertive without being offensive?

"I've noticed the dynamics at work. I see that some women are overly assertive to the point it comes across as offensive, especially when they're working with groups of men. Ironically, these women hold very senior management positions. I'd like to attain their level of achievement, but don't want to come across that way. **What do men think is the best way to be assertive in a work relationship with a man without being offensive?**" —Terri, age 54, married

What the men say

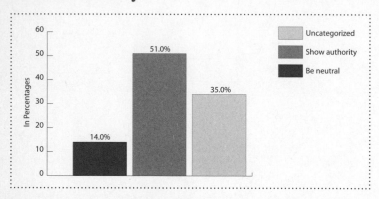

What men are really saying

Fifty-one percent of men responded that the best way to be assertive without offending a man is to keep your emotions, conversation, and demeanor professional. A woman should hold her ground without getting too emotional and show she knows what she is talking about.

"Hmm, I would say, choose your words carefully, but stand your ground. Make your rationale clear and why you are taking your stand. Above all, use common sense when choosing your words, not 'Your idea is dumb,' etc." —Thomas, age 33

"Speak your mind. Listen. State what you agree with and what you disagree with. Listen. Hold your ground if you believe you are right and not just making a stand on principle. Be prepared to compromise." —German, age 40

Forty-nine percent of men also point out that it's not just what you say, but how you say it. Tone of voice and overall approach make a difference in how men will react.

"Have a neutral tone in your voice and have the same behavior toward everyone in the workplace." —John, age 25

"Just be up front with a nice tone of voice." —Xavier, age 35

What to look out for: Believing that men accept women becoming emotional when they assert themselves.

Men believe that women really need to take emotion out of the workplace. They shouldn't worry if they offend or hurt anyone's feelings. If they are professional but polite, and don't overreact, not many men will take offense to that approach.

Are men intimidated by women in a higher position?

"I work in a group of six people in the telecom industry. We seem to be friendly with each other, but one of the two guys in our group really has a problem with taking a direction from our supervisor. I wonder if it's just him not taking direction well or if it's because our boss is a woman? **Are men intimidated by a woman in a higher position?**" —Staci, age 28, single

What the men say

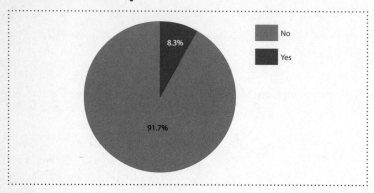

No

Yes

8.3%

91.7%

What men are really saying

An overwhelming 92 percent of men say they enjoy having a woman for a boss. If a woman works hard and gets promoted because of that, men respect that and look up to her.

"I am not intimidated by a woman in a higher position than me. I actually enjoy it because they usually get along better with me than male managers, and if they're hot, they are also fun to flirt with." —Burt, age 28

"She earned it. She performs at a higher level and has shown, more than me, that she is capable of working above me. Now, through my work performance, I have to show my value, and hope I too can move up the corporate ladder." —Ralphie, age 38

The other 8 percent said they are usually intimidated by their boss, no matter if it's a male or female.

"Any person in a higher position than me intimidates me, not just females. I strive to be the best." —Cole, age 18

"I find it difficult to predict their actions." —Reed, age 23

What to look out for: Thinking that men dislike reporting to a female boss.

Almost all men told us that women who work hard will be recognized for their advancement and not be ostracized because of their gender. Men no longer think they are the superior gender in the workplace. This is great for women, as most men no longer think that the women did anything but perform their way to the top.

Can my success be a threat?

"Last month the announcement went out that I'd been promoted to a very senior management position. I'm pretty happy with my promotion, but I also noticed that not everyone shares my happiness. I know some of this is expected. It stands to reason that some people who have been there longer would be a little upset. What puzzles me is that a guy who started about six months ago is now treating me differently. **Why do men feel threatened when women get a promotion or bonus before them?**" —Sara, age 26, married

What the men say

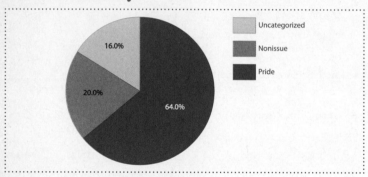

What men are really saying

For men it's a matter of pride. Sixty-four percent of men say they are the provider and should be the one getting promoted over a woman. They still tend to feel they are the dominant gender, and it really brings them down a notch if a woman outperforms them.

"Men feel threatened by women getting a promotion because of cultural reasons. Men are trained from birth to think things come easier for them in society than for women. Also some men feel bad to be taking orders from a woman, saying 'my boss is a woman' is something not too many men are proud to say." —Carlton, age 29

"I believe it has to do with ego. Throughout the ages, you will find that in almost all societies, men were the ones in charge. This seems to be the case still today. I assume that even if a woman is as qualified as a male, the male would most likely get the promotion. One reason for this is that men are conditioned that they should be the provider and not the woman." —Vince, 56

Thirty-six percent of men really don't feel threatened by a woman getting promoted if she deserved it.

"I'm not like this especially if she deserves it." —Kurtis, age 35

"I don't get threatened. Some men have a male ego that is easily injured." —Jeff, age 48

What to look out for: Presuming that men easily accept women advancing at work faster than the man might.

Men still struggle with their pride in the workplace. They're naturally competitive and feel they need to be the best at everything they do. As advancement goes, when stacked against a woman, male insecurities remain.

Ask men your question at www.wtfarementhinking.com

Who's more qualified?

"I worked at a company for six years and have a great working rela-tionship with everybody. Like most companies, we have a few men who will joke about how great they are at work. They feel that they're so qualified and skilled at what they do. My problem with this is that they always seem to do this when in the company of women, and I think it's to show some sort of dominance. In general, **do men secretly believe they are more qualified than women in the work-place?**" —Annette, age 27, single

What the men say

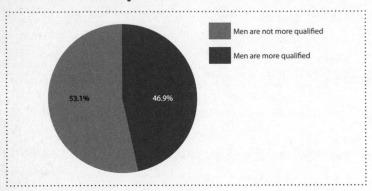

Men are not more qualified

Men are more qualified

53.1%   46.9%

What men are really saying

While the results are close, 53 percent of men do not think they are more qualified than their female coworker counterpart at their jobs. They say that whoever can get the job done the most efficiently, no matter the gender, is the most qualified.

"I believe that women can be just as qualified as men. They are on a level playing field; it just depends who the better person is for the job. There are certain places that I would give preference to a male over a woman, such as in a public safety position." —Brian, age 29

"That is a fairly large generalization of men in the workplace. There will always be a group of men within the workplace who feel superior to others, be it women, minorities, etc...I feel that most men want professional, well-qualified, competent, and hard-working coworkers, regardless of gender." —Jonathan, age 26

What about the 47 percent of men who do feel they are more qualified? Is it a belief based on old stereotypes or a warranted thought?

"Not really a secret but men don't take time off during key years to raise a family." —Kevin, age 28

"Sometimes men believe that we work harder and women are placed in power just for the appearance of equality." —Pearce, age 45

What to look out for: Believing that men see women at work as typically less qualified than they are.

The male's mindset of women in the workplace is changing, and women are more accepted as equals and superiors in the workplace.

A hard-working woman will be respected as much as her fellow male coworkers and is no longer just a pretty face at work.

Equal cash?

"I was discussing two coworkers with my husband the other day. They both do the same job, but one is a woman and the other is man. The woman found out that she makes a little less than he does, and they have the same tenure, experience, and position. I told my husband, and his reaction was, 'Well, didn't she have three kids in four years? She's always out of the office. Wouldn't it make sense that he would make more, since he is there more?' This set me back, so I'd like to know: **do men think that women should get the same pay as men if they are both doing the same job?**" —Janice, age 43, single

What the men say

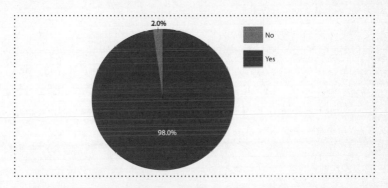

What men are really saying

An overwhelming 98 percent of men believe that a woman deserves pay equal to a man when they share the same job title/functions. A discrepancy in pay means they are discriminating against the woman for her gender which men feel is unfair.

"Absolutely! I think if it's the same job, it should be the same pay no matter who is working it. Period!" —Cam, age 28

"Women who have the same education and job experience that men have should be paid the same hourly wage or salary as men. Paying women less than men would be unfairly discriminating against women based on their gender." —Scott, age 33

The 2 percent of men who answered no didn't justify their reasons why, so we can only assume it was either because they just felt a man deserved more or were just narrow-minded in thinking.

What to look out for: Not much. Overwhelmingly most men agree: equal work, equal pay.

When it comes to pay, men see women as equals in the workforce and told us that their pay should reflect that. If a woman and a man do the same job, have the same tasks, and the same job title, there should be no reason why a man should make more. It looks like strides have certainly been made in this regard, and almost everyone agrees. We think it's about time.

Would a man choose a man's idea over a woman's?

"As a man in the workplace, if you were presented with two different ideas, both good ones, **would you choose the man's idea versus a woman's, even though they are both very similar?**"
—Suzy, age 27, single

What the men say

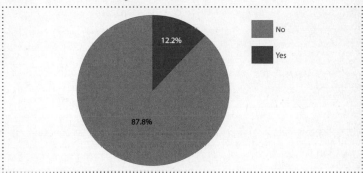

No

Yes

12.2%

87.8%

What men are really saying

The overwhelming majority of men, 88 percent, say that they never base their decisions on the gender of the person who brought an idea to the table. They do consider that person's experience and look at the details of each idea, and that's what helps them decide.

"I would weigh both ideas, then use the best. Ideally, I could bring the two people together and the three of us discuss the pros and cons, then arrive at a unanimous decision." —Phil, age 67

"As a man, I'm not too proud to admit that a woman has a better idea than a man. I believe in giving credit to whom credit is due. So if the woman came up with the idea first, I would give her credit." —Scott, age 33

The 12 percent who said they would automatically choose the man's idea are a little more narrow-minded in their thoughts of women in the workplace. When asked for a reason on why they felt that way, most said simply that men work harder.

"Because men excel in hard work [more] than women. They are strong, and others surely know that he has the willpower to finish the job." —William, age 20

"A man's idea would be better than a woman's idea." —Manjot, age 20

What to look out for: Believing that men prefer male viewpoints to female.

Men don't see gender typically playing a factor when making a decision for a project at the workplace. Most men take into account the pros and cons of both ideas and try to see which option edges out the other one, no matter what gender.

How can a woman make her boss take her more seriously?

"My boss is an older gentleman who is a 'boys club' type of guy. I feel like all he expects/wants from me is to 'get the coffee.' **How can I get him to take me more seriously in projects that I'm involved with?**"
—Deborah, age 31, married

What the men say

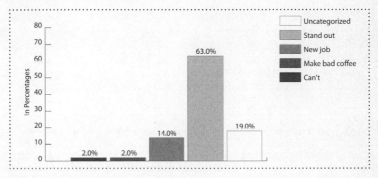

What men are really saying

The majority of men (63 percent) say that a woman who is treated like the coffee girl needs to "man up" and make herself stand out and set expectations about her role.

> "Start to do the job she wants to do without being asked; it's easier to show you can handle responsibility if you take on the tasks expected of a position of higher responsibility."
> —Brenden, age 27

"If she shows initiative and/or ability, her boss will recognize her as equally as capable. She may just have to work harder to get her boss to notice it. If not, you need to discuss it with him and make it clear what you are there to do. He might be totally unaware of how he's coming across." —Nic, age 31

Some bosses are just set in their ways and see women as nothing more than glorified secretaries. When that happens, sometimes you have to leave to improve your situation.

"Go get a job where they appreciate you, and quit working for that old sexist pig asap!" —Wolf, age 35

"She should put in a reasonable amount of time to find out if it can change. If not, go find a job working under a person who is more reasonable." —Ben, age 33

What to look out for: Assuming that men are always aware of how they come across to women.

If Deborah wants to be perceived differently, she needs to prove she's as good as the job she wants. Taking on more for a little bit will show her worth and reinforce her knowledge to her archaic boss. Men also mention that they're not always in tune with how their behavior comes across, so having a discussion to reveal that is not only a powerful move, but also shows that you're in control and confident about yourself and your abilities.

Is he tempted to cheat with someone from work?

"My husband is a little younger than I am and is still working. He's been working a lot lately, and while I'm not overly concerned, I still wonder that it could be 'not all work.' **Do men get tempted to cheat on their wife with someone from work?**" —Shirley, age 66, married

What the men say

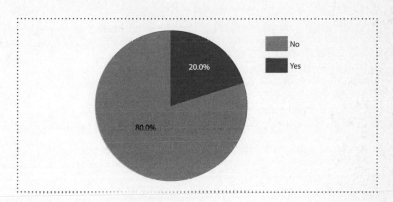

What men are really saying

Men said that once they are in a committed relationship, they see no reason to cheat. Eighty percent of men say they wouldn't want to ruin their current relationship on a work fling that would ruin their home life, and if the fling went south, it would cause complications at work.

"Work is a professional place and shouldn't be a place where you are finding someone to have sex with. Men typically focus on

the task at hand. While they may fantasize, the workplace would be very problematic if it became known or if things went south."
—Nali, age 31

"It would make life and work very hard. Not only would it mess up life at home, it would also affect work life. I view coworkers in a different light." —Leo, age 21

Out of the 20 percent who said yes, some said they have actually gone through with cheating because the relationship they were in was bad, while others said they fantasized and were tempted, but it never went past the fantasy.

"My first relationship was one with a very controlling woman, and it was unhealthy. The relationship was tanking, and both of us knew it would never last. It was near the end of this relationship and so it was not a huge deal to me." —Anthony, age 19

"Sometimes I fantasize about other women but never have gone through [with it] because I loved the person I have been with. I have never cheated on anybody." —Cassidy, age 29

What to look out for: Assuming that men see the workplace as a potential "meat market."

Most men stated that they are too faithful to their wives or significant others to actually cheat on them. They view an office fling as just that, a fling, and not worth the risk of ruining something meaningful.

Ask men your question at www.wtfarementhinking.com

How can a woman ask a man to tone down his guy talk?

"I work with these two men in their early twenties who constantly talk about their weekend sexual conquests. While I could ignore it if I wasn't working directly with them on a regular basis, I can't avoid it because I do work with them quite a bit. **How can I ask them to stop without seeming like a prude?**" —Tennille, age 31, married

What the men say

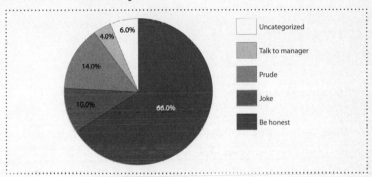

- Uncategorized
- Talk to manager
- Prude
- Joke
- Be honest

6.0%
4.0%
14.0%
10.0%
66.0%

What men are really saying

Sixty-six percent of men think women should be honest and up front about stuff that bothers them. If the men think she is a prude, so what? At least she got them to stop talking about the topic.

"Be direct and let them know that that kind of discussion is not appropriate for the work environment." —Gabe, age 23

"If it bothers you, say something or shut up. You not saying anything encourages them to continue because they know
if it bothered you, you would have said something already."
—Edward, age 27

Fourteen percent of men say that if something like that bothers
a woman, she is being a prude. People like to talk during work and
have some fun; not everything can be serious. If she's bothered by
what people say, she can just wear headphones and tune them out.

"Just ignore them or get an iPod. Better yet, just suck it up and
quit complaining!" —Max, age 35

"Just ignore the topic." —Phanindra, age 28

What to look out for: Presupposing that passive-aggressive behavior is an effective approach in the workplace.

In Tennille's case, if she's not willing to ignore the men or listen to
music while they are talking, she should just be up front about it and talk
with them. She shouldn't avoid it. She needs an environment where she
can be productive, and she needs to teach these men how to act around
her. Your approach and attitude toward handling it can alleviate you
sounding like a prude. Men think your only other option is to simply
deal with it.

Chapter 7

MEN SOUND OFF

This last chapter is a little different. Up until now, every question that was asked in this book was done so by women who posed their questions to us via www.wtfarementhinking.com. But for this chapter, we cut out the women altogether.

We offered no specific questions, no prompting, and very little direction. We simply gave men the opportunity to reveal their thoughts in a free forum.

Their insights, answers, feedback, and thoughts await you.

The Top Five Mistakes

Listen, we get it. Some of you will disagree and say "They're crazy! What woman does that?" or "No way. This isn't me," but trust us, some of you (you know who you are) will somewhere in the back of your head say "oh crap, I've done that" and "ooh, I do that too." Remember, this is the honest and most raw truth we can give you. It is not our interpretation, but instead is just the visceral feedback that men have for women in general.

So here it is: our top five list of what annoys men about you ladies (in no particular order), plus an extra miscellaneous category. In some cases, you even get a bonus "why."

1. Sex/Physical
2. Money
3. Attachment/Relationships/Baggage
4. Communication/Nagging/Emotions
5. Control/Change

Sex/Physical
Sex

Sex, sex, sex. This topic came up quite a bit, and simply put, men have a beef about sex for a few reasons. While there are a slew of different takes and ideas about how to handle sex, there were a few themes that bubbled up to the top. Highlights of this are:

Unless men ask you, *do not* **volunteer your sexual past.** Keep him guessing as to how you learned that special technique of yours. If your man does want to know, he will ask you. If he does ask, then tell him. But remember, generalities are better than specifics. Otherwise, some things are better left unsaid.

> "Telling us all about your sexual past (very whorish, in some instances). We don't need to know...because we will always use it against you, always!" —Trey, age 36

"Don't volunteer information on sexual things you've done. If we don't ask, we don't want to know. And if we do ask, lie and minimize it." —Ronnie, age 20

Don't make men ask for sex. After reading this book, you know that men are sexual creatures. There have been several studies that have shown that men think about sex every so many seconds of the day. The men we contacted said that just because you are okay with not putting out, it does not mean they are okay with it. Besides, making men work for sex is silly, and taking a little initiative is very appealing to men.

"I've been married for five years, and I will start cheating if you don't start being more interested in sex." —Chuck, age 33

"Don't ask us if we want to have sex, just jump right in and start. It's a lot sexier that way." —Keith, age 33

Don't fake an orgasm. Maybe you want your man to feel like he is a stud. Maybe you want to fake it so he will get more excited and finish earlier. If that's the case, and it's a persistent thing, you have bigger issues than just faking it. Keep this in mind: men have told us countless times that they want to satisfy you. If you fake it, they will not learn how to satisfy you.

"Don't fake it. We want to know better how to pleasure you, and if you give off fake signals, we will likely continue to make the same mistakes, and no one will be happy about that. Be honest, and teach us." —Matthias, age 37

Be aware of bisexuality. Here is a quick test for you. Without reading the passage below, what would you think if we told you that we got more than just a few comments regarding bisexuality? Be honest, was your first thought that we're going to talk about you and another woman? As men, we would bet it was. Below is a quote from a man about bisexuality. Some things are better explained by the quote itself.

"I knew Rachel for about five months, and she wasn't down with me hooking up with other men. I told her to move on with her life because I'm sexual. She should have been more accepting and down for new things in the bedroom." —Justin, age 23

Physical

After reading this far, you should have a pretty good grasp as to how men view physical beauty.

As we went through all of the comments, there was one thing that stood out that we felt compelled to include: to men, one thing that will affect change in your physical appearance is your attitude. You may have heard this countless times before, but it bears repeating. What we heard loud and clear is that your confidence will carry you, even if you're not on the cover of every magazine at the newsstand. If you feel sexy and act like you are, that exudes that attitude, and you will turn heads. Trust men on this.

Oh, and one more thing. Asking questions like "does this make me look fat?" or "which looks better?" and so on is asking for trouble. There is no right answer, no matter what you think, and men consider it a trap. This includes fishing for compliments by saying something along the lines of "I think my butt is getting bigger" or "I'm getting too old for those (you fill in the blank)." In these situations, men may not always pick up on your need to be reassured that you look fine, and you'll end up getting upset because of it.

> "I've been with Caitlin for three years, and she isn't sexy just because she's with me, it's her attitude that makes a huge difference in her appearance." —Adam, age 23

> "Asking for an opinion on which dress looks better when there is no way to explain that without getting into comments on which looks worse and why." —JR, age 43

> "They worry too much about how they look. Men may find other women attractive, but in the end, they are sensible enough to know what women they can get." —Fred, age 51

> "Always think they're fat, no matter what we say." —Joshua, age 29

Money

How does the saying go? "One step forward, two steps back?" Many of you and countless women before you have fought hard for equality and the chance to be independent. It seems puzzling to men, however, that with that one step forward, why in this day and age would some women choose to take two steps back by expecting the guy to pay for everything? Some of the major money themes are best summed up by the guys themselves.

"My friend thinks men should pay for everything, but men are struggling in the economy as well." —Kyle, age 23

"I've been dating her for two years, and she expects me to buy dinner every single night we go out to eat." —Jeff, age 30

"They think just because a man is not driving a fancy car, he has little or no money." —Mark, age 53

"My latest girlfriend's (dated for six months) biggest mistake was thinking that money was more important than commitment and honesty." —Ivan, age 37

"I met a girl just after she moved to Nevada from school in California. We dated for about a month, and I learned real fast that staying with her would be a huge mistake. She always wanted the latest and greatest. Not too bad, except she wanted me to foot the bill for her wants. Another month of that, and I wouldn't have been able to afford rent, and I know she would have been out the door." —Todd, age 26

Attachment/Relationships
Attachments

What man doesn't love a woman who is into him? No man. It feeds their ego, etc. There is a limit, however, that you should be aware of when it comes to how attached you get. Getting too clingy is a big no-no. It's not flattering, and sometimes it's downright scary. Let's break it down based on what we know. Why isn't it flattering? You are an independent woman. You have things going on in your life that require your attention. Taking care of these things will make you a better person. You don't have time to text like crazy. You shouldn't have time to call a million times, and you really don't want to say "I love you" to your man too soon. Keep in mind, men find it attractive when a woman is independent and doesn't need a man to complete her life.

"First mistake that women make is becoming too attached or clingy. I hate it when they always want to know what you're doing or who you're with." —Jordan, age 18

"If you wanna keep your man, I prefer you don't be so clingy. Don't try and make the man love you, but let him love you. If he wants to, he will. There's no way to make a person fall for you." —Jerry, age 23

"Don't be too needy, show some independence. Some men may like a woman who depends on them for everything, but most men really like a girl with some spirit and independence." —Jefferson, age 26

"Another thing is the clinginess. I dated a girl named Samantha for just four months, and she would keep tabs on me throughout the day. If I did not answer texts she would call; if I did not answer, she would message me on Facebook. It was horrid!"
—Greg, age 26

Relationships

Relationships—and romance, for that matter—aren't always what you read about in some of the popular magazines and romance novels. Reading those is perfectly fine, but we need to keep the message in perspective. Relationships take time to develop, and they require an openness that comes from knowledge that you too could be making the mistake of judging men by ridiculous criteria.

After reading comments from the men in our surveys, we feel compelled to share that "Prince Charming" comes in all sizes and isn't always drop-dead gorgeous. He may very well be the everyday nice guy you would never think to give a second look to, all because you think you can do better. Let's face it, that one hot guy you think is up to par thinks he can do better than you too. Men's feelings about how women approach relationships are summed up by the guys:

"They expect too much. Life isn't a romance novel. Try having some fun instead..." —Baxter, age 51

"The last girl I dated (only two weeks)—her biggest mistake was that she felt like there was no man in the world good enough for her." —Dominick, age 37

"I've known my friend for five years, and she always just assumes the nice guy is too much of a dork for her. She doesn't understand that the dorks are the most faithful and caring." —Kyle, age 23

Baggage

Another area where men felt obligated to comment centers around bringing baggage into the relationship. Baggage, while a necessity when on a vacation, is a real turn-off in a relationship. Don't think for a moment that men are delusional and believe that all emotions, memories, etc., end with the relationship and walk out the door with your ex. But keeping them in check to be shared at the appropriate moment is expected. Remember, you're starting a new chapter in your life. Learn from past bad experiences, but don't presume every guy is going to behave exactly the same—don't take your past out on others who had nothing to do with those experiences.

Lastly, while some would say that keeping your ex as a friend is okay, if you keep your ex as a friend, you should take care in making sure that your new guy is okay with it. If he isn't, it will be a real source of trouble in your new relationship.

"They bring baggage into the new relationship. They linger on the bad experiences from the past and hold it against us when we become the next guy in their life. I had a friend many years ago who wouldn't go certain places or do certain things with me because the previous guy mistreated her. While I have sympathy for people who suffer emotional abuse, I think that it's unfair to have to suffer the penalty for something that another guy did." —Roger, age 39

"One big mistake that happens a lot is when a women stays in contact with an ex. Men want to be the only one, and for them to think they are talking to an ex is not a good thing, so get rid of that ex. He's an ex for a reason." —Kynaston, age 37

Communication/Nagging/Emotions
Communication

Talk, talk, talk. During the course of compiling the data for this book, we received questions from women like "Why don't you ever listen to me?" or "Why don't you ever talk to me about your feelings?" Sound familiar? In asking men these questions, it became clear that according to men, women are talkers. Men said that women processed information through talking it out. It's no secret that men do not process information this way.

The nice way to put it would be that men have a tendency to want the quicker version. The truth is that men really don't want to hear about every last detail. They want to hear the main points, and if more info is needed, they will ask.

So you're saying to yourself, "No! I don't mention every last detail." Really? Here's a quick anecdote.

A friend of mine was retelling a story from his wife. The story starts with her explaining how it took longer for her to get to work because of the way some guy was driving while she was on her way to work. I thought this was going to be an "I almost got into an accident" story. But she continued on to talk about how she went to Starbucks for her daily coffee. So now I'm thinking that the story is going to be about some over-the-top order from someone who wants everyone to know they graduated from "coffee." It turns out that after all that buildup, the story was about how a vice president and an intern in her company were arguing in the vice president's office. The argument started because the vice president just found out that their affair resulted in her being pregnant. Despite hearing this really shocking story, I couldn't shake the thought and asked my friend why he didn't just get to the best part of the story. He laughed and said, "That's how she told the story to me."

> "Men don't like talking for very long, usually, or listening for that matter too. If you've been talking for ten minutes straight and your boyfriend hasn't said anything, you're talking too long."
> —Bert, age 26

Men tell us that they are not mind readers, no matter how long they've known you. It's not fair for you to think otherwise. Quick tip: If you want us to know something, please, by all means, say it. If you have a question, ask it. And if you want something, tell us. Remember, men are problem solvers and want to provide for you.

> "They think that men are mind readers; instead just explain what you want, and don't drop hints." —Zach, age 19

> "They fail to be one hundred percent truthful about their expectations and expect us to be mind readers. I was once in a relationship with a woman who felt that if I loved her, I should know exactly what she wants from me. Granted, at some point, as I get

to know her likes, dislikes, etc., then I'll be able to anticipate some things. But I do not communicate telepathically." —Roger, age 39

"The biggest mistake women make is assuming that we can read their minds. Women tend to not talk about certain things, get all pissy, then assume we know why without saying a word." —Howie, age 26

"I've been married for a year and a half, and one thing that really bugs me is that she wants me to read her mind!" —Jed, age 21

But wait, there's more.

"A woman can never lose an argument. How come if I'm right you just change the subject? It's like a black hole that you don't want to get stuck in." —Emilio, age 19

"We don't like to be tricked or backed into a corner with questions. I've been married for five years, and my wife still asks me if I like the dress she's wearing or if I like her new haircut. First, if I like it, I'm going to say I like it, so you don't have to ask me. Second, I'm a smart guy, so I know the answer you're looking for. You're looking for an answer a woman would tell you—I like the color, it gives great shape to your body, the fabric looks like it breathes. Men don't care about that stuff. We're going to say 'Yes, we like it' because that's what you want to hear, but we really don't care—unless we're trying to sleep with you." —Todd, age 30

"My wife's first mistake is not being direct when communicating what she wants—the whole 'I don't care if you go golfing,' although she is actually pissed." —Fred, age 32

"I've been with the same woman for six years, and the worst thing she does is bring up old arguments that have nothing to do with the current argument!" —Bjorn, age 21

Nagging

Rarely has a subject been covered as often, whether through joke or heated arguments, as nagging. Yet despite the commentary so little has been gained. But you don't nag. Okay, we believe you. Regardless, if you take one thing from this section, let it be that nagging simply does not work!

So, what constitutes nagging? What are its forms? And why doesn't it work?

First, nagging, according to the dictionary, is a verb meaning continually faultfinding, complaining, or being petulant. It comes sweetly and innocently at first, but as your aggravation grows, so does your tone. (We're not giving the men a free pass and letting them off the hook, but remember, this is about mistakes women make with men. Their "mistakes" book is up next.)

Why doesn't it work? Because, quite frankly, men see this as a positive reinforcement for bad behavior. Given the submissions below, the message is clear. Stop!

"I've known Caitlin for three years, and she doesn't understand that nagging me constantly will result in me not doing what is being asked of me, because doing the action will reinforce her belief that nagging is a valid method." —Declan, age 23

"My ex-wife's (married for ten years) biggest mistake was her belief that she could nag me into changing." —Myron, age 37

"I've been married for seven months, and she nitpicks every little thing I do." —Nick, age 24

"Nagging, nagging, nagging!…and nag some more!…Plain and simple, please stop." —Trey, age 36

Emotions

When it comes to emotions, the men we surveyed made it clear that they want you to please keep them under control. They understand you are an emotional being; they just don't see that as an excuse to take it out on them. For example, men inherently know that women like to talk things out. So there is no question in doing it. From their perspective, it's how you do it that's important. Talk with your man, but remember to do so in a rational way, attempting to not get too frazzled or crazy if the conversation is emotionally charged. These men sum up the feeling about emotions from the man's perspective:

"Girls get too emotional and tell you all their problems and expect you to have answers and always have answers. Maybe if they weren't so emotional, they wouldn't have these problems in the first place." —Jordan, age 18

"I've been dating my fiancée for two years, and she gets very moody seven to ten days before her period, and she says very harsh things to me that if I had said to her, she would drop me in a second." —Porter, age 30

"Why is it my fault that you had a bad day? Oh wait, it isn't, you're just going to take it out on me. It isn't my fault your employees hate you." —Spike, age 19

Control/change
Changing me

One of the men we surveyed said, "Women are always looking to change you. It's like they're saying, 'We like you just the way you're going to be when we're done with you.'" This sums up the feeling from many of the men we surveyed. In fact, we'd go as far as to say that men almost anticipate that some degree of change will come when you get involved with women; it's just a degree of tolerance for how much.

Are you one of those women who wants to change the one you're with? If so, why do you feel the need for the change? You picked him for a reason. Was there a caveat when you started dating? Meaning, "He's a nice guy, but he needs to get a better car," or "I wish he would learn how to match his clothes better." Unless you purposely chose him as a "fixer-upper," then you fell in love with him for a reason.

Focus on why you fell for him and build on that. Here's what the male sentiment is in that regard:

> "A big mistake women make is try and change men! We are fine just the way we are at first to them, right? Wrong! In the back of your woman mind, you are already planning the little tweaks that you want to do to make us your (fantasy land) ideal man!...Don't do it, okay?!?" —Stan, age 36

> "Women need to stop telling us how to dress. They already dominate every facet of our lives; can we at least dress ourselves?" —Ora, age 19

> "They always try to change a man into something that he isn't." —Zach, age 19

Control

Understanding control is a key element to all aspects of how you interact with men. Control as in knowing when not to say "I told you so." Control as in knowing when it's appropriate to get involved with various situations. The majority of men told us that this is a deal breaker for them. It causes some to withdraw, and even resent the woman they're with. If you understand control, you stand a good chance at finding a relationship you both will be very happy in.

> "For over a year and a half, this girl has to know where I am all the time!" —Valentin, age 21

"They try to control everything. When men feel they're not being listened to, they withdraw." —Fred, age 51

"Always up my ass." —Bob, age 41

Miscellaneous

There were a few miscellaneous comments that we wanted to mention here. The comments came up quite a bit in our research to the point that we wanted to include them, but they couldn't be categorized in any one particular area of the book. We'd like to share them with you:

"No matter how much we say it, we hate it when you drive. My wife cannot drive, and letting her drive more will not make her get better at it. Also, we don't want to have a conversation with you, especially if there's a good song on the radio. Men want to get from point A to point B as quickly as possible. We don't want you to point out every nice house or cool billboard. We want you to sit there and maybe even join in as I'm singing along to the radio at eighty miles an hour." —Todd, age 30

"Don't laugh too much. It becomes annoying, and eventually it just seems fake. Try adding something to the conversation that's intelligent and interesting." —Nick, age 20

"One of the biggest turn-offs is smoking. It doesn't look cool, you smell terrible, kissing you tastes gross, it's a waste of money, and it's a waste of time. It's definitely a deal breaker." —Keith, age 33

"Shoes. No lie, women. I once had a girl I dated who had so many shoes, I literally had to place my clothes in a bin instead of in my closet. Needless to say, with the spending habit on those shoes and the sheer madness of it, the relationship did not last long." —Blaine, age 26

"Not trusting our opinion can also cause problems. You ask us our opinion, and when we give it to you, you don't take it for what it is worth, and we ask ourselves why we bother to give you the very opinion you asked for in the first place." —Bryon, age 37

CONCLUSION

We get thousands of questions each month on every topic imaginable on our website, and with this book, we've shared the top questions and answers with you.

Even though you've just finished reading our book, we consider this book a continual work in progress. We think that sharing with you the reactions from men will bring some debate. Some answers you'll agree with. Some you will absolutely not. That's really our point.

We would welcome your questions for men, your feedback on what you agreed with and what you didn't. Visit us online at www.wtfaremen-thinking.com and share your thoughts and questions. Don't forget to sign up for our email newsletter too. When we start writing the book for men, this time, *you* can supply the answers!

As we've mentioned before, our goal all along is to provide a guide to why men think the way that they do, so you can make better, more informed decisions about the men you deal with in your life. We hope we've achieved that. We look forward to hearing from you.

METHODOLOGY

How we did it

Through our company, Solavista Inc., we maintain a research panel of respondents. We used this Solavista research panel, consisting of over two million men, to identify samples of women and men who would participate in online surveys that generated the data for this book. In October 2010, we surveyed U.S. and Canadian women, ages eighteen to seventy-two, to gather information on the questions they would most like to ask men regarding relationships, dating, sex, communication, and more. Over one thousand women submitted their responses through an online survey or directly to our website, www.wtfarementhinking.com, which we created as a forum that allows women to ask questions that we can take to men for answers. (www.wtfarementhinking.com is now the digital companion to this book.)

Then, in November 2010, we conducted an online survey of U.S. and Canadian men using the questions submitted by the women. Responses came from men, ages eighteen to sixty-six. Each question

(250 in total) was asked of a unique group of one thousand men, over 250,000 in total.

The results of our surveys comprise the book you are now holding.

Survey respondents were remunerated for participating in our surveys. To encourage candor, survey respondents were assured that only their ages and first names would be used in the published results, unless otherwise authorized.

The goal of this project was not to conduct a scientific study of all aspects of the male-female dynamic. As such, the sampling methodology was not weighted to be representative of the North American population. In addition, the online survey approach excluded individuals who lacked Internet access.

Our goal was to develop insights into and a better understanding of the beliefs and attitudes men have regarding the questions women raised through our survey.

ABOUT THE AUTHORS

Christopher Brya is the founder of Solavista Media, and he has worked for twenty years in marketing research, emerging mobile and SEO technologies, and user experience research for brands such as Revlon, Motorola, and Choice Hotels International.

Miguel Almaraz is the chief research officer at Solavista Media and a user experience and online research professional. He has conducted hundreds of studies to unlock the story of what truly motivates people and has worked previously at Fortune 1000 companies such as Motorola, Pearson, and Thomson NetG.